C000103188

THE
ZEEBRUGGE
AND
OSTEND RAIDS
1918

THE
ZEEBRUGGE
AND
OSTEND RAIDS
1918

DEBORAH LAKE

Pen & Sword
MILITARY

First published in Great Britain in 2002 by Leo Cooper

Reprinted in this format in 2015 by
Pen & Sword Military
An imprint of
Pen & Sword Books Ltd
47 Church Street
Barnsley
South Yorkshire
S70 2AS

Copyright © Deborah Lake, 2002, 2015

ISBN 978 1 47383 796 6

The right of Deborah Lake to be identified as Author of this work
has been asserted by her in accordance with the
Copyright, Designs and Patents Act 1988.

A CIP catalogue record for this book is
available from the British Library.

All rights reserved. No part of this book may be reproduced or
transmitted in any form or by any means, electronic or mechanical
including photocopying, recording or by any information storage and
retrieval system, without permission from the Publisher in writing.

Typeset in 10.5/12.5pt Plantin by
Phoenix Typesetting, Auldgirth, Dumfriesshire

Printed and bound in England by
CPI Group (UK) Ltd, Croydon, CR0 4YY

Pen & Sword Books Ltd incorporates the Imprints of Aviation, Atlas,
Family History, Fiction, Maritime, Military, Discovery, Politics, History,
Archaeology, Select, Wharncliffe Local History, Wharncliffe True Crime,
Military Classics, Wharncliffe Transport, Leo Cooper, The Praetorian Press,
Remember When, Seaforth Publishing and Frontline Publishing.

For a complete list of Pen & Sword titles please contact
PEN & SWORD BOOKS LIMITED
47 Church Street, Barnsley, South Yorkshire, S70 2AS, England
E-mail: enquiries@pen-and-sword.co.uk
Website: www.pen-and-sword.co.uk

For
Joe Hibbert
With Thanks

CONTENTS

PREFACE AND ACKNOWLEDGEMENTS

The actions at Zeebrugge and Ostend in the spring of 1918 have been strangely neglected in recent years. An event, hailed at the time by the Allies as a war-winning operation, has faded into a vague obscurity.

The intention was to render the two ports useless as bases for the Imperial German Navy. The Kaiser's submarines and destroyers of the Flanders Flotilla were, in the opinion of the Royal Navy, an unmitigated menace. The best way to overcome them was to render the harbours unuseable.

British historians have, by and large, ignored German accounts of the action. German writers have rarely checked the British version.

Both sides used the raids as propaganda material. The British trumpeted their achievement from the moment the raid took place. German reaction was more leisurely. It was not until after 1933, during the Hitler Years, that the affair became a useful tool. Documents from that era provide a particular challenge to the researcher as words can take on a meaning different to their everyday use.

It would be presumptuous to claim that this book is a totally definitive version of the events of 23 April 1918. I believe, though, that it lays various myths and legends to rest, possibly to the chagrin of some readers.

Two conventions are observed.

Firstly, the familiar Bruges is used throughout as opposed to the more correct Brugge. There is a decent precedent as even the Belgian Tourist Board uses it for British customers.

Secondly, imperial measurements are used except when German sources are utilized. Without being patronizing or chauvinistic, it is absurd to insert equivalent measurements in the middle of an eyewitness account. Very few British participants in the affair would have recognized a centimetre if it had poked them in the eye. The seventy-five metre width of the Mole was obviously eighty yards to the British sailors and Marines. That is what they were told and so it should remain.

Similarly, their opponents would have been equally perturbed to learn that their 88mm guns were really 3½ inch calibre.

The help I have received, both from public institutions and private sources could not have been bettered.

The hard-working staff at the Morpeth Branch of Northumberland County Library deserve special thanks. They processed my requests for an increasingly eclectic selection of books without a murmur. The British Public Library system has been sadly neglected for some years but it still serves an invaluable purpose. Luckily, councils and central government are now recognizing its value.

No writer on matters warlike can ignore the Imperial War Museum who have, as ever, been unfailingly helpful. In particular, Tony Richards of the Department of Documents and Colin Bruce of the Department of Printed Books met my various requests with considerable adeptness.

The same is true of Allison Wareham at the Royal Naval Museum in Portsmouth who answered my e-mail demands and dealt with my personal visit with charm, efficiency and knowledge. She has made a major contribution to this book by drawing my attention to the unpublished manuscript the Library holds, written by Captain H. C. Grant and filed under Royal Naval Museum, Ad Lib MSS 217.

Matthew Little at the Royal Marines Museum at Eastney was equally helpful even though my visit was interrupted by a false fire alarm. He not only found some rare photographs which are reproduced in this book but offered some German material in his archives which is probably unique.

Alison Marsh of the Chatham Historic Dockyard resolved my queries with aplomb.

In Bruges, the staff of the Town Archive and Library were most helpful in producing some extremely rare documents about the Zeebrugge Raid from the German viewpoint. Any fault in translation from the Flemish and German is entirely down to me.

Peter Elliot of the Royal Air Force Museum dug out logbooks and made photocopies without demur. Again, the greatest courtesy came from him, as it did from all the museum staff.

The Mersey Maritime Museum was also of great help and readily supplied photocopies in response to my request for information.

I owe a debt of thanks to Luuk Jonkers and Caspar Nijland in the Netherlands who tracked down photographs and made telephone calls on my behalf. Caspar and his wife Anja also did a check translation of material that I drew on from the *Adolfzeit* to ensure I had not fallen prey to some strange shades of meaning.

Max Stead on the Isle of Man traced a significant newspaper piece for which I am grateful. I owe Nick Kelly, also on the Island, my sincere thanks for his help.

Janet Hall of the *Northumberland Gazette* displayed valour beyond the regular call by tracking down the fragile 1918 files of the newspaper. She also made photocopies of crumbling pages without complaint.

Johan Ryheul of Jabbeke and Alain van Geeteruyen of Knokke-Heist in Belgium were of particular help. Between them, they probably have more knowledge about the Imperial German Navy and Marines in Flanders during the First World War than anybody else.

Johan very kindly read the manuscript and put me right on various points. He freely shared his knowledge as well as providing photographs which are duly credited elsewhere. His own book about the *Kaiserliche Marine* is a valuable source for anybody who wishes to study the First World War.

Alain provided, amongst much else, an extremely rare and previously unpublished photograph which is published for the first time. His enormous generosity in making it available instead of hoarding it for his own work shows a noble and selfless spirit indeed.

James Hayward, whose claim to fame is not only that he owns his own Lewis gun but is also most knowledgeable on the subject of the Great War, diligently ploughed his way through the text and made some very useful suggestions.

Being a computer illiterate, I have to thank Jim Kelly and Keith Rodwell for their assistance. Keith, in particular, did wonders in rescuing faded photographs from oblivion as well as explaining various mysterious computer processes.

Russell White, in Australia, supplied the photograph of Sandford on board his submarine.

The Liddle Collection in Leeds very kindly made available an account by Lieutenant Berthon of the Royal Navy for the chapter dealing with the 23 April attack on Ostend.

Thanks are made to Colin McKenzie for permission to use extracts from a letter written by his great-uncle Able Seaman Albert McKenzie, VC; to the present Lord Kennett for permission to quote from the recollections of Lieutenant Hilton Young; to the Earl of Wemyss and March; to the Library of the House of Lords; to Lord Keyes and to Earl Haig to use extracts for which they are the copyright holders.

Great efforts have been made to trace all holders of possible copyright material but not always with success. Anyone who feels that unacknowledged and inadvertent use of copyright has happened in this book is requested to contact me so that the matter may be resolved.

As usual, I acknowledge the enormous help given to me by Vanessa Stead who not only proofread the manuscript several times but also ensured that my domestic life did not descend into chaos during the writing of the book.

All of the staff of Leo Cooper have been totally charming and extremely helpful. Their courtesy is old-world and has been much appreciated by this particular harassed author. Brigadier Henry Wilson patiently dealt with my various requests while Susan Econicoff deserves a special pedestal as a stunningly competent and helpful editor.

In conclusion, I have to acknowledge a large white cat of distinguished Turkish descent by the name of Beyaz Aslan for keeping me company most of the time during the writing of this book. He is, I believe, the only feline to have an intimate knowledge of North Sea Naval Operations during 1917 and 1918.

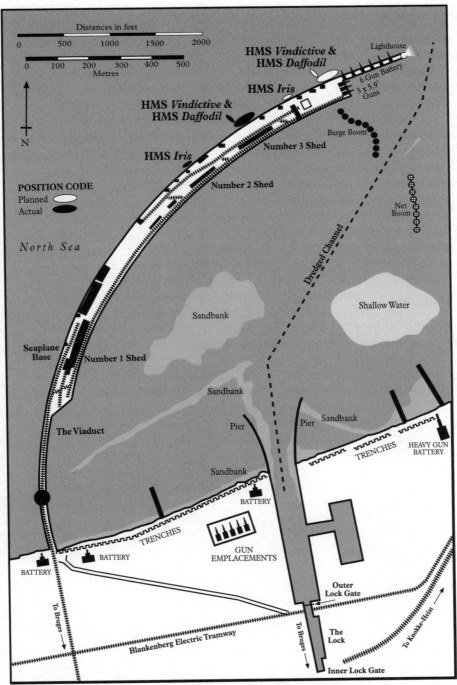

Distances in feet

0   500   1000   1500   2000

0   100   200   300   400   500
Metres

N

North Sea

POSITION CODE
Planned
Actual

HMS *Vindictive* &
HMS *Daffodil*

HMS *Iris*

HMS *Vindictive* &
HMS *Daffodil*

HMS *Iris*

Lighthouse

6 Gun Battery
3 x 5.9"
Guns

Barge Boom

Net
Boom

Number 3 Shed

Number 2 Shed

Dredged Channel

Sandbank

Shallow Water

Sandbank

Seaplane
Base

Number 1 Shed

The Viaduct

Pier

Sandbank

Pier   Sandbank

TRENCHES   HEAVY GUN
BATTERY

Sandbank

BATTERY

TRENCHES

GUN
EMPLACEMENTS

Outer
Lock Gate

BATTERY   BATTERY

BATTERY

To Bruges

Blankenberg Electric Tramway

To Bruges

The
Lock

To Knokke-Heist

Inner Lock Gate

Port of Zeebrugge, 1918

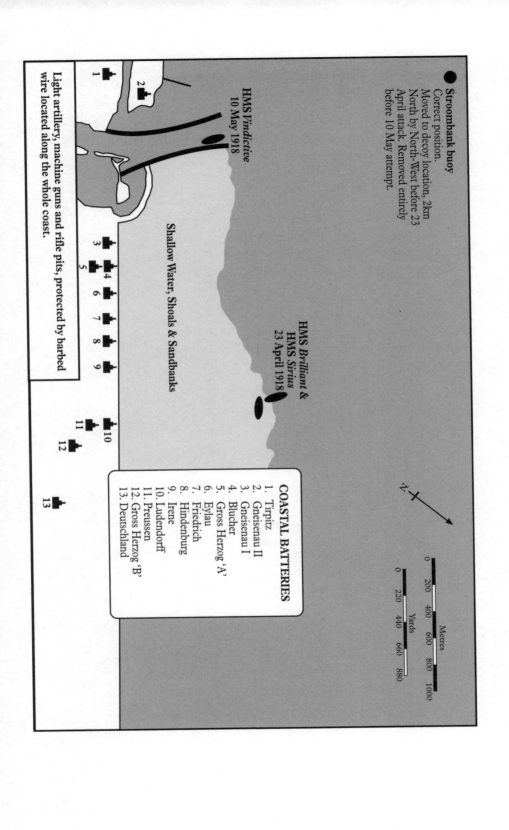

Stroombank buoy
Correct position.
Moved to decoy location, 2km
North by North-West before 23
April attack. Removed entirely
before 10 May attempt.

HMS *Vindictive*
10 May 1918

Shallow Water, Shoals & Sandbanks

HMS *Brilliant* &
HMS *Sirius*
23 April 1918

Light artillery, machine guns and rifle pits, protected by barbed
wire located along the whole coast.

COASTAL BATTERIES
1. Tirpitz
2. Gneisenau II
3. Gneisenau I
4. Blucher
5. Gross Herzog 'A'
6. Eylau
7. Friedrich
8. Hindenburg
9. Irene
10. Ludendorff
11. Preussen
12. Gross Herzog 'B'
13. Deutschland

Metres
0 200 400 600 800 1000

Yards
0 220 440 660 880

N

CHAPTER ONE

An incensed *Kapitänleutnant* Kurt Tebbenjohanns spluttered angrily when dragged from the chilly waters of the Irish Sea on 4 August 1917. His beloved charge, *UC 44*, one of the Kaiser's specialist ocean-going minelaying submarines sat at the bottom of the sea for no reason other than the crass inefficiency of the Royal Navy.

The *Kapitänleutnant* enjoyed a considerable reputation in the closed world of U-boat mariners. He was not merely a fine seaman but a cunning opponent. Tebbenjohanns had been the first to divert stalking surface forces by discharging a mixture of oil and debris through the torpedo tubes. Satisfied that they had made a kill, the jubilant hunters departed, leaving Tebbenjohanns to continue his mission.

Now, *UC 44* rested on the seabed in shallow water near Waterford off the Irish coast after only her sixth patrol. She had released just eight mines before she hit one laid previously by a sister boat, *UC 42*. Tebbenjohanns waxed wrath about British carelessness. The Royal Navy's minesweepers should have made the waters secure for his submarine. It was an exceedingly exasperated U-boat commander who went ashore to spend the rest of the war gazing out through the wrong side of the barbed wire.

Rear Admiral Sir Reginald Hall of the Naval Intelligence Division was somewhat less annoyed. Cornered U-boats had the annoying habit of going down in deep water, taking their secrets with them. One which could be salvaged was a prize worth having. Fortunately, boastful claims in an Irish pub by a drunken mariner of a cleared German minefield reached the Wilhelmstrasse with little delay. One untouched patch was no accident. Another steel shark had silently arrived to restore the field but instead sailed into waters bristling with danger. Tebbenjohanns learned that ungentlemanly low cunning still played a part in warfare.

It was not until October that *UC 44* was towed into harbour. The salvage team, bulky and clumsy in their diving suits, encumbered by lead weights, protected by surface ships against another marauding

U-boat or inquisitive fishing vessels, had finally delicately disarmed the mines and torpedoes nestling in their captive's hull. With one eye on the worsening weather as winter approached, it was a race against time. The divers won. Tebbenjohanns' pride was brought to the surface to yield a rich haul of information.

The code books went to the patient men and women of Room 40 who spent their days and nights listening to the German Navy's crackling wireless messages. The boat's logs became a source of great attention to interrogators for they gave an insight into the morale of the U-boat service.

Hall himself read the various reports with interest. *UC 44* was built in the Vulcan yard at Hamburg. Eighteen mines were released through six separate chutes. She carried seven torpedoes and sported a 3.5-inch gun on her deck – the Admiralty's experts thoughtfully transformed the notorious *88mm Kanone* into a more innocuous beast. Two diesel engines gave her 160-foot long hull an estimated surface speed of twelve knots. Underwater, the experts believed the two electric motors drove her at a steady seven knots.

Even more absorbing to Hall were the captain's instructions. Tebbenjohanns carefully kept them in oilcloth to counter the endemic dampness of U-boat life. One directive, in particular, confirmed the Admiral's fears. *UC 44* had set off on her final mission on 31 July 1917. She had made good time to the Irish coast from her German base and the reason was quickly revealed. Tebbenjohanns' order stated:

> It is best and safest to pass through the Straits of Dover on the way to the Atlantic seaways. Pass through at night and on the surface, as far as possible through the area between Hoofden and Cherbourg, without being observed and without stopping. If forced to dive, go down to forty metres and wait. Avoid being seen in the Channel . . . on the other hand, those craft which in exceptional cases pass around Scotland are to let themselves be seen as freely as possible, in order to mislead the English.

Royal Navy Intelligence had long suspected that U-boats operating out of the *Kapersnest* – the 'Pirates' Lair' – of Zeebrugge and Ostend entered the Atlantic shipping lanes by way of the Channel. Their assessments were brushed aside by an overworked Board of Admiralty. No sea raiders passed the obsolete battleship, two light cruisers, twenty-four destroyers, eight patrol boats, fourteen monitors and the motley selection of drifters, trawlers and requisitioned yachts which formed the front line of the Dover Patrol.

Apart from the surface craft, an elaborate system of mined nets, suspended from buoys, deterred intruders. To help the Allied vessels, some buoys were illuminated to aid navigation, a thoughtful procedure much appreciated by the U-boat commanders. Below the nets, deep minefields waited to snare any submariner foolish enough to run the gauntlet.

Unfortunately, most British mines did not work. Both firing and mooring gear was faulty. Moorings chafed and parted. Mines floated away. Their porous casings eventually sent them to the bottom where they posed no threat at all. One estimate suggested that, out of 20,000 mines in store, only about 1500 would function on demand.

British mines were a treasured souvenir in the U-boat service. Mounted on a polished wooden block, they were proof positive of passing the best defences the enemy could offer. So poor was the performance of British mines that German submariners simply treated them with contempt. A German Admiralty pamphlet stated flatly that British mines did not explode.

Hall sent a copy of Tebbenjohanns' instruction to Vice Admiral Sir Reginald Bacon, commander of the Dover Patrol. Bacon was a conscientious, ingenious and most talented officer. He had his own fierce opinions on the operation of his command. He categorically disbelieved assertions that at least one German submarine passed through the Straits every night. In his opinion, the big ocean-going boats went round the north of Scotland. Only the smaller minelaying submarines attempted the Channel passage.

It was not an impossible task for any U-boat. On a dark night, submarines could run on the surface. It needed a particularly alert and keen-eyed lookout on one of Bacon's patrol craft to distinguish the dark prowling shape at anything over half a mile. The submarine crew saw their hunters at a much greater distance and took discreet avoiding action. On nights of a full moon, U-boats passed semi-submerged, virtually disappearing in the waves of the Channel. With the lamentable mines, the danger was minimal. Only two German submarines had fallen foul of British technology since November 1915.

Bacon had pressed for a new and improved minefield for many months. He initially produced a scheme for building a wall of mines laid at varying depths from the Varne Shoal to Cape Gris-Nez. Later, he amended it to extend the barrage all the way to Folkestone. In September 1917, he added a third refinement of a shallow minefield and four lightships to help the surface patrols.

The new H 2 mines – based on their German counterparts – finally became available in quantity in November 1917. The minelayers of the Dover Patrol finished the first part of the new field on 21 November 1917. Bacon had no doubts that any U-boat, ocean-going or coastal, which hit one would certainly be wrecked.

Tebbenjohanns' piece of paper was just another Whitehall diversion. The necessary action to deal with the threat had already been taken. The Vice Admiral filed away the assessment.

In any event, Bacon considered, rightly enough, that the major task of the Dover Patrol was protecting the Allies' cross-Channel supply lines. German destroyers and torpedo boats, snarling out of Zeebrugge and Ostend in the dark of the night, were more of a menace than the occasional U-boat which was under orders not to create a disturbance. Fast, manned by highly skilled crews, the German surface vessels were always seeking a chance to wreak havoc on the patient supply ships plodding across the Channel.

The route the U-boats took to reach the gloomy waters of the Atlantic was almost a secondary matter. Once there, the raiders ravaged Allied shipping. German propaganda on the point was succinct. British yards took three months to build a merchantman. A U-boat destroyed it in three minutes.

In February 1917, the German Government declared unrestricted U-boat warfare. In April that same year, 866,610 tons of shipping slid under the surface as the U-boats roamed the nervous sea lanes. 'We will frighten the British flag off the face of the waters,' the Kaiser boasted. The Supreme War Lord spoke for his nation. Most Germans were convinced the U-boats would win the war.

Unwilling to hazard his popularity by introducing full rationing the Prime Minister, Lloyd George, prompted the King to issue a Royal Proclamation:

> We, being persuaded that the abstention from all unnecessary consumption of grain will furnish the surest and most effectual means of defeating the devices of our enemies, earnestly exhort . . .
> Our loving subjects . . . to practise the greatest economy and frugality in the use of every species of grain.

The loving subjects should reduce their normal consumption of bread by one-quarter. Those who could afford to purchase 'articles of food other than wheaten corn' were asked to do so, a suggestion which greatly cheered the clientele of the more expensive grocery outlets. They patriotically spent their money on candied chestnuts and fresh truffles from France. These had braved the Channel crossing rather than the

4

perils of the Atlantic. It would help win the war. The King had said so.

On 20 June 1917, the First Sea Lord, Admiral Sir John Jellicoe, silenced a War Cabinet meeting with a single pessimistic remark. The politicians and the military were debating Sir Douglas Haig's proposals for the Army's 1917 Flanders Offensive. Lloyd George, reluctant as always to put British troops into the firing line, was deeply unhappy with the idea. Offensives meant casualties. Dead men could not vote. Worse, their distraught relatives might blame the politicians rather than incompetent generals. It was a simple equation.

Like his successor in the Second World War, the Prime Minister cherished the doubtful military virtues of the indirect approach. Beating Bulgarians in the Balkan mountains would, by some feat of alchemy, crush the German Army on the Western Front. That his own generals repeatedly insisted that the only way to win the war, *any* war, was to vanquish the main body of the enemy on the main battle front, merely confirmed Lloyd George in his belief that they were both stupid and incompetent.

The War Cabinet dithered. The discussion went back and forth without any decision being reached. Finally, Haig recalled:

Jellicoe . . . stated that owing to the great shortage of shipping due to German submarines, it would be impossible to continue the war in 1918. . . . Jellicoe's words were 'There is no good discussing plans for next Spring – we cannot go on'.

Haig believed his Flanders campaign would clear the Belgian coast of the enemy. This promised much. To adapt the homespun comment of Woodrow Wilson, to swat individual hornets on the farm took more energy and was less effective than destroying their nest. The nest was at Bruges and its satellites of Zeebrugge and Ostend. Even if the British Expeditionary Force did not take all of its objectives, there was a clear chance that the ports would come within range of the Army's big guns. The U-boats would seek another home. Evacuation of the North Sea bases would transform the whole U-boat war.

Lloyd George had little option. He grudgingly agreed that Sir Douglas could proceed. His support was, even so, equivocal. The War Cabinet gave its final approval a mere six days before the offensive opened. Haig went into battle like 'a man with a rope around his neck' in the telling phrase of the Chief of the Imperial General Staff, Sir William Robertson.

The Dover Patrol and Commodore Reginald Tyrwhitt's Harwich Force mounted a series of joint operations against Zeebrugge and

Ostend during the three years that Bacon had been in command at Dover. A succession of air attacks had done little damage. Mines laid outside the harbours failed to explode. Monitors – nothing more than enormous artillery pieces mounted on cumbersome hulls with the seagoing capability of a rhinoceros – had fired very large and expensive shells at the Belgian harbours. Most of the time they had excavated large and expensive craters in the sand dunes or produced enormous splashes in the water. The problems of hitting targets which the gunners could not see, exercised Bacon's mind considerably. Using spotter aircraft was the obvious solution except that the Germans had already thought of it. *Seeflugstation Zeebrugge* was the home of some exceptionally aggressive fighter pilots who rather enjoyed splashing British machines into the sea.

Despite the mines, despite the bombs, despite the shells, little had been achieved. The German submarines, ships and seaplanes of the North Sea harbours retained in the words of the Official History 'a great capacity for mischief'. The enemy forces were a constant threat to the vital cross-Channel links and the shipping routes to the Netherlands.

The Dover Patrol had suffered a severe humiliation on 26–27 October 1916. The German 3rd and 9th Destroyer Flotillas, some twenty-four ships in all under the command of *Kapitän* Andreas Michelsen, slipped out of Zeebrugge in the blackness of the autumn night for the Straits of Dover. The 3rd Flotilla dispatched seven of Bacon's precious drifters and the destroyer HMS *Flirt*. Not to be outdone, the 9th Flotilla accounted for a transport ship, damaged three Tribal Class destroyers and mauled a trawler.

One of the unfortunates was HMS *Nubian*. Her bows were blown away. She was beached near Dover. By chance a sister ship, HMS *Zulu*, had lost her stern to a mine. The two wrecks were joined together by the ingenious Dover salvage team. The second-hand, low-mileage result – claimed to be as good as new – joined the Fleet under the name of HMS *Zubian*. The hybrid earned her keep. In February 1918, she attacked and destroyed *UC 50*.

Bacon, asked to explain the disaster, defended himself vigorously. He told the Admiralty, with some justification, that it was 'as easy to stop a raid of express engines with all lights out at night at Clapham Junction, as to stop a raid of 33-knot destroyers on a night a black as Erebus, in waters as wide as the Channel'.

Setbacks are rarely in isolation.

In January 1917, Admiral Hall's Intelligence Division learned that another German destroyer flotilla would arrive at Zeebrugge on the 22nd of the month.

Harwich Force and the Dover Patrol pooled their resources to intercept the new threat. Tyrwhitt commanded a total of six light cruisers, two flotilla leaders and sixteen other destroyers. The Commodore kept the six cruisers, split into two groups, under his immediate command. The destroyers patrolled the chill waters off the coast of the Netherlands. Midnight came. It was 23 January 1917.

The German flotilla, commanded by *Korvettenkapitän* Max Schultz in *V 69*, was spotted at 02.45 hours by the first cruiser group, led personally by Tyrwhitt in HMS *Centaur*. The cruisers switched on their searchlights and opened fire. The Germans promptly made smoke. The majority fled into the night under its blanketing shroud.

Schultz suffered. Her steering damaged, *V 69* collided with her sister ship, *G 41*. A third destroyer, *S 50*, lost touch with the flotilla in the confusion. Tyrwhitt signalled his forces that he had engaged and scattered the enemy but failed to add any orders. Some of his ships immediately headed for the scene. Others remained on patrol. By 03.30 hours, the British ships were well littered across the North Sea as they hunted for the foe.

Schultz, limping away from the first cruiser section, ran into the second at 03.40 hours. One destroyer is severely outgunned by a single cruiser. To face three of them invites unrelenting punishment. The British ships raked the unfortunate *V 69* at close range. Convinced that they had destroyed her, the cruisers switched off their searchlights and departed to seek more prey.

V 69 retreated painfully into the healing darkness and headed for Wilhelmshaven. The other damaged vessel, *G 41*, made for Zeebrugge which she reached without further incident.

The third casualty was *S 50*. Out of touch with the rest of the flotilla, she fell in with some other destroyers at about 04.00 hours. To her captain's horror, they flew the White Ensign. A sharp engagement followed. *S 50* displayed a fierce pugnacity. Accurate shellfire dissuaded the British ships from closing in for the kill. To add insult to very definite injury, *S 50* put a parting torpedo into the hull of HMS *Simoom* before heading back to Germany.

Tyrwhitt searched until dawn for the enemy who were now well clear of his questing ships. As the pallid light of a winter morning dawdled across the North Sea, he scuttled the waterlogged *Simoom* and went home.

The ambush had failed. The Admiralty was not pleased.

7

On the night of 25–26 February 1917, Zeebrugge-based destroyers made another incursion into the Straits. Eleven raiders evaded the patrolling British, although HMS *Laverock* later intercepted six of them shortly before midnight. The lone British ship engaged them without hesitation. Lieutenant Binmore of the *Laverock* fought and manoeuvred with such skill that the Germans thought they were fighting three destroyers. They withdrew before reinforcements arrived. The other five German ships shelled Margate, Westgate and the North Foreland wireless station before retiring.

Bacon and the Admiralty were not at all displeased with these results. They optimistically decided that the whole affair clearly showed the Dover Patrol was strong enough and well enough handled to confine the Germans to nothing more than harassing raids.

One month later, *Korvettenkapitän* Werner Tillesen bluntly shattered such complacency. He took seven vessels of his 6th Flotilla, on the evening of 17 March, to search for Allied merchantmen in the Channel. Five destroyers of Z Flotilla led by *Korvettenkapitän* Albrecht with a further four Z Flotilla ships commanded by *Kapitänleutnant* Zander accompanied him.

Four British destroyers patrolled near the light buoys in the middle of the Channel. Reinforcements stood by at Dover and Deal.

At 23.00 hours, HMS *Paragon* met the 6th Flotilla in full cry. She was shelled, then hit by a torpedo. Fiercely aflame, she did not survive the blast when her depth-charges exploded. A mere ten British sailors lived to recount the details of the one-sided action.

Tillesen was a patient man. He waited in the gloom. The noise and flames were guaranteed to attract more British vessels.

HMS *Llewellyn* and HMS *Laferey* duly arrived. Neither saw the German destroyers. A single well-aimed torpedo did for *Llewellyn*. Both British commanders assumed a U-boat lurked in the forbidding waters. They hastily wirelessed Dover. Bacon, well aware of the problems of finding a submarine in the dark, immediately ordered them back to base. They arrived just in time to learn that Zander's half-flotilla had shelled Ramsgate and Broadstairs and destroyed a drifter for good measure.

The Prime Minister and the War Cabinet were not impressed.

Bacon's report which stressed that 'the enemy can vary the time of attack at will and choose the night. They can predetermine whether to "shoot or scoot" or to carry out a more or less prolonged attack' sounded more excuse than reason.

The next raid gave the British press something to crow about. On the evening of 20 April 1917, the 3rd Flotilla, directed from ashore by

Korvettenkapitän Kahle, slipped out in the gloom to attack Channel shipping. At the same time, *Korvettenkapitän* Gautier with his 5th half-flotilla went to bombard Dover and gobble up stray craft that crossed their path.

South-west of the Goodwin Sands, Gautier met HMS *Swift* and HMS *Broke*. The *Swift*, under Commander Peck, was quickly damaged. Her captain still made a desperate attempt to ram a German destroyer. The *Broke* succeeded. Commander Evans crunched his ship into an astonished *G 42*. The Germans mounted a boarding party in retaliation. It fell back after a short and very bloody hand to hand action. That problem resolved, *Broke* shivered clear. The 5th half-flotilla left *G 42* to her fate. Evans gave chase but lost the disappearing Germans as his engines faltered down to half power.

Broke returned to the sinking *G 42*. Close by, *G 85* was having difficulties in making way. Although the *Broke*'s boilers had virtually expired, Evans engaged the German destroyer in a broadside battle reminiscent of the days of Nelson.

British reinforcements arrived at 01.15 hours on 21 April in time to take the *Broke* in tow as her two opponents slid beneath the dark water. Seventy German sailors died. *Broke*'s crew took forty casualties. *Swift* had five.

Evans became a hero overnight. One over-excited journalist hailed the combat as 'the greatest sea victory since the Battle of Trafalgar'.

The War Cabinet, less easily swayed, demanded more decisive action. They wanted offence not defence. Lloyd George was pugnacious from the safety of Downing Street. He had little concept of what it was like to sail perilous seas in the worst of weather.

Bacon had not, in truth, been idle. He was as anxious as anyone to curb the German threat. On the night of 7 April 1917, an air raid persuaded some of the destroyers at Zeebrugge to leave harbour until the excitement was over. British coastal torpedo boats, forewarned, lingered outside the port, waiting for their chance. They claimed one destroyer. *G 88* was hit by a torpedo. She sank in shallow water after being towed into harbour but was later repaired.

Bacon bombarded Zeebrugge in May 1917. He believed firmly in the power of the heavy gun and the value of the monitor. Five of his monitors had gone to the mouth of the Thames for a brief period early in 1916 to deter Zeppelin raiders. Their presence achieved little but mightily reassured an apprehensive civilian population for whom the threat of bombs dropping through the clouds far outweighed the perils of the Western Front.

Sir Reginald was a resourceful officer, greatly involved with the science of gunnery and its problems. He had produced many improvements to the mounting, elevation, traversing and transport of heavy calibre naval guns. He had a tremendously inventive mind. Every operational quandary, no matter how insignificant, was tackled with the same methodical approach. Security minded, Bacon insisted that his classified orders should be typed only by a commissioned officer. If one was not available, he did it himself.

The operation on 12 May took three months of careful preparation. Weather conditions had to be absolutely right to ensure success. Bacon needed the correct tidal direction along the coast, no low cloud to hamper the artillery observation aircraft, no mist over the target and no wind to disperse the smokescreen laid round the lumbering monitors.

Two cruisers, twelve destroyers borrowed from Tyrwhitt, three monitors each with a 15-inch gun, thirty-eight other ships and launches from the Dover Patrol duly arrived at the aiming point.

Early morning haze silenced the monitors until nearly 05.00 hours. By this time, the spotter aircraft were running low on fuel. Their task was made no easier by the arrival of the *Marine-Fliegerabteilung Zeebrugge* in some considerable numbers. Their *Hansa-Brandenburg W12* fighters were very superior machines. In the fierce combat which followed, target observation became very much a secondary consideration for the pilots and observers of the Royal Naval Air Service. The monitors fired without correction. It later proved that their range-finding was seriously amiss.

The support ships circled the monitors, creating a smokescreen to hide the hulking gun platforms. From Knokke, the 30.52-centimetre guns of the *Matrosen Artillerie Regiment 1* in the *Batterie Kaiser Wilhelm II* thundered a formidable reply. Their own spotting aircraft quickly joined the action, directing the battery's fire.

Bacon's force fired 200 shells from a range of thirteen miles. Forty of them were in the general area of the target. Fifteen landed within forty-five yards of the lock gates which remained serenely undamaged behind their concrete shelters.

Three weeks later, on 4 June, Bacon went to Ostend. His ships hurled 115 shells towards the harbour. Twenty exploded in or around the dockyard. They damaged one destroyer, *S 55*, and a handful of smaller vessels. Despite Bacon's denials, his gunners damaged several private houses. Some civilians died. German propaganda made full use of the funeral photographs.

No British ships were actually hit when the German shore batteries replied with swift ferocity. The defences were both very much alert and accurate, straddling the attackers thirteen miles away, with successive salvoes. Once shells dropped either side of a ship, a direct hit was usually not far behind. Several bombarding monitors had been hit in the preceding months. Their captains had learned to be cautious. Yet again, the heavy coastal batteries enjoyed the skills of their specialized spotting aircraft.

The British ships withdrew under cover of more smoke. Bacon waited impatiently for the aerial reconnaissance photographs. They were a severe disappointment. Ostend continued to function without a hitch.

The Admiral was not deterred. He produced a scheme involving the use of three monitors, each armed with a massive 18-inch gun on a special mounting designed by himself. These vessels – of which none actually existed – would open fire from fifteen miles away – outside the range of the enemy's shore batteries – in an attempt to destroy the lock gates at Zeebrugge. The gates were shielded by hulking concrete shelters. The chances of a direct hit were minimal. As the modified gun mountings could not be produced for some months, the plan was gently shelved.

Bacon believed that the problem of Zeebrugge and Ostend could only be resolved at long range. Despite his convictions, though, he was always prepared to consider other options. His own motor boat officers suggested that specially trained crews could penetrate the harbour at high speed during daylight, dash to the canal entrance and fire torpedoes at the lock gates.

This suicidal plan was actually approved at an Admiralty meeting but held in abeyance in the hope that something less despairing might be proposed.

The decision greatly disappointed the young men of the Coastal Motor Boat crews. They agreed that casualties might be heavy if the enemy was not taken by surprise but argued that, even then, the speed of the tiny fragile craft would keep them out of danger.

Everybody was certain about one point. The menace of Bruges had to be wiped out. Britain was bleeding to death on the high seas.

CHAPTER TWO

Lloyd George knew the answer to the thorny question of the North Sea bases. More and better bombardments would solve the problem. He dismissed Bacon's response – via Jellicoe – that specific conditions of tide, visibility and wind were necessary. Impatient to a fault, he demanded that the Grand Fleet batter Zeebrugge and Ostend into rubble. He wrote in his *War Memoirs*:

> No attempt was ever made by our powerful Navy to turn its great guns on the submarine nests of Flanders. When I ventured to suggest such an idea it was turned down peremptorily.

Despite this indignant post-war claim, the Celtic firebrand had been clearly told why such an operation was impossible. Two or three British battleships arriving off the North Sea coast would attract every U-boat commander and German surface craft captain who could fire a torpedo. Instant glory was guaranteed for the officer who sent a British dreadnought to its doom.

The Grand Fleet would need its own destroyer screen. Worse, the battleships had an enormous draught. They were always at hideous risk from mines. The Germans mapped their fields with precision but strangely failed to tell their enemy where they were. More Teutonic mines would sprout within hours of a single attack by British ships. One discouraging feature of warfare is that the enemy usually takes steps to thwart repeat attacks or quickly finds countermeasures to new threats.

Some German coastal batteries had a formidable range. They enjoyed the benefit of dedicated *Küstenstaffeln*, artillery observation aircraft whose sole purpose was to direct their fire. Bacon's monitors were well accustomed to retreating as soon as enemy shells arrived. A first salvo over the top, a second salvo falling short, was a sure indication that the next shell would probably land with a loud bang on the quarterdeck.

Lloyd George frequently alleged that advice from his military and naval experts was wrong. He subsequently claimed, with his typical flair for modest understatement, that the Admiralty was full of men who were 'in a condition of utter despair . . . men whose caution exceeded their courage'.

Jellicoe made it acutely clear that bombardments were fraught with danger. The loss of even a single capital ship from the Grand Fleet would crush British morale, both service and civilian. The First Sea Lord would risk neither his nor the Navy's reputation by pursuing suicidal actions. There was only one Grand Fleet. Without it, Britain was defenceless.

Lloyd George was already at loggerheads with Jellicoe over the introduction of a convoy system to protect Allied shipping against the depredations of the confident U-boats.

The Admiralty mustered several arguments against convoys. They were, for one thing, desperately short of escort and anti-submarine vessels. The Navy estimated a convoy of more than twenty-two ships needed at least eight destroyers; between sixteen and twenty-two merchantmen, seven were required. Small convoys of less than sixteen ships could manage with a mere six escorts.

The Admiralty's specialists firmly believed that the primitive instruments in most merchantmen would prevent their skippers keeping station at night. The customary lack of a voice-pipe between bridge and engine room inhibited precise speed alterations even if the engines could take the strain of constant changes. Merchantmen were designed for economical plodding, not eternally tinkering with the ship's speed. Additionally, a single careless tramp could endanger an entire convoy by smoke billowing from her funnels.

Convoys were necessarily restricted to the speed of the slowest ship. Slow ships were easy targets for the U-boats. If the whole convoy dragged at a snail's pace, the enemy could destroy it with ease. Nobody suggested dividing the ships into slow and fast convoys.

The Admiralty calculated that much time – about twenty per cent or more of cargo space – would be lost in assembling convoys. This was a valid argument. Instead of a merchantman sailing as soon as her holds were full, she would be forced to wait until sufficient others were ready. This could take as long as a week, a week of shipping time completely lost, a week in which perhaps 3000 tons of supplies could have crossed the Atlantic instead of remaining in harbour. Some pessimists suggested the space lost was as high as fifty per cent.

Putting a gaggle of merchant ships together was the equivalent of spreading honey near a termite's nest. The U-boats would flock to the killing. An Admiralty pamphlet declared authoritatively:

It is evident that the larger the number of ships forming the convoy, the greater is the chance of a submarine being enabled to attack successfully, the greater is the difficulty of the escort in preventing the attack.

In fact, this did not happen. Poor communications stopped the U-boats forming wolf-packs. It was not until a later war, in which the same problem gnawed at the Allies, that the potential weakness of the convoy system was cruelly exposed. In another twenty-five years, the U-boats, faster, equipped with long-range radio, able to submerge for long periods, would hunt in groups, picking off the ships in slow-moving convoys with an almost contemptuous ease. *Ultra*, sufficient escorts and long-range anti-submarine aircraft finally turned the tide of that particular struggle. Jellicoe had simply got the wrong war.

Finally, the Admiralty argued, collisions and straggling were inevitable. This argument had merit. Interestingly the enemy agreed. A German manual, based on the experience of the U-boat captains during 1917, tartly commented on the 'indescribable irregularity in station-keeping at the point of assembly'. This, however, changed as the merchant skippers learned the system.

The Prime Minister disagreed with Jellicoe and the admirals. He believed that convoys restricted the U-boat commander's ability to find targets. Without convoys a German submarine only need wait on a shipping lane until a plump merchantman appeared.

One great advantage of the protected convoy, as a memorandum by Sir Maurice Hankey, Secretary to the War Cabinet, made clear, was that:

The enemy can never know the day or the hour when the convoy would come, nor the route which it will take. The most dangerous and contracted passages can be passed at night . . . The most valuable vessels can be placed in the safest part of the convoy . . . The enemy submarine, instead of attacking a defensive prey, will know that a fight is inevitable.

In short, the convoy system forced the submarines to come to the hunters rather than force the hunters to roam all over the ocean looking for the U-boat.

Hankey's memorandum was pushed under Jellicoe's nose on 13 February 1917. Lloyd George was certain that any attempt to stem the losses was better than none at all. Jellicoe replied with his previous arguments but it was clear that something had to change.

The First Sea Lord finally agreed to experiment with a convoy system in May of the same year. He was well aware that even if it worked, it would not do so immediately. Its introduction might be too late to be effective. His decision was not totally without an important outside influence. Rear Admiral William Sims of the United States' Navy arrived in England to command US Navy Forces in Europe and to study the best way of cooperating with the Royal Navy.

Sims and Jellicoe were old friends. What was more important, Jellicoe trusted the American.

The US Admiral bombarded Washington with demands for destroyers to help fight the U-boats:

> . . . history records few spectacles more heroic than that of the British navy fighting this hideous and cowardly form of warfare in half a dozen places with pitifully inadequate forces, but with undaunted spirit which remained firm against the fearful odds.

The first six destroyers from the United States arrived in early May 1917. Two weeks later, twelve more docked to join the forces guarding the Western Approaches. The U-boat crews were in for a hard time.

This was not good enough for Lloyd George. Jellicoe, he thought, was not vigorous enough. It is true that the admiral was desperately tired, worn down by the heavy responsibilities of his office. His recalcitrance, and the inability of the First Lord of the Admiralty, Sir Edward Carson, to impose the political will, sealed both their fates. Jellicoe's continued refusal to order the Grand Fleet to shell the U-boat bases merely confirmed Lloyd George in his opinion of the Admiral:

> I was dissatisfied that our Navy with all its tremendous power could do so little against the Belgian harbours . . . I asked Jellicoe whether, if the German Fleet had the same preponderance over ours as we and the Americans together now enjoyed over theirs, they could not make Dover or Harwich untenable for our fleets. He denied we had an overwhelming preponderance, except in battleships, and further stated that even if the Germans held an overwhelming preponderance, they could not render either Harwich or Dover untenable. Harwich was defended by navigational conditions, in which respect it resembled Zeebrugge and Ostend. Dover could be bombarded, but our ships could come back as soon as the bombardment was over. You could not render

a harbour so unpleasant that ships could not use it. Our Grand Fleet could not go nearer to Zeebrugge than 18,000 yards range; and if monitors, which were unarmed, closed to that range, they would be sunk.

The First Sea Lord was, perhaps, aware of the rumours which were sweeping London. Wild allegations were made. It was murmured that he had been court-martialled for treason for deliberately allowing the German Fleet to escape after the Battle of Jutland. Found guilty, he had been briefly imprisoned in the Tower of London before being led out at dawn to be shot. A convincing embellishment alleged his wife was herself a German spy. The treacherous pair had stood, blindfolded, side by side, to face a firing squad from the Grenadier Guards.

At Dover, Bacon conceived an ambitious scheme for a large-scale landing on the Flanders shore. A specially built pontoon would carry a massive gun, seventy-foot long and weighing 150 tons, to Westende village, some miles from Zeebrugge. The gun would be dragged by teams of sweating sailors – or possibly motor-tractors if they could be had – to the local Palace Hotel. Installed inside the building, it would destroy the lock gates with ease. A firm base would give the monster an undreamed-of accuracy. The Admiral may have known that his enemy had lodged a similar creature inside a hotel on the Ostend sea front. Only when in use did its snout poke out of an upstairs window.

Bacon designed an enormous lighter, displacing 2500 tons. Several of these would carry, aside from mere soldiers, artillery, tanks and the gun tractors. The lighters would be fastened to the bows of monitors by strong chains and pushed towards the shore under cover of the ubiquitous smokescreen. A full division and its equipment could be landed within twenty minutes.

Sir Reginald's plan, detailed in the extreme as to how the brute would be transported and installed, needed only one small gesture from the BEF. Before his 'Great Landing' could take place, the flank of the German Army in Flanders must be turned. Sir Douglas Haig and his men had been trying to achieve this for some time with no success. Bacon's scheme remained no more than a pipe dream.

Neutralizing Zeebrugge, Ostend and Bruges had exercised the Navy's brains ever since the ports were taken by the enemy in the autumn of 1914. The occupied Belgian coastline was a heavily-defended Military Zone, commanded by an extremely energetic Admiral Ludwig von Schröder. Called back to service upon the outbreak of war, von Schröder set about making his mandate a constant challenge to the

16

Allied supply lines which crossed the English Channel and the North Sea.

He succeeded. Zeebrugge, Ostend and Bruges were a perpetual nightmare to the Admiralty. Making them harmless became a major preoccupation.

The dossier on how to render the North Sea harbours innocuous grew and grew. In 1916, Admiral Sir Lewis Bayly, who commanded the Western Approaches, produced a detailed plan for landing troops in occupied Belgium to seize Ostend and Zeebrugge. Ambitious in the extreme, it demanded men and equipment which were already in short supply. The idea was shelved.

Interestingly, it was this very prospect of an attack on the German rear which von Schröder most feared. His three divisions, stretched along the beaches and sand-dunes of the West Flanders coast, spent long hours gazing out to sea waiting for a British Fleet to appear on the colourless horizon.

A short while later, Commodore Tyrwhitt proposed destruction of the lock gates with a blockship. This vessel, crammed with explosives, would enter Zeebrugge harbour protected by a heavy bombardment, a smokescreen and a rolling cloud of poison gas. Hidden by smoke, and with the defenders disabled, the blockship would enter the canal, triumphantly ram the gates and be scuttled in the channel.

Ingenious though this scheme was, its detractors quickly pointed out that even the slightest change in the wind would be disastrous. The gas might blow back on the attackers. Worse, a freshening wind would send it further inland than intended. Chemical warfare against German Marines and sailors was one thing. Phosgene and chlorine clogging the throats of innocent Belgian civilians was quite another.

The Commodore refined his plan. He incorporated his first ideas into a project which envisaged not merely an assault on Zeebrugge Mole but the capture of the town itself. The lock gates could then be destroyed at leisure. Tyrwhitt suggested, perhaps too optimistically, that Zeebrugge could be held permanently as a base from which to attack the Germans on their flank. The numbers of infantry needed to achieve this Nirvana was left uncalculated but it would clearly have been considerable.

Bacon, as commander of the Dover Patrol, was asked for his opinion. He considered the military operation was impracticable although he conceded that a raid to destroy the gates was a possibility. His assessment, though, remained the same. The best chance of success lay in long-range bombardment.

17

In Downing Street, Lloyd George brooded. He had become Prime Minister on 7 December 1916 when political support for his predecessor, Herbert Asquith collapsed. Asquith's direction of the war effort was undoubtedly less than dynamic. His oft-quoted remark when faced with any crisis of 'Wait and see,' had brought him a certain notoriety amongst the cynical troops on the Western Front. French matches, whose compound was such that a full second passed before they burst into flame, were widely known as 'Asquiths'.

Lord Haldane, who had served as Minister of War when Lloyd George was Chancellor of the Exchequer before the war, succinctly defined the difference between the two men:

Asquith is a first-class head of a deliberative council. He is versed in precedent, acts on principle and knows when and how to compromise. Lloyd George cares nothing for precedents and knows no principles, but he has fire in his belly and that is what we want.

Margot Asquith, wife of the outgoing Premier was, understandably, rather more waspish. 'Show Lloyd George a belt,' she observed acidly 'and he will hit below it.'

Lloyd George had one objective – to win the war. The change was described by the Clerk of the Privy Council as 'the substitution of dynamite for a damp squib'.

The dynamite was made more effective by the new Prime Minister's personal blend of cunning, influence, inspiration and instinct. A timorous few feared he dabbled in curious Celtic spells. He was not, they felt, called the Welsh Wizard without good reason.

Anxious to create an irresistible impetus and, at the same time, settle old scores, Lloyd George appointed new men. Sir Eric Geddes, already a member of the Board of Admiralty as Controller of the Navy, replaced the Ulsterman, Sir Edward Carson, as First Lord of the Admiralty, the political head of the Navy in July 1917.

Geddes had been Deputy General Manager of the North Eastern Railway before the war. The Prime Minister praised him highly. 'He had the make of one of their powerful locomotives. I knew he was a find.' Lloyd George found no difficulty in allowing the innocent reader of his memoirs to assume that he had been the genius who had plucked Geddes from the relative obscurity of a railway company.

It was actually Haig who winkled out his fellow Scot to reorganize the Army's railway system in France. Haig arranged for Geddes to take the rank of Major General. Immediately and inevitably, he acquired the nickname of 'The Railway General'.

18

In early 1917, Lloyd George put Geddes in charge of the national shipbuilding programme. He was made a Vice Admiral which at least gave him a choice of uniforms to wear. He soon became a familiar sight in shipyards across the country, striding about with his cap at the operational angle popularized by Admiral Beatty, commander of the Grand Fleet.

Now, Lloyd George decided he had a greater purpose to fulfil. The Prime Minister made one thing abundantly clear to his new First Lord. Sir John Jellicoe was to go within the not too distant future. Lloyd George was reluctant to carry out assassinations in person but was happy enough to hand the blade to an accomplice.

In much the same way, he was to send the South African General Jan Smuts, accompanied by Maurice Hankey, on a mission to find a replacement for Sir Douglas Haig. The Prime Minister even grilled foreign generals for their opinion of the commander of the BEF. Smuts duly reported that the Army was utterly convinced that Haig was the best man to lead the British forces on the Western Front. Lloyd George was deeply disappointed. It says much for his personal antipathy towards Haig that he should feel dismay that the best man available was already doing the job.

All of Lloyd George's malevolence towards the military sneaks out in his account of Smuts' mission:

> It is a sad reflection that not one amongst the visible military leaders would have been any better. There were amongst them plenty of good soldiers who knew their profession and possessed intelligence up to a point.

That 'up to a point' reveals much. Lloyd George equated intelligence with fluency of speech. Silver-tongued himself, he considered the often taciturn generals and admirals to be his intellectual inferiors. 'Had we removed Haig,' Lloyd George continued without apparent irony, 'we might have set up in his place a man who had not his mastery of the profession, and with no greater gifts to make up that deficiency.'

Unwilling to risk upsetting the Navy, public opinion and some of the press – Lloyd George considered *The Times* to be 'the mere kettledrum and the mouth-organ' of the General Staff – if Jellicoe was removed immediately, he modestly suggested that if Geddes found it impossible to work with Jellicoe, the First Lord of the Admiralty would have to replace his First Sea Lord.

In his memoirs, Lloyd George is remarkably bland:

Geddes, in his acceptance of the position of First Lord, stipulated that Jellicoe should not be immediately removed. Geddes knew that Jellicoe had the confidence of the senior officers in the Navy and that it would therefore be a distinct advantage to secure his co-operation if that were at all possible. He promised to tell me without delay if he found that he could not work with or through him.

Geddes accepted the concept without demur. He was a brilliant administrator. He was also ruthless. He told Douglas Haig after the 20 June meeting that Jellicoe was 'feeble to a degree and vacillating.'

As a first step, Geddes created a brand new post. Sir Rosslyn Wemyss, a descendant of one of William IV's illegitimate daughters by his 'divine Mrs Jordan', became Deputy First Sea Lord. The economist, John Maynard Keynes, dismissed Wemyss as a lightweight, a man with 'a comical quizzical face, and a single eyeglass'. He was, Keynes noted with disapproval, 'pleasure-loving, experienced and lazy'.

Keynes was not totally fair. It was true that Wemyss enjoyed life and he preferred compromise to confrontation. He was, though, a hard worker when the need arose and capable enough. No man who commanded warships at sea was a total fool. What was more, and this was something that politicians found hard to understand, Wemyss, along with the vast majority of his contemporaries, was devoted to the Service. Duty, loyalty, honour held much greater importance for a professional officer than political wishes.

Wemyss had, it must be confessed, hardly suffered in his career by being related to the Royal Family, albeit on the wrong side of silken sheets. Through his father, he laid claim to descent from one of Scotland's noblest families. One ancestor, Lord Elcho, had quarrelled with Bonnie Prince Charlie on the field of Culloden. Sir Walter Scott recorded the famous occasion:

> After the left wing of the Highlanders was repulsed and broken
> . . . Elcho rode up to the Chevalier and told him all was lost and
> that nothing remained except to charge at the head of two
> thousand men, who were still unbroken and either turn the fate
> of the day or die sword in hand as became his pretensions. The
> Chevalier gave him some evasive answer and turning his horse's
> head, rode off the field. Lord Elcho called after him . . . 'There
> you go for a damned cowardly Italian' and would never see him
> again, though he lost his property and remained an exile in the
> cause.

Wemyss had steel in his ancestry. Even more importantly, he was in the same term at the Royal Naval College as the two royal princes, George and Eddy. Wemyss became a great friend of them both. Eddy died but Prince George continued in the Navy. Wemyss had served with him on more than one commission. This Royal connection was no bad thing especially as Prince George was now the King-Emperor.

Lloyd George heartily approved the appointment. The small town solicitor turned professional politician considered 'Rosie' Wemyss to be 'not a man of outstanding ability' and, most usefully, amenable to political direction. He was unlikely to oppose the Prime Minister's habit of asking even the most junior officer for ideas on how to win the war.

Jellicoe had objected strongly to this quirk, pointing out that ideas should be submitted through official channels. Lloyd George found this risible, maintaining that a politician was not bound 'by any rule of honour or etiquette from sending for any person either inside or outside his office, whatever his rank, to seek enlightenment on any subject affecting his administration'. Sir John would soon learn just how thoroughly Lloyd George dispensed with honour and etiquette.

Wemyss had his own favourites from amongst those with whom he served. This was not unusual amongst the core of professional officers who served in the pre-War Army and the Navy. Both services were small. The career officers, in consequence, knew each other very well. There were, inevitably, likes and dislikes, cabals and cliques. Wemyss had steered a careful course, never allowing himself to become closely associated with any particular group. As a result, he was on good terms with everybody.

Wemyss lost no time in sending for Rear Admiral Roger John Brownlow Keyes to join him at the Admiralty as Director of Plans. Wemyss believed fervently that the Admiralty had lost the will and the urge to fight. The battle had to be taken to the enemy. Keyes was a man of the same opinion. On the 28 September 1917, Keyes took up his new appointment, six days before his forty-fifth birthday.

Slim, of medium height, shy, Keyes had always wanted to go to sea although his father was a soldier. Sir Charles commanded the Punjab Frontier Force and so Keyes spent the first five years of his life in India. He was a delicate child. By the time he entered the Navy, his health was still precarious. His general appearance was little better. A broken left arm had been badly set. Throughout his life, Keyes had a crooked forearm. Amateur psychologists can speculate that both he and the Kaiser made up for a physical shortcoming by an eager desire for military glory.

The new Director of Plans was not universally liked. Jellicoe dismissed him as not 'blessed with much brains'. Some contemporaries felt that Keyes did not possess really adequate administrative skills. He delegated responsibility freely, it was true, but his detractors claimed that he rarely checked if the subordinate had fully carried out his instructions. Keyes had a reputation as a thruster, someone who met a challenge head-on, smacking down any opposition with fierce determination. He was a firebrand and fire scorches. If he skimped on detail in his staff work, that was the price to be paid for an officer who, in Winston Churchill's opinion, had 'more knowledge and feeling for war than almost any naval officer I have met'.

Keyes went to the Britannia Royal Naval College in 1885 when he was thirteen. A contemporary cadet later described him as 'a miserable little squirt'. He never achieved anything better than a Second Class pass in any subject. He only just scraped through his professional pilotage certificate. His future as a full time seagoing officer appeared less than bright.

He was serving on the Africa Station two years later. His first command, in 1898, was HMS *Opossum*. He then distinguished himself mightily during the Boxer Rebellion in 1900. Commanding, prophetically, HMS *Fame* he captured four Chinese destroyers, albeit that Great Britain was not at war with China, destroyed a fort after a successful land assault and was first into the besieged British Legation at Peking. The thinnest man at the head of the Relief Column, he squeezed through a sluice-gate onto the lawn. He received accelerated promotion for his exploits which put him four or five years ahead of his contemporaries. In a service in which seniority counted for almost everything, Keyes was set fair to make his mark. Napoleon would have approved. He too believed in officers making their own luck.

On his return to Britain, Keyes became second in command of the Devonport destroyer flotilla. An embryo Naval Intelligence Department claimed his services in 1905. Prince Louis of Battenberg selected him to go to Rome as the Naval Attaché. After short stints at Vienna, Athens and Constantinople he came home in 1908. He was freely spoken of as an officer with a glittering future. Already, he had made powerful friends. A polo devotee, he got on particularly well with another enthusiast – Winston Churchill was also determined to rise to the top.

Keyes became the youngest captain in the Navy when he took command of HMS *Venus*. In 1910, he participated in exercises which involved the Navy's minute submarine force for the first time. Soon afterwards Keyes was appointed Inspector General of Submarines although he was not a specialist in underwater craft nor, in particular, an expert on their main armament – the torpedo.

He was, though, energetic and active. No technical genius but a self-confessed 'salt horse', he had the invaluable ability to choose first-class officers. Submariners rapidly became an elite branch of the Service.

Promoted Commodore, and controlling the whole submarine service, Keyes concluded that the submarine was more than just a means of defending harbours or sailing in the shallows of coastal waters. With the enthusiastic support of the First Lord of the Admiralty – Winston Churchill – Keyes commissioned larger submarines. He also introduced depot ships. They not only had full repair facilities but also provided accommodation for crews not on patrol. Until then, officers and men slept on board in the most squalid conditions. The surface Navy joked that a keen nose could smell a submariner at 100 yards distance.

It was as Commodore of Submarines that Keyes showed his weakness in checking detail. Having decided, with his usual enthusiasm, to send some British submarines to Russia after war broke out in 1914, he neglected to tell the Russians. Neither did he mention the matter to the Admiralty nor the Foreign Office. Admiral von Essen, the Tsar's Commander-in-Chief at Petrograd maintained a distant politeness when he informed the British Naval Attaché that 'he would have been more pleased had he received timely notice of their coming, or been informed as to whose orders they were intended to be subordinate'.

Nor had Keyes arranged for the British vessels to receive fuel, stores, torpedoes or ammunition. Nothing, either, had been done to arrange adequate docking and maintenance. All in all, it was a sorry story of omission and mishap.

In February 1915, Keyes went to the Mediterranean Fleet as Chief of Staff. Admiral Sir Sackville Carden, its commander, was in failing health. He was invalided home. Keyes remained as Chief of Staff to the new Admiral, Sir John de Robeck.

Keyes had a front view seat when the Dardanelles campaign opened. The Navy failed to force the Narrows to Constantinople in this adventure so ardently advocated by Winston Churchill. Keyes had his own opinions as to what went wrong.

The use of troops was agreed. Keyes worked with Wemyss who was the naval officer responsible for the landings on the Gallipoli Peninsula. They became close friends.

By October, when it was excruciatingly clear that the Dardanelles expedition had failed, Keyes again put forward a plan he had originally suggested in August. He proposed a new naval attack. A strong fleet would force the passage through the Dardanelles and anchor off Constantinople. The Ottoman Empire would be defeated in short order. He was strongly supported by Wemyss. De Robeck would have none of it. Forcing the Dardanelles by ships alone had already proved a costly failure. De Robeck saw no major change from the plans which had been so disastrous in the spring. The only difference, he thought, was that the new scheme was prepared to accept calamitous losses to win through.

In November, Kitchener, the Minister of War, left London for the Gallipoli Peninsula to judge the situation for himself. He had agreed to meet Commodore Roger Keyes at Marseilles to discuss his plan. Keyes was unable to make the appointment. Kitchener sailed on. Keyes ended up in London. Keyes' diary makes it clear that he told his Admiral that he was impelled to push his ideas for a new naval attack. De Robeck apparently agreed that it was his duty so to do but emphasized that he personally did not agree with them.

While Keyes was in London, de Robeck received a telegram from the then First Lord of the Admiralty, Arthur Balfour. It proposed that he should take a holiday after all his hard work. He should, the First Lord suggested, hand over his command to an officer who would be prepared to reopen the naval offensive if so directed. The message stressed that de Robeck would return to his command at a later date.

De Robeck knew all about Keyes' influential friends. Not unnaturally, he thought that there was a conspiracy to replace him with his ambitious junior. He was neither the first nor the last officer to come to that bitter conclusion.

Keyes claimed that he was invited to explain his plan to the Board of Admiralty. Balfour asked him who he thought should command the effort. Keyes replied that Wemyss would be ideal as overall commander but that the actual forcing of the passage would do very well under his supervision.

One could question Keyes' loyalty to his Admiral. He had offered, according to his own account, to resign before he went to London but states firmly that de Robeck told him that it was his duty to push his case.

It was a curious incident. Keyes did not believe he was disloyal even though he was suggesting that his superior officer should be replaced by someone else, albeit for a limited period. De Robeck, according to Keyes, let the incident pass but he did not take kindly to rumours in the more excitable press, which suggested that the Navy would have done better if he and Keyes had exchanged places.

Wemyss did not take over.

Kitchener, appalled by what he saw, dithered but finally decided that withdrawal from Turkey was essential. The option of a new attempt by the Royal Navy to seize Constantinople vanished into thin air. Keyes never changed his belief that the Dardanelles withdrawal was 'one of the most disastrous and cowardly surrenders in the history of our country'.

With the collapse of the Gallipoli expedition, de Robeck reorganized his forces. One of Lloyd George's favourite fantasies, that of defeating Germany by entering through a back door, was well under way. Bulgaria had entered the war on the side of Germany. Britain and France sent troops to Salonika in response to pleas from Greece and Serbia. The Prime Minister's hope of a casualty-free advance through the Balkans to Berlin swiftly withered. The Bulgarians could dig trenches and man machine guns too.

Despite this setback, the enterprise had to be fed, supplied and cared for. Keyes was dealing with the sea communications for the Salonika front when de Robeck was asked to release him.

Keyes arrived in London to learn that his recall was a consequence of the Jutland battle. Casualties had pushed him to second on the captains' list. He could anticipate promotion to Rear Admiral in the very near future. It was suggested that he accept the command of HMS *Centurion*, serving with the Grand Fleet under Jellicoe.

If promoted, he could remain in command of his ship until an admiral's position became available. If he did not take a ship, he could not be freshly appointed to command one as a Rear Admiral if promotion arrived before the ship was ready. In such a case, he would have an indefinite period of unemployment.

Keyes went to *Centurion* at Scapa Flow. In November, Jellicoe was appointed First Sea Lord. Sir David Beatty replaced him. Admiral de Robeck took command of the 2nd Battle Squadron, an appointment which put Keyes under him once more.

Strangely, rumours began to circulate, early in 1917, that as soon as Keyes was promoted, he should take over the Dover Patrol. Nobody knew where they came from or how they started. Keyes himself was adamant that he wanted to stay with the Grand Fleet.

He was promoted Rear Admiral in April 1917. In June, the task of second in command of the 4th Battle Squadron fell to him. On leaving *Centurion*, the officers and warrant officers presented him with a teak casket containing a huge ensign made of silk. It was, the donors hoped, 'to be flown in battle'.

Although Keyes was confident that there would be a great fight between the British and German Fleets, in reality the chances of action were slim. Only if the High Seas Fleet ventured into the cold, dark waters of the North Sea would the Grand Fleet sail to meet them. Beatty might wish to sally out to trail his coat but Jellicoe would not risk the Fleet. The possibility of a German invasion, something which only the Grand Fleet could prevent, was never far from his mind. Then Wemyss was appointed to the Admiralty.

CHAPTER THREE

Keyes very quickly came into contact with the Zeebrugge problem during his first days in Whitehall. Haig's Flanders offensive, known to history as the Third Battle of Ypres or, more emotionally, Passchendaele had failed to throw back the Germans. The North Sea coast was still occupied by a determined enemy.

In addition to their ships and aircraft, Bruges, Zeebrugge and Ostend maintained substantial repair facilities. They were a safe haven for thirty or more destroyers and torpedo-craft and a similar number of submarines. The Imperial German Navy had fortified the triangle Bruges-Zeebrugge-Ostend to create a valuable asset. Extensive and well-equipped dock facilities returned severely damaged ships to sea in a very short time.

The ports were also a springboard. If the German High Seas Fleet ever did sail, Zeebrugge and Ostend could provide a host of support craft from minesweepers to torpedo-boats. Finally, their position, well into waters that the hard-pressed Harwich Force fought to keep under Allied domain saved the U-boats time and fuel, chopping off some 600 miles of return journey if they were forced to use bases in Germany.

Keyes was appalled when he saw the results of the U-boat onslaught on the Allied shipping. In general terms, seventy-five U-boats were at sea at any one time. They destroyed more than half a million tons of Allied and neutral shipping every month, losing no more than two of their number in the process.

To beat the menace two tasks were necessary. The first was the immediate job of stopping enemy submarines from passing through the Straits of Dover into Atlantic waters. The second was to root out the problem at source – to deny the Kaiser's Navy the use of the North Sea ports.

Keyes took his ideas to Jellicoe who passed them to Admiral Bacon for his comments. The First Sea Lord told Keyes to produce a proper Staff Appreciation to detail the resources necessary to implement his ideas. In the interim, Bacon was asked for his comments and proposals for offensive action against the harbours.

His response contained the germ that became the Zeebrugge Raid. Bacon suggested that the Mole, a long curving breakwater, be stormed from the seaward side. Assault parties would rush ashore to destroy the lock gates and anything else of use to the enemy that they found. How this could be done became the subject of another of the Admiral's incredibly detailed and well-considered proposals. Bacon thought a heavy monitor – he named the *Sir John Moore* as the ideal choice – could be fitted with a hinged ramp eighty feet long and ten feet wide. This would weigh some twenty tons. The ramp would be hinged at a point thirty-four feet from the inboard end. It would be held upright at a sixty degree angle when the monitor put to sea, kept in place by substantial cables. The *Sir John Moore* would have false bows able to withstand a thousand-ton shock.

Approaching Zeebrugge Harbour at a steady four knots – naturally behind a smokescreen – the monitor would ram the Mole head-on, the false bows acting as a fender and collapsing to absorb the impact. The crew would slacken the cables. The ramp would ease down onto the parapet which Bacon estimated would be about fifteen feet above the monitor's deck. The hinge of the ramp would rest on the parapet itself, allowing an enormous assault party to charge, eight abreast, up the thirty-degree slope of the first half of the ramp. They would then clatter down the forty-degree slant of the second half onto the Mole. The men would be heavily armed and laden with equipment. Many were to carry half-filled sandbags to set up defensive shelters from the anticipated enemy fire. Their progress down the steep slope on to the Mole would have been, without doubt, rather hasty. 'The impetus of the men down the slope,' observed Bacon solemnly, 'would have been an asset in launching the attack.'

To lessen the odds that the fearsome contraption would be chewed at by every piece of ordnance that a hard-faced enemy could muster, Bacon proposed a diversion. Bombarding the battery at Knokke might persuade the Germans that a landing was imminent there. The surmise and wild reactions that this would induce would allow the monitor to reach her target with little interference.

Bacon emphasized one point. Trying to put soldiers on the Mole by bringing a ship side-on to it would be useless. The swell of the water, even on the calmest sea, would be catastrophic to any attempt to land troops quickly. Swaying, narrow, shuddering gangplanks would not work. A huge bow ramp was the quickest way to get men ashore. Along with the untutored Confederate general, Nathan Bedford Forrest, Bacon knew that the essential was 'to git thar fustest with the mostest'.

Bacon suspected, not without cause, that Keyes coveted the command of the Dover Patrol. He had, in fact, been told by a friend in October 1917 that a clique at the Admiralty were conspiring for his removal and replacement by Keyes.

Bacon could console himself, though, with the knowledge that the Navy never appointed the officer who criticized another's performance, to take his place. It was a long-held and extremely practical custom. The Service could not function effectively if plotting held sway. British military organizations are not commercial firms in which successful scheming to remove the chief executive showers rewards upon the slaughterer.

Geddes began delicate moves to achieve his ends. In November, he set up the Channel Barrage Committee with Keyes as its head. This organization was tasked with examining ways of denying the Straits to enemy vessels. Bacon called it 'irresponsible'. Admirals commanded, not committees. As far as he was concerned, the Committee was 'a fifth wheel on the carriage' and of no use at all.

The Committee solemnly decided that a brilliantly lit and closely patrolled Channel would force the U-boats to dive below the shallow mine nets and into the deep minefield.

Bacon objected fiercely. He disliked Keyes and it showed. He did not mince his words. Illumination, he explained icily, would expose his own patrols to submarine or destroyer attacks. Neither did he have enough ships to patrol en masse along the approach to the Straits. A new minefield was being laid under a proposal which harked back to the previous February. Because of the erratic supply of mines it was only now that the new field was being put down.

On 15 December 1917, the Committee directly ordered the Vice Admiral to institute their ideas. The strongest guard possible, using ships withdrawn from Dunkirk if need be, with illuminations, must police the Channel entrance.

On 18 December, at the Admiralty, Bacon presented his plan to attack Zeebrugge. The idea of landing troops on the Mole itself immediately appealed to Keyes. The Board of Admiralty approved the plans. They told Bacon, officially, that he was to command a determined operation against Zeebrugge. The attack was to take place on 22

29

February 1918. The Vice Admiral returned to Dover to produce detailed proposals. There was no time to lose.

Keyes immediately hastened to Scapa Flow to arrange for volunteers from the Grand Fleet. Beatty, he knew, would be a fervent supporter of the scheme. Officers, seamen and stokers were needed. The Grand Fleet, spending most of its days swinging idly at anchor, was the place to find them.

The new flare and searchlight patrol brought immediate and dramatic results. On 19 December 1917, *UB 56* was driven into the mines and destroyed. Keyes was jubilant. Bacon was not convinced. The Committee might like to claim the credit but it was no more than the anticipated result of the plans previously made by Jellicoe and himself.

Christmas came closer. It would not be merry for some. Food shortages bit deep. Butchers slammed down their shutters. They had no stock. Several thousand people queued in the snow outside Smithfield Market from two in the morning in their hunt for meat. Housewives were urged to try horseflesh. Its consumption had bred several generations of gallant Belgians.

Not only meat was in short supply. Butter, plentiful in France, had almost disappeared from British tables. Soldiers sent packets home to their desperate relatives in England. It melted during the journey. Postmen complained of slimy packets with illegible addresses. Recipients accused postmen of stealing the contents when a flat, greasy package was finally dumped in their hands. Sir Douglas Haig issued a specific order to every man in his Army. No provisions or foodstuffs were to be posted home.

One irate mob of women besieged a local Food Control Office. Not even margarine was available. They were dispersed by the local police with the curt message that things were worse in Germany.

This was true. Britons might be hungry but Germans starved. Despite the privations, racehorses in Britain munched their way through the same generous amount of oats as they had before the war.

Geddes, urged on by Wemyss, decided that Bacon should go. Jellicoe objected. On 24 December 1917, the First Lord of the Admiralty showed his teeth. He solemnly informed the Prime Minister that he found it impossible to work with the First Sea Lord.

Lloyd George commiserated. And waited.

Geddes used the stiletto with the practised ease of a mediaeval assassin. On Christmas Eve, Jellicoe, the First Sea Lord, the professional head of the Royal Navy, discovered a letter on his desk. It was from the First Lord of the Admiralty. After the initial preamble, it stated baldly:

> After very careful consideration I have come to the conclusion that a change is desirable in the post of First Sea Lord. I have not, I can assure you, arrived at this view hastily or without great personal regret and reluctance. I have consulted with the Prime Minister and with his concurrence I am asking to see The King to make this recommendation . . .

Geddes had already arranged to motor to Sandringham the next day to take Christmas dinner with the King.

Jellicoe replied at once:

> You do not assign a reason for your action but I assume that it is due to a want of confidence in me.
> Under these conditions you will realise that it is difficult for me to continue my work . . . I shall therefore be glad to be relieved as soon as possible.

Wemyss took over. And Wemyss knew exactly what he was required to do. He sent for Keyes. The conversation between the two men was short and to the point:

> Well, Roger, you have talked a hell of a lot about what ought to be done in the Dover area. Now you must go down there and do it all yourself!

The Dover Patrol was no small command with more than 300 vessels. Dover itself supplied a harbour and workshops, a seaplane base, a Royal Naval Air Station and a collection of non-rigid airships for anti-submarine work. Across the Channel, a joint French and British force at Dunkirk came under Keyes' command.

Amongst the other odd remnants to which Keyes, immediately promoted to Vice Admiral, succeeded were two siege trains, equipped with extraordinarily large guns, manned respectively by the Royal Navy and the Royal Marines. The Dunkirk command also included a respectably sized aerodrome which was home to ninety aircraft.

Bacon was summoned from Dover again. He believed he was to present his final Zeebrugge plan to the assembled Sea Lords and politicians. Instead, he was brusquely told by Geddes that he was to hand over to the man who had plagued him with suggestions for the last three months. Like Jellicoe, Bacon was forced to accept an unholy breach of one of the Navy's most dearly-cherished beliefs – that while the system may allow an officer to bring about the downfall of another, it will not tolerate him benefiting by the other's misfortune.

Bacon was simply abandoned. It was customary for an Admiral, on leaving office, to receive a Letter of Appreciation from the First Lord. There was none. Neither did Bacon receive the accepted courtesy of an interview with the Sovereign on relinquishing his post. It might have been interesting. Bacon, like Wemyss, had been in the same entry as King George at the Naval College. The new First Sea Lord stayed discreetly out of the way while his old classmate was sacrificed.

Less than twenty-five years later, Air Chief Marshal Hugh Dowding, who commanded the fighters of the Royal Air Force during the Battle of Britain, suffered the same brutal fate. His successor, too, was generally thought to have conspired and schemed to inherit the post as C.-in-C., Fighter Command. Churchill had never forgiven Dowding for refusing to send his last remaining Hurricanes to support a rapidly crumbling France. Subsequent victory over Herman Göring's Luftwaffe was not enough to save him.

Both Bacon and Dowding failed to realize that politicians will embrace expediency in preference to tradition. Keyes wrote later with what could be interpreted as stunning naivety or total hypocrisy but what was probably simple honesty:

> . . . it seemed hardly decent that I should be sent to fill a vacancy which my own relentless efforts had caused . . . Admiral Bacon . . . came back to my room apparently quite unperturbed and as friendly as ever. He said he thought the change had better take place at once – could I come down to Dover the following day? I felt so fearfully sorry for him, and greatly admired the way he took his knock.

Bacon may have looked apparently quite unperturbed but Keyes had made a lifelong enemy. It was not until 1934 that Bacon was finally awarded a pension. Not surprisingly, the first captain of HMS *Dreadnought*, a former and well-respected Director of Naval Ordnance, turned his back on the Navy which he had loved and served loyally. Bacon recorded later:

> If a country is to get the best from its Admirals and Generals it should see that they are treated with at least as much consideration as is usually accorded to domestic servants . . . A First Lord, handicapped by possessing neither political nor departmental

experience, was set over a Service of peculiar traditions and sentiments; for as the sea differs from the land, so the ruling of sea officers differs from that of railway servants. Suddenly to supersede a First Sea Lord and install in his office his assistant is without precedent . . .

Exactly a fortnight before the day on which the First Lord informed me of my supersession, he expressed to me his sense of the great work I had done at Dover and the hope that nothing would ever cause a break between the Admiralty and myself.

Neither did Bacon countenance the criticism of the manner in which he commanded the Dover Patrol:

We had maintained sea communications with the Armies in France without intermission in spite of destroyers, submarines, mines and aircraft, and our commerce had passed as freely and with almost equal security to and from the Thames as it did in peace time.

Sir Reginald could point to the undisputed fact that, during his three years as Commander, 120,000 merchant ships had passed through the Straits. Fifty had been destroyed by mines. A mere five had been torpedoed. Just one had been destroyed by German gunfire. It was a remarkable record.

Lloyd George showed his satisfaction with the turn of events. 'Among the fruits of this rearrangement,' he observed, 'may be reckoned the carrying through of the attack on Zeebrugge and Ostend by the Dover Patrol Force under Keyes – one of the most gallant and spectacular achievements of the War.'

The reader of his *Memoirs* was allowed to draw the obvious conclusion. Without a farsighted Prime Minister, there would have been no Zeebrugge Raid. Like many politicians who came after him, Lloyd George enjoyed basking in the reflected limelight of military success.

Mendacity and double-dealing aside, Lloyd George had the perfect reason for preferring expediency to tradition. He had to win a war or, at the very least, end it on reasonably favourable terms. With the sometimes reluctant assistance of the War Cabinet, he expanded the bounds of political control over the conduct of the fighting. Lloyd George's reasoning was simple. The end always justifies the means.

The belief that politicians can intervene in the actual conduct of the war, as opposed to providing the means by which to wage it, became firmly rooted in the twentieth century. Prime Ministers and Presidents, after all, can tell themselves they hold office because of the enthusiastic will of the populace. Generals, admirals and air marshals reach eminence only by showing a modicum of professional ability.

Abraham Lincoln had been ready to let his generals see to the combat whilst he dealt with the politics. Lloyd George believed that war was too momentous a matter to be left to the military. He meddled in matters which were the province of generals and admirals. His belief that a Prime Minister had the right to decide on such matters encouraged his successors to interfere in the conduct of later wars.

It was common gossip among US pilots in Vietnam that their President sat up in bed at night to choose the ground attack targets for the next day. Their military value was often negligible but that mattered little. The generals were told how to fight the war. Lloyd George, one suspects, would have approved.

On New Year's Day 1918, *The Times* filled three-and-a-half pages of small print with recipients of awards in the newly created Most Excellent Order of the British Empire. Described as 'Democracy's Own Order', it nonetheless retained the five classes of more established orders together with an innovation. A medal was introduced, intended essentially for munitions workers.

The new Order, with its motto *For God And Empire*, was the first to admit women on equal terms with men. It introduced a rank for women, equivalent to that of knight. Women could now aspire to the title of Dame.

Amongst the recipients of the Order of the British Empire was an obscure Wing Commander in the Royal Naval Air Service. His name was Frank Arthur Brock. He had founded and still commanded the Royal Naval Experimental Station. To the Navy, he was a very important man. Still young, he had a mind which embraced the needs of a scientific war. He got his award because the Navy needed him and wanted to show its appreciation.

The uneasy wind of a bitter New Year's Day sent grubby scraps of litter scurrying along the quayside at Chatham Royal Naval Dockyard. An aged light cruiser swayed gently at anchor in the greasy water. HMS *Vindictive*. Built at Chatham, commissioned in 1898, she was considered too old for front line service. Most of the dockyard workers thought that Chatham would be not only her birthplace but her graveyard.

She was not alone. *Thetis*, *Iphigenia*, *Brilliant*, *Intrepid* and *Sirius* were also on the Admiralty's list of outdated vessels. New technology had done for them.

To the north, on the Mersey, two fat civilian ferry-boats, *Daffodil* and

34

Iris bustled about their daily business. Double-hulled, broad of beam, they were built to last.

Vindictive, Thetis, Iphigenia, Brilliant, Intrepid, Sirius, Daffodil, Iris. Their names were hardly known to the general public. But Roger John Brownlow Keyes, commanding the Dover Patrol, would change all that.

CHAPTER FOUR

Keyes had no illusions about his new command. His hold on it depended on how quickly he got to grips with the U-boat problem. Block the Channel passage. Close off the North Sea ports. It was not a great deal to ask.

He had a cool reception at Dover. Not all of his officers were happy with the sudden change of command. Bacon was far from unpopular with his staff. He was widely respected as being a fair-minded man with an even temper – not necessarily common qualities amongst senior officers of either the Army or the Navy.

Some officers of the Dover Patrol suspected that favouritism and skulduggery had played a part in his replacement. A few believed that there had been a squalid and disgraceful conspiracy.

Keyes' first objective was to make the Straits impassable to the enemy. The plan was simple. Discard the nets. Illuminate the area with searchlights and flares. There would be new minefields, laid at varying depths, whilst the Straits would be patrolled by every surface craft available. Keyes' suggestions were not a million miles away from those proposed by his predecessor. Most were already in effect. Bacon, though, had been adamant that too much illumination would not merely indicate the limits of the minefield but put the patrolling vessels in danger from hit-and-run raids. Bacon preferred searchlights which would not blind the lookouts. Keyes decided flares were the answer.

Keyes claimed that he was greeted with no little hostility by the destroyer captains who maintained firmly that the U-boats preferred not to chance the Channel passage. The new Admiral, by his own account, produced the intelligence report, quoting heavily from the document retrieved from *UC 44*. He made his attitude very clear. He would, as he was fully entitled to do, get his own way, come what may.

Keyes alleged that the memorandum citing the *UC 44* instructions came as a surprise and disconcerted the captains of the Dover Patrol. Bacon had, Keyes suggested, simply dismissed it. It was the first instance of what became a regular habit of denigrating his predecessor to his close staff.

Captain Herbert Grant, his Staff Intelligence Officer, had been a cadet at *Britannia* with Keyes. He had detested him then. The passing years had not changed his opinion. On hearing of Keyes' appointment to replace Bacon, Grant wrote, 'I thought the Admiralty had gone mad. Later (when I was) at the Admiralty, I was convinced that Sir Reginald had been ousted by as despicable an intrigue as ever occurred in the annals of war . . .'.

One always has to be careful in assessing the remembrances of an officer who freely admits that he disliked his superior. Even so, Grant's comment that 'Keyes seemed to delight . . . in belittling his predecessor's views' is borne out by others in the Dover Patrol.

It is peculiarly difficult, in the middle of a war, for an officer to resign purely because he disagrees with his superior. His duty is clearly to the Country and his Service. One, though, did feel strongly enough to ask to leave. Evans of the *Broke*, promoted captain to serve as Bacon's Chief of Staff, displayed a fierce loyalty to his former chief. Like Grant, Evans was convinced that Keyes' appointment was the result of some extremely distasteful manoeuvres. He asked for an immediate transfer. Keyes agreed on the ostensible face-saving grounds of sickness.

Other officers, especially the more junior ones, were quite content to let the in-fighting go on without them. Dover was a good posting. A married officer could live contentedly on shore; single officers had London within their grasp. Better Dover than Scapa Flow or some benighted port on the Northumbrian coast.

The new procedures went into effect. Supported by Admiralty directives, Keyes requisitioned every mine he could find. Wing Commander Brock was instructed to develop more and better flares.

Brock deserved to be described as a genius. Aged just thirty-four, he was from the family which had created Britain's largest firework concern. He did more than create excellent pyrotechnics. He played rugby for Richmond, was an authority on antiquarian books and prints, an excellent shot and an enthusiastic stamp collector. He was both inventor and engineer.

Pretending to be an American tourist, he went to Germany in 1914 to take a close look at the Zeppelin airships. The result of his investigation was an incendiary bullet with which to shoot them down. He produced remarkably good and powerful signal flares and developed the flameless smokescreen for the Navy. Before Brock looked at the problem, the Navy's apparatus produced large flames which lit up the ship, a disconcerting habit which was particularly inconvenient during a night action. Brock's smoke did have the discouraging side effect of being mildly poisonous but this was a small price to pay for a suitable product.

In the first four weeks that Keyes commanded the Dover Patrol, five U-boats were destroyed in the Channel. One was spotted as it submerged. A series of depth charges sealed its fate. The other four, pinned in the searchlights or flares dived into the minefield with the inevitable result.

The Intelligence Department forbade any details being released. Admiral Hall wanted the Germans to be kept in the dark. If they had no idea whether submarines were trapped in the Channel, destroyed by Q-ships or sunk by destroyers, the morale of the U-boat crews would slide downwards at a fast rate. He knew that the U-boat Officers' Club in Bruges had a motto prominently displayed. *One lives but a short time and one is a long time dead. Enjoy life while you may is the counsel of the wise.* Hall was determined that German submariners should view every trip as their last.

Keyes was not unhappy with his first month's work. He felt he could now fully concentrate on his plan to reduce Zeebrugge and Ostend. The routine of the Dover Patrol was handed to his new Chief of Staff, an old friend from Boxer Rising days, Captain the Honourable Algernon Boyle. At Keyes' request, Boyle was gazetted Commodore.

Another old acquaintance joined Keyes from the Grand Fleet. Captain Wilfred Tomkinson came south to become, as far as official-dom was concerned, Destroyer Fleet Captain. In practice, he was the trusted aide of the new commander of the Dover Patrol.

Tomkinson had been Keyes' First Lieutenant on HMS *Fame* during the Boxer War. He was with Keyes when the four Chinese destroyers were captured. He was at his captain's side when the Taku Fort was blown up and he took command of *Fame* when Keyes slid through the Peking sluice-gates into the British Legation.

Eight years later, Tomkinson was Keyes' First Lieutenant again, this time on HMS *Venus*. When Keyes moved on to become Inspector-General of Submarines, Tomkinson was a Flotilla Leader before taking command of HMS *Lurcher*. This was the destroyer Keyes chose as his flagship as Commodore.

Although they served in different theatres when Keyes was in the Dardanelles, it was Tomkinson who became captain of HMS *Colossus* which was Keyes' flagship in the Grand Fleet.

Even while Keyes was settling in, the Admiralty had proceeded on the basis of Bacon's plan. On 8 January 1918, the 4th Battalion of the Royal Marines was raised. They would form the major part of the striking force to land on the Mole. Keyes had to work out how this could be achieved.

Important though the attack on Zeebrugge was, other events demanded Keyes' full attention. On the night of 14–15 February 1918 the German Navy showed it was uncowed by the arrival of a new and thrusting commander at Dover. More specifically, the new flare barrier in the Straits was a massive inconvenience to the Zeebrugge boats. After urgent appeals from the *Flotille Flandern*, the destroyers of *Nr II Torpedobootsflotille* were detached from the High Seas Fleet to deal with the situation.

Kapitän zur See Heinecke led two half-flotillas down to the Straits. At 00.55 hours they struck like hungry panthers at both ends of the line of patient trawlers and drifters patrolling the entrance to the Straits. One trawler and seven drifters went to the bottom; a paddle steamer and three more drifters were severely damaged. The German destroyers linked up in the middle of the line and snarled home. The night's activity cost the Dover Patrol seventy-six officers and men killed and thirteen wounded.

Keyes had created an elaborate plan for a series of warning signals if the Germans came. These would unleash his own destroyers. The system failed. His fury was uncontrolled perhaps not least because the casualties of the German raid were as bad as anything that Bacon had endured. There was also, in Keyes' opinion, a whiff even of cowardice. That was something he would not tolerate.

A Court of Inquiry was convened into the conduct of the commanding officers of HMS *Termagant* and HMS *Amazon*. Both officers had made a series of errors. Their Admiral determined they would suffer.

The findings of the Inquiry decided Keyes. He informed the Admiralty that there would be a court martial. For good measure, he wanted to dismiss the commanding officer of the monitor *M 26* which was in the vicinity at the time. There was little or no evidence against him but Keyes detested any suggestion of a lack of fortitude. He was dissuaded from this course of action when he learned that the monitor's captain had a double DSO, one of which had been awarded for a Q-ship action. Being a decoy for U-boats was no task for the faint-hearted. Even so, Keyes vented his spleen to Beatty in a letter, giving it as his private opinion that the monitor captain had no stomach for action.

The unfortunate Lieutenant Adam Ferguson, a regular officer, of

HMS *Amazon* was duly tried. The evidence stated that *Amazon* reported to *Termagant* that three Allied destroyers, without lights, had just passed, steering east. *Termagant*'s watch officer enquired how *Amazon* knew that they were friendly vessels. He received the startling reply that they had not replied to *Amazon*'s challenge.

The court considered its verdict. Lieutenant Ferguson was found guilty of being 'negligent in the performance of his duty' and sentenced to be severely reprimanded. The court also voiced its disapproval of *Termagant*'s captain who, they believed, should have turned his ship towards the intruders and investigated the strange vessels.

Keyes was not prepared to accept the sentence. He badgered the Admiralty for a harsher punishment. Ferguson was dismissed his ship. For all practical purposes, his seagoing career was finished.

A frisson of distaste and outrage rippled through the officers of the Dover Patrol. They had yet to understand that their new Admiral was a man of single-minded purpose. He had only one design – to utterly destroy the enemy. Nothing would be allowed to impede that aim. Keyes judged both superiors and subordinates in the same way. They either agreed or disagreed with him. Seniors who disagreed were either obstructionists or incompetents or both. Juniors were removed or browbeaten into acquiescence.

The British military throws up such obsessive characters with unbroken regularity. Douglas Bader was one. Orde Wingate was another. James Wolfe, the hero of Quebec, was reputedly a third. Usually, they are either loved or detested by those who serve with them. One thing, though, is certain. They carry out the fight with unremitting vigour.

The new Vice Admiral had other worries than the devastated career of a junior officer. If the Zeebrugge attack was to succeed – and even if it never happened – something had to be done about the abysmal standard of the coastal bombardments by the monitors. There were no systems of ranging available which did not depend on somebody being able to actually see the target and log the fall of each round. Neither was gyroscopic direction control in use. It was, sadly too often, a matter of by guess and by God.

The same problem had dogged the Dardanelles operations. The infantry's opinion of Naval support was markedly rude. A Commander Henry Douglas of the Hydrographical Department had worked wonders there. Assisted by Lieutenant Commander Francis Haselfoot, he had produced a most effective method of establishing the relative positions of ship to target. The gun crews had learned and their accuracy improved remarkably. The infantry continued to grumble but were less unkind about the Navy's ability to hit the target.

The need to develop a similar skill within the Dover Patrol was essential if the German batteries on the Belgian coast were ever to be brought under control. Keyes asked. Keyes got. Douglas, now a Captain, and Haselfoot arrived at Dover and went to work.

They very soon discovered that the available navigational charts were of little use for their black art. They needed detail. That meant large-scale charts. The French and Belgians, as well as the Admiralty, all had bits of information. Douglas and Haselfoot accumulated every snippet and produced their own maps. Within a very short while, they were spending dark nights in a motor launch off the Belgian coast, plotting the position of every German battery they found.

Once that was done, Douglas drew up a table and diagram from which range and bearing could be worked out very quickly from given data. This was what they had done at Gallipoli. The theory was that the German batteries would learn a harsh lesson.

Better was to come. On a visit to Dunkirk, Keyes spoke with a Commander Altham, who commanded a monitor. Altham mentioned that he had invented a gyroscopic director, a device which made it possible for guns to be laid on any true bearing without the fiddling need for aiming marks. The invention had gone to Admiral Bacon for approval. Bacon was warm in his praise but replaced before he could take further action. Keyes resurrected the device. Within two months, the new system was ready.

Keyes had already begun to assess the difficulties of an assault on the harbours in his short time at the Admiralty. What he now had to do was to produce a plan which would have the backing of Wemyss.

Bruges was the operational headquarters of the German Military Zone which extended from the Dutch frontier down to the Allied front lines at Nieuwpoort. The thrusting and vigorous commander of this zone, Admiral von Schröder – dubbed the 'Lion of Flanders' by an admiring Press – commanded a formidable array of troops and gun batteries to defend his fiefdom.

The town was one tip of a triangle Bruges-Zeebrugge-Ostend. An eight-mile long canal linked the town to Zeebrugge. Ostend was reached by an eleven-mile long canal. Along the Bruges-Zeebrugge route, the Germans had dug out a series of submarine shelters. Roofed with corrugated iron covered with turf, they deceived the cameras of the RNAS reconnaissance aircraft.

Bruges itself was safe from attack from the sea. It was eight miles inland. Any attempt to get close enough inshore to bombard it would be met by the resistance of the 173 guns which were the armament of the forty-four *Matrosen* and *Marine Artillerie* batteries which ran along the shoreline from Nieuwpoort to Knokke. The guns ranged from a modest 3.5-inch calibre to 15-inch monsters. They could accurately deal with any intruder up to fifteen miles out to sea. The Germans had added heavily to the modest Belgian defences of 1914. Wretched, half-starved, ill-treated Russian prisoners of war had laboured in appalling conditions to create concrete bunkers and emplacements. Elsewhere, German and Belgian contractors, some with forced labour but all making handsome profits, had built substantial fortresses for even more guns. The Germans made it very clear that they had come to stay.

The battery names alone sounded like the crack of doom. *Tirpitz*, *Preussen*, *Eylau*, *Freya*, *Württemberg* and, inevitably, *Kaiser Wilhelm II*. Because gunners are sentimental men at heart, they named the individual guns for wives, daughters, sweethearts and tiny children. *Erica*, *Heidi*, *Marlene*, *Maria*. Some guns – those with the loudest bark – were nicknamed *Schwiegermutti*, for mothers-in-law are the same the world over.

Machine-gun nests spotted the long miles of dunes. Barbed wire menaced intruders. German marines and sailors manned the positions. These were no second- or third-rate troops. Well-trained, well-equipped, they were formidable opponents. Admiral von Schröder's Marine and Naval Infantry Regiments supported the artillery. All of them were spoiling for a fight.

The easy answer was to put the ports out of action. The difficult question was how it could be done. Keyes decided that at Zeebrugge, the lock-gates, the canal-mouth and the basin were vulnerable. Ostend could be closed by blockships.

Applying the solution was not easy. The first snag was the distance between Dover and Zeebrugge. The two harbours were seventy-two miles apart. This was a considerable journey for an attacking force. Some of the crossing would inevitably be in daylight. A single German aircraft, a lone U-boat, a fishing smack flying neutral colours, was enough to alert the defences.

An attempt to block the Bruges-Zeebrugge canal or ram the lock-gates demanded big ships. These would, of necessity, be of fairly deep draught. Unfortunately, the coast off Zeebrugge was riddled with sandbanks on which a large vessel could go aground. Each tide changed the layout.

Before the war, the banks were surveyed continually. Marker buoys were constantly repositioned as the sand swirled into new positions. It was said that a harbour pilot who took a month's leave had to spend a week on his return learning the alterations.

The occupying Germans blithely removed the buoys or let them drift free. One channel from the Zeebrugge lock-gates to the open sea was kept dredged. The Imperial Navy used vessels of shallow draught – nothing bigger than a destroyer – and sat back with their collection of guns and hard-faced Marines to await anybody who was crazy enough to try to attack.

Keyes looked at the aerial reconnaissance photographs. He studied charts of the harbour approaches. He consulted Belgian refugees who knew the harbour. Reports trickled in from spies around the harbour areas although the valuable *Knapen* network was rounded up by the Germans at the beginning of February. Despite this intelligence blow, slowly a plan formed.

The distances were formidable. The mouth of the Zeebrugge canal where it reached the coast was 116 yards, the length of a full-size football pitch. Each side of the mouth two curving piers, both about 270 yards in length, extended into the harbour. A ship entering the mouth between the two piers was still some half-mile from the lock-gates inland.

Keyes only reluctantly discarded thoughts of a ship ramming the lock-gates despite all odds. He did, in fact, return to the idea more than once. Every preceding plan had made the same point. The only reliable way to cut Bruges from its satellite port was to damage the lock-gates beyond easy repair.

The single route was along an unreliable dredged channel. Slow running and careful navigation – quite possibly in the dark – was essential. All in all, the defenders would have plenty of time to destroy an intruder.

Keyes at last decided that, instead of trying to ram the lock-gates, the canal entrance could be blocked. The raiders would still need to sail between the piers. Rather than proceed the full half-mile to the lock-gates, however, they need only to reach the coastline, less than half the distance. Once there, the blockships could neatly turn through ninety degrees and sink themselves across the entrance channel.

Potential disasters stalked through this seemingly easy alternative. Turning a 300-foot long ship in a 350-foot wide channel is rather difficult. Car drivers may consider it to be no more than the equivalent of a three-point turn. In fact, with no brakes, steering that responds only slowly, a pitch-dark night and the inhabitants of the banks on either side doing their level best to kill the crew, the whole enterprise was strictly dubious.

Blocking the entrance channel, in Keyes' opinion, nonetheless offered distinct possibilities. Aerial photographs revealed that the German occupiers, either by intent or lack of enthusiasm, had allowed silt to build up on either side of the dredged channel at the canal mouth. Keyes decided that blockships could be sunk at an angle in the mouth, their bows and sterns driven as far as possible into the sandbanks. More silt would then accumulate around the hulls until the full width of the entrance was blocked.

Accurately positioning the blockships was a major difficulty. Keyes was confident it could be done. It was true that the Navy had never, in its long and honourable history, placed a blockship in the exact spot required but there was always a first time.

Sailing into Zeebrugge Harbour to set a ship in a precise location on an evilly black night required seamanship and navigation of a very high order. If the defences were anything more than a very aged soldier eating a spiced sausage sandwich, life for the intruding crews would suddenly be exceptionally hazardous. Nevertheless, the basic idea was formed in Keyes' mind. Blocking the channel rather than destroying the lock-gates, he decided, was the easier option.

The blockships needed a diversion to give them a good chance of reaching their target. Otherwise, the defences would simply concentrate on blowing the intruders out of the water. If the diversion worked and the blockships reached the canal, they could go like fury towards the lock-gates. A study of the aerial pictures would have shown Keyes that the canal banks were less heavily defended than many observers believed. The defences were not geared to the concept of a blockship getting that far. Once in the canal, the chances of reaching the gates were very much enhanced. Reaching the canal was the difficulty.

Keyes adopted Bacon's idea of assaulting the Mole itself. This would certainly attract the attention of the defences. An air raid, as an additional item, would add to the confusion.

The Zeebrugge Mole, the largest in the world, was formidable. As any fluent speaker of classical Latin will immediately explain, the word comes from 'moles' which means 'massive structure'. This was a most accurate description of the enormous breakwater which jutted out into the North Sea to protect the harbour.

It began at the coastline about a half-mile west of the canal entrance, a great concrete finger, curving north-east in an arc one-and-a-half miles long and of approximately one-mile radius. Its total length was a little under two miles.

The Mole had four main sections. Its first 300 yards consisted of a causeway which carried a footpath, a roadway and a twin-track railway. These continued onto a steel viaduct also about 300 yards long. The viaduct served a vital purpose. The tide raced between the web of supporting steel girders to scour the harbour and prevent it silting up.

At the end of the viaduct came the Mole proper. Eighty yards wide, paved with granite, it was more than a mile long. On the seaward side was a concrete wall, about sixteen feet high and ten feet thick. Along the top of the parapet ran a nine-feet wide road. This was protected from the wind by another parapet, this time four feet high, on the seaward side.

Even at high tide, the top of the second parapet stood thirty feet above the surface of the water. The most optimistic estimate suggested that a ship's deck would be at best, a minimum of fifteen feet below the parapet.

At the end of the breakwater was the Mole extension. A narrow stone pier, 1000 feet long, continued to carry the upper roadway – still protected by its own four-foot parapet – to the lighthouse which marked the harbour entrance.

Aerial photographs confirmed that across the approach to the extension, facing the land, were concrete emplacements which undoubtedly housed machine-gun posts.

At least six guns sat on the extension. Two were thought to be 3.5-inch, four were 4.1-inch. A suspicious object near the lighthouse was probably a large 6-inch cannon to fire star shell. If this guess was correct, it could light the whole harbour with a certain emphasis.

Three 5.9-inch guns on the end of the main section of the Mole guarded the harbour and entrance. Any unauthorized vessel steaming blithely past the lighthouse would be within point-blank range. It took no great imagination to realize that any intruder would be blown out of the water in short order.

To the Mole's peacetime buildings of a railway station, two large goods sheds and docking and unloading facilities, the Germans added four aircraft hangars, a long submarine shelter, a seaplane base and living quarters for the permanent garrison of the Mole.

There were more guns on the Mole itself. Some were 'Quakers' or dummy guns. Even the keenest eyes could not tell which was which from the reconnaissance photographs brought back by the air service.

45

Distinguishing between real and fake was a job that could only be done on the ground. Something nasty could be lurking on the concrete.

No great tactical brain was needed to decide that an assault party must land as close to the batteries as possible and, ideally, behind the concrete emplacements which faced down the Mole. Surprise was essential. That alone meant that the invading ships needed a most efficient smokescreen. The attackers had to be ashore so rapidly that the defence could not react quickly enough. Keyes estimated that the Mole garrison could be as large as 1000 men. They would not, thankfully, be congregated at the end of the Mole. A swift attack there would probably face no more than a bunch of gunners with a handful of support troops.

Keyes decided that a concrete building near the end of the Mole was the way in. The roof looked as if it was level with the parapet roadway. The building, which Keyes thought was probably a barrack room was close to the guns at the end of the Mole and the batteries on the extension. It was behind the machine-gun nests. It had to be the place to strike.

Keyes reviewed his decisions.

The solution to the Zeebrugge problem was blockships in the mouth of the canal. There were clear navigational problems in getting them to the correct position with the addition of a sinister unknown factor. Mines. The Germans would undoubtedly have mined the approaches to the harbour. Keyes was sure that the Navy would find a clear channel to the canal mouth and sweep a path through any minefield.

The assault must be at night if the blockships were to have any chance of reaching their target, preferably when there was little moon. Timings had to allow the escorting vessels to be safely out of range of the coastal guns by first light.

The blockships, inhibited by their draught, needed to enter the Zeebrugge canal approximately ninety minutes either side of high tide. With this restriction, and the requisite darkness, an attack was possible only between 22.30 hours and 01.30 hours on four or five nights in the lunar month. Even then, favourable weather conditions were vital. A light onshore wind was essential to blow the smokescreen towards the defences to foil the inevitable searchlights, flares and star shells.

Navigation to both Zeebrugge and Ostend would be by dead reckoning. No lights, no marker buoys, no aids. The attacking flotillas would have to cope with cross-currents in an area of minefields and shifting sands. It was another area in which specialist knowledge would be useful.

If landing parties attacked the junction of the Mole end and the extension, some could advance seawards along the roadway to the lighthouse and destroy the guns there. Others could dash across the roof of the apparent barracks, then drop fifteen feet or so to the Mole surface to attack the Mole end batteries from the rear. Having rendered the 5.9-inch guns useless, and being inside the fortified zone, they could rush the machine-gun posts before advancing down the Mole. By destroying the Mole installations they would divert the defenders on the shore from noticing a threat to the canal mouth. The raiding troops, Keyes calculated, should finish their work within an hour.

With perfect conditions and absolute success attending the attack on the Mole, the blockships could be inside the canal before the Germans realized what was happening.

The plan, to become reality, required only a large assault ship capable of transporting several hundred men with all their equipment. It should draw little water to minimize the hazard of mines. It needed armour for, although it would approach the seaward side of the Mole, there could be heavy defensive fire. In a perfect world, if complete surprise was achieved, not a shot would be fired by the enemy before British bayonets were piercing their throats.

Keyes had already decided that the coastal batteries could be lulled into a sense of acceptance if monitors attacked them in a series of night engagements. If they began at the same time and fired for a set period each night, the enemy would soon assume it was normal practice. This would slow their reactions and leave them unprepared for the close-quarter action of the assault.

Keyes made one vital addition to the plan for Zeebrugge. The noise and confusion would undoubtedly attract enemy reinforcements to the scene. Destroying the viaduct would create both short- and long-term difficulties. Most important of all, it would stop the arrival of fresh troops from the shore garrison.

The plan relied not only on achieving surprise. It also assumed that the defence would be less than alert. This is a dangerous assumption when Germans are involved. No credible assessment of the opposition appears to have been made. The men manning the guns were not weary reservists dreaming of home and pension. They were the products of a harsh school of training. They were all very competent young men who were, of course, prepared to die for their country. They did, however, consider it infinitely preferable if they ensured that the enemy died for his.

Ostend was less complicated. There was no Mole. The harbour

defence relied on its coast artillery. Thirteen batteries guarded Ostend – the *Friedrich*, *Ludendorf* and *Irene* batteries of 11-inch guns, together with a daunting companion in the form of the *Jacobynessen* battery with 15-inch guns were within 5000 yards of the harbour entrance. A selection of light artillery and machine-gun nests, including a pair of ancient Gatling guns on the piers at the mouth of the Bruges-Ostend canal, dotted the area. Either side of the harbour entrance, scattered along the sands which had been so attractive to Belgian society before the war, were clusters of machine-gun and searchlight posts. Ostend was no easy target either.

Even so, as long as the blockships found the harbour entrance, they could sail directly into position. There were, of course, sandbanks and other impedimenta but there was, in Keyes' view, neither a need nor the possibility, of a diversion. An attack on Ostend would have to rely on surprise alone.

Only one thing was certain: the dock facilities of Zeebrugge and Ostend must be destroyed.

CHAPTER FIVE

Keyes' ideal assault ship was a fast, shallow draught vessel. A steam packet, able to fit snugly against a stone quay, was the perfect answer. None of a sufficient size, though, were immediately available. Keyes had no time to waste. If obstructions and difficulties could not be demolished without delay, one simply took another route. If a suitable civilian ship could not be commandeered, he would find something from within the Navy.

The search had begun in January. Wemyss sent a personal note. There were six light cruisers, built in Victoria's reign, which could certainly become blockships. One of them might serve as the assault vessel. Of the six available, the 5600-ton HMS *Vindictive* was close to hand at Chatham. She was a coal burner, well able to make the return trip to Zeebrugge with less than full bunkers.

Keyes inspected her. She would do. He was well familiar with the class. A sister ship, HMS *Arrogant*, was under his control, serving as a mother ship to the motor launches and 'E' class submarines.

Vindictive was far from perfect for her new role. She had led an undistinguished career. Launched in 1897 and commissioned one year later, she served with the Mediterranean Fleet until 1904. After that, she moved with her crew of 430 men to the Dockyard Reserve. She then went to the Nore Division of the Home Fleet before successively being part of the 3rd and 4th Divisions. Her last active service was as tender to HMS *Albion* and HMS *Vernon*, the torpedo school.

She was not outstandingly elegant. Three pompous funnels poked skywards from a huddle of gigantic ventilators. Two slender masts suggested that her designer was not totally convinced that the age of steam had arrived. They implied canvas could be hoisted if ever the coal ran out. Her looks, though, were not the drawback. That was her draught. She grounded in less than nineteen feet of water. If she ran into a shallow minefield – and nobody was at all sure which areas outside

Zeebrugge had been mined by the resourceful enemy – her bottom would be ripped apart.

Keyes knew his predecessor had also been offered the old ship as the assault vessel. Bacon had turned her down without discussion. Apart from her draught, she was able only to go alongside the Mole, not hit it bow-on. The flood of troops which Bacon considered essential for a successful attack would be reduced to a mere trickle. Worse, she did not have enough space to carry all the assault troops nor anywhere for them to shelter before they stormed ashore. One can only assume that Keyes either did not consider, or did not believe that, a bow-on assault was necessary. He was the admiral. It was his judgement. His eagerness to get the operation under way pushed aside any objections. As it was, he had to find auxiliary assault ships to carry the rest of the men.

Keyes certainly knew Bacon's thinking. His predecessor had sent a long memorandum about the problems associated with an attack on the North Sea harbours. Bacon may have been smarting at his brusque dismissal but he was fiercely loyal to his country and to the Navy. He warned Keyes about the difficulties of the tides and the need for perfect navigation. The North Sea had its own particular treacheries. Bacon passed on his hard-won experience without rancour.

If Keyes had any reservations about *Vindictive*'s suitability, he certainly did not reveal them in a letter to Sir David Beatty. On 4 February 1918, he had written in enthusiastic terms both about the ship and the operation:

> . . . her boat deck is level with the Mole, her lower fighting top stands 12 feet above it – other machine gun positions will be fitted aloft – also liquid fire ejectors and flammenwerfers – I have been urged to use gas but am not going to.
>
> A thousand thanks for your promise of help, without it I don't think we could take it in with any great confidence – now I am absolutely full of it! And am delighted to know that the Grand Fleet is going to share in an enterprise, which if it fails even, and it is not going to, can only bring credit to the Service.
>
> Anyhow, I'd much rather go under or be superceded (*sic*) having tried it, than sit here content to act on the defensive.

Suitable vessels with a shallow draught were an urgent requirement. Large packet ships might not be to hand but smaller ships could be requisitioned.

Grant, despite his antipathy to Keyes, was a loyal officer who did his duty to the best of his considerable ability. He recalled that Mersey ferries would probably be suitable. He remembered two by name. He suggested to Keyes that the Admiralty promptly requisition the *Lily* and the *Rose*.

Keyes decided that Grant should visit Liverpool in person. Civilian authorities were notoriously touchy about handing over their property to the military. There was always the vexed question of compensation should they be damaged during their Service careers. It would be better if the ferry company were asked to help rather than ordered to hand over their ships.

Grant acquiesced with some reluctance. Dover to Liverpool was a tiresome journey. He had more than enough work to do. But an admiral's order is equivalent to an instruction from the Almighty or, at the very least, a senior archangel. Grant packed his bags and caught a train.

It was not until 24 February 1918, that Keyes was ready with his revised plans. With a refreshing lack of subtlety, he named his proposals Operation ZO. Used in close proximity to an aged cruiser under the aegis of the Dover Patrol and equipped with a vast array of weaponry and defensive protection, the meaning could be described as obvious. That it disguised nothing would soon become apparent.

Even in 1918, a general consensus existed that codewords, by definition, obscured the details of the operation to which they referred. Codewords did not reveal the purpose of the mission to an eaves-dropper. Not much is lost if a reference is made to Operation Pippin. Codewords should not be confused with nicknames which are given to operations widely publicized before the event. Desert Storm was, tech-nically, a nickname, Overlord was a codeword. Keyes' choice simply underlines the essentially amateur approach that runs like a thread through the planning.

Keyes presented his scheme with his normal ebullient optimism. A single attack would, in the opinion of the Vice Admiral, deny that hated triangle to the Germans 'for an indefinite period'. It would bar the oceans to 'the forty or fifty submarines that would probably be resting or refitting at these places'.

The essence of the diversion was that the landing parties would scramble ashore between the Mole batteries and defences guarding them. This required the most precise placing of the assault ship. The storming parties would wipe out the machine-gunners and other defenders before destroying the battery guns. This accomplished, they would advance down the eighty-yard wide, one-mile long Mole in an orgy of destruction. Seaplane sheds, barracks, gun batteries would all

51

be reduced to rubble. It was hinted that they might even reach the canal entrance. It was heady stuff. If it was not quite a question of the war being won in a single hour, Keyes' fervour made it sound so. The enterprise was daring and risky but the Royal Navy had undertaken many such ventures in its long history.

Despite his Dardanelles experiences, one gets the impression that Keyes did not fully grasp the perils and dangers of modern industrial warfare. For him, it was, apparently, still a matter of boys' adventure stories. Even if the landing parties were led by those two fictional heroes Jack Harkaway or Ralph Steadfast, both of whom quelled foes with a single shot and overcame difficulties with a moment's lightning thought, the operation would still need the most careful planning.

Keyes was a product of his age and upbringing. Almost every young British male believed in the Empire and the superiority of the men who made it. Boys who came to manhood in the late Victorian era and the years before the First War considered it not only their birthright but their bounden duty to maintain and even expand Imperial rule if the chance arose.

This was not simply a matter of class. Although it was true that the public schools specifically imbued their pupils with the ideals of service to the Crown, boys who would get no closer to Eton or Westminster except as delivery urchins on bicycles, knew about the demands and obligations of Empire.

They read magazines full of derring-do. *Pluck* was a typical example. Its masthead informed the reader that it contained '. . . the daring deeds of plucky sailors, plucky soldiers, plucky firemen, plucky explorers, plucky detectives, plucky railwaymen, plucky boys and plucky girls and all sorts of conditions of British heroes'.

There were no plucky Germans, no plucky Frenchmen, no plucky Spaniards and no plucky Italians. Chinese were invariably sinister, black men comic but loyal. Sikhs and Gurkhas attained an honorary Englishness when led by British officers. Foreigners, when not funny, always plotted evil. No matter how desperate the situation, though, the gallant quick-thinking Briton always won through.

The boys' papers – and *Boys Of England*, *Union Jack*, *Young Britons* and the determinedly middle-class *Boys' Own Paper* were among the dozens available – preached patriotism in large type. They were, according to Alfred Harmsworth who published many of them, one of the best recruiting agencies ever devised. Even when Harmsworth had become Lord Northcliffe, an influential newspaper magnate, he still extolled the values displayed in his boys' magazines.

One of the more malicious of modern myths is that the men who went off to fight in 1914 were victims. They were not. They never thought it either. They believed in what they were doing. Neither did they criticize the men who led them. That was a later introduction, largely promulgated by a handful of highly literate middle-class writers. They never spoke for the vast majority who served.

Admiral Sir Reginald Bacon detested plans which assumed that gallantry on the part of the officers and men would overcome any shortcomings in the scheme. He also condemned the lack of respect for any opposition: 'That wretched idea that the British nation owned the world's supply of pluck, and that foreigners were wanting in that virtue, has ever been a stumbling-block to progress in our Navy.'

It was little wonder that he and Keyes were at opposite ends of the table.

The Board of Admiralty, under Geddes and Wemyss, looked, listened and pondered. The Sea Lords, as was their duty, commented on the proposals before them. Despite Wemyss' thoughtfulness in providing *Vindictive*, the Board considered it a poor choice. Without exception, each one queried the suitability of the aged cruiser for her intended role. Keyes explained he had little option. It was the *Vindictive* or nothing.

It is never sensible to attempt an operation when the main tool available is generally considered to be unsuitable. Keyes, however, ignored the objections. Wars, he knew, are not won by doubters.

The Board of Admiralty, aware that Harkaways and Steadfasts might not be readily available, were unanimous in underlining what they saw as a major obstacle. The vital requirement, which Keyes had not fully faced, was to get the storming parties on to the Mole as quickly as possible. The Third Sea Lord summed it up simply: 'The essence of these storming parties being successful' he commented, 'is celerity in actually getting ashore.'

This was, without doubt, absolutely essential. Any delay in getting men onto the Mole would jeopardize the whole diversion.

Their Lordships were also extremely unhappy with Keyes' idea of a night attack. Naval actions at sea, fought in the dark were fraught with the danger of collision. The Board considered that land fighting had the same potential for confusion. They suggested that 'morning twilight' would be a far better time to attack. Not only could one see the enemy but defenders at dawn were often less alert, thinking more of a warm bed than a hostile onslaught.

The Second Sea Lord was not at all sure that the assault ship would be able to successfully anchor against the Mole. He suggested that two motor launches could push her against the quay during the whole operation.

But Keyes won his approval. He received formal notification on 4 March 1918. There had been little doubt that he would get it. There was, though, one very important rider. The attack was to go ahead as soon as possible.

Urgency stalked the wooden panelled rooms of the Admiralty. The submarine peril was still potent. Limited rationing of essential food-stuffs had already been introduced in London. Within the Cabinet, it was known that it would be nationwide by April. Lord Lee, the Director of Food Production, remembered that the spring of 1918 was the worst period of all. There was only two weeks supply of food in the whole country. 'This was the deadliest secret of the war at that stage, and to the very few of us who were in the know it was as ceaseless and nerve-wracking (sic) an anxiety as the powers of hell could devise.'

The assault, Keyes agreed with the Board, demanded a moonless night. High water must be within ninety minutes of midnight. There must be 'fair, settled weather, with the wind in the right direction for ensuring a serviceable smoke-screen.' The first suitable period was a clearly impossible 12 March. After that, the next relevant date was 9 April.

The Board and Vice Admiral Keyes concurred. The armada to destroy the *Flotille Flandern* must be ready by 8 April, prepared to sail up until 13 April on the first afternoon upon which the weather was opportune.

The task of preparing *Vindictive* went to a Lieutenant Commander Robert Rosoman. Posted to the *Arrogant* as First Lieutenant, he was interviewed by Keyes who took an instant liking to the forty-two year old. He had the slightly unusual qualification for a career Royal Navy officer of a civilian Master Mariner's Certificate. The Admiral cancelled Rosoman's posting to make him First Lieutenant of the *Vindictive*.

Rosoman hurried to Chatham to make his new ship ready in all respects for the operation. He had just four weeks. To help him, he had Engineer Lieutenant Commander William Bury. Commander Seymour Osborne, a gunnery expert on Keyes' staff at Dover, revamped *Vindictive*'s armament.

None of the three had extensive experience of landing men in the face of determined opposition. Very few naval or military officers did. The only immediate and not very useful example was the Gallipoli campaign. In any event, it was not their job to do other than what they were asked. They set to with determination.

Six of the existing 6-inch gun positions on *Vindictive* were removed. To replace them, Osborne requisitioned an assortment of extra armament. An 11-inch howitzer arrived for the quarterdeck. A 7.5-inch variant found a home on the forecastle. When Osborne later discovered that a false deck would run along the port side to get the assault parties ashore, he promptly found another 7.5-inch howitzer to go there.

The howitzers were to silence the batteries on the Mole. Osborne concentrated, though, on equipping the ship as an infantry support vessel. Six Lewis gun positions were established in the foretop. These were high enough to fire over the Mole parapet. They were joined by three pom-poms. Osborne believed that this collection of weaponry, going at full blast, would deter even the most dedicated opposition.

The foretop would be the only part of *Vindictive* visible when she was alongside the Mole. Its occupants would be able to rake the quayside with their guns. It was obvious that the enemy would have no hesitation in returning the favour. To protect the foretop crew, Osborne transformed it into a gigantic armoured mushroom. Metal reinforcing plates ran around the sides. Lewis guns and pom-poms peeped from sinister slits. The whole was covered by a large circular curved plate in best rolled steel.

The gun positions on the decks were less well protected. They were hidden from the enemy's view once *Vindictive* docked.

On the fore and aft decks, Osborne arranged Stokes mortars to lob bombs at enemy gun positions or ships in harbour.

The new First Lieutenant faced the problem of getting the troops onto the Mole. Eight hundred men had to get ashore as quickly as possible. The Navy would contribute a Bluejacket Assault Party of 200 men. The remainder were Royal Marines. Each man carried at least eighty pounds of equipment. Demolition experts had gun-cotton, detonators, fuses and other dangerous impedimenta. The General Post Office was duly asked to yield up some wicker parcel baskets on wheels. The 'wreckers' would be able, in theory, to run them ashore with consummate ease.

Rosoman and Bury started from Admiral Bacon's plan for a ten-foot wide ramp. It certainly allowed a lot of men to charge on to the Mole. The two officers agreed that it was too heavy and unwieldy for *Vindictive*. However, all was not lost. One ten-feet wide ramp could be replaced by lots of lesser ramps or landing brows. The end result would be the same or even better. Nobody seemingly realized that there was a world of difference. Charging down a ten-feet wide ramp held firmly in position was one thing. Trying the same manoeuvre on a twenty-seven inches wide gangplank, described as 'a sort of light draw-bridge with a hinge in the middle', from a heavily rolling ship was quite another.

It was at this point that the scheme of assembling a false deck on *Vindictive* was conceived. It was essential to get the troops as close as possible to the top of the parapet for the landing. If they were higher up, they would not have so far to climb. The deck stretched along the port side of the *Vindictive* from the forecastle to the quarterdeck. Three wide ramps led to it from the starboard side. The false deck served another purpose. The massed troops could shelter under it on the original upper deck. It was no match for artillery but they would be reasonably safe from shell splinters and small-arms fire. It also became home to an extra ten Lewis guns.

The next stage was the construction of the landing brows. The 'toe' of the Mole presented a dilemma. A projection on the bottom support of the causeway, it prevented *Vindictive* from anchoring tightly to the quay-side by fouling her keel. With an additional gap caused by her fenders, the hull might be as far away from the parapet as thirty feet, a very long way for heavily-laden men. A very, very long way indeed if the ship was rolling in the swell.

The dockyard carpenters hammered together eighteen wooden ramps, each thirty feet long and twenty-seven inches wide. Each one was hinged about one-third along its length. Folded, hauled upright, they ran along the port side of the ship. Assuming the attack took place at high tide, the parapet top would be, at most, seven feet above the false deck. It might even be as little as four or even non-existent as Keyes had enthusiastically told Beatty. On arrival at the Mole, the ramps would simply crash down into place.

Captain Grant had, in the interim, found two suitable ships at Liverpool. He was greatly aided by the fact that the manager of the Ferry Company was a former Naval officer. Like Grant, he had served on the China Station. Having established a warm relationship, the Staff Captain faced an inquisition of Ferry Company officials and local councillors. They demanded to know precisely why the Navy wanted their ships.

Grant concocted a tale that they were needed to ferry US troops from landing jetties to ocean-going liners in New York. The two chosen vessels would cross the Atlantic and be away for some time. His audience was reluctant to agree. There were other ports, other boats.

Grant asked if any of the meeting had sons in the trenches. Receiving affirmative growls, he enquired gently if they would countenance an officer accepting second-best for their sons. Grant got his boats.

The *Lily* and the *Rose* were not, though, as suitable as two newer vessels on the Mersey, plying the choppy waters between Wallasey, New Brighton and Liverpool. Grant pressed them into service instead. The *Iris* and *Daffodil* joined King George's Navy.

They were an excellent choice. Both drew less than nine feet of water which allowed them to cross almost any minefield. Even if they did hit a mine, their double hulls would probably survive the detonation. Built on the Tyne in 1903 by Robert Stephenson and Co., their Liverpool-made engines worked all day without complaint. They had served peacefully on the Mersey for twelve years. Now they would go to war.

The two fat ships, each 154 feet long, joined the Navy as HMS *Iris II* and HMS *Daffodil IV*. *Iris* for some inscrutable shipyard reason was nine tons heavier than her sister. A scratch crew sailed them from Liverpool to Portsmouth. A swarm of workers painted them grey and armour-plated their sides. Mattresses and sandbags gave splinter protection. As with *Vindictive*, it was done in a rush.

Daffodil and *Iris* solved another conundrum. Rosoman had been trying to decide the best way of keeping *Vindictive* close against the Mole throughout the action. The normal methods were obviously un-available. It was generally accepted that there would be no helpful loiterers on the quayside, anxious to loop a heavy rope around a handy bollard. The Sea Lords, it will be recalled, had already noted that particular dilemma. They suggested two launches be detailed for the task.

Derricks were built fore and aft on the *Vindictive*. Two huge grappling irons hung from them. On arrival, the contraptions would be lowered over the parapet. The wires would then be hauled taut, the grapnel arms would bite into the concrete and secure the ship fast to the Mole.

The new arrivals allowed an extra possibility. *Daffodil* would be placed under the orders of *Vindictive*'s commander. If necessary, he would order her to butt the assault ship hard against the Mole until she was firmly in position. *Daffodil* would substitute for the motor launches.

Both ferries collected smoke apparatus, grappling irons to fasten them to the Mole and a set of scaling ladders. With decks substantially lower than that of *Vindictive* it was accepted that, in emergency, they could come alongside the bigger ship and land their troops over her sides.

It was another compromise solution. The project would accept yet more. Military operations rarely go according to intent, especially when a determined and skilful enemy is involved. A commander must consider all possibilities, including the risk of disaster. The likelihood of events going sadly wrong increases with every failure to analyse the task properly. Compromises over equipment and personnel eat away at the viability of the enterprise. And the compromises were increasing in number.

What was more, the diversion – landing troops on the Mole – was fast becoming the main event. Plans, ideas and energy were devoted to that rather than anything else. No thought seems to have been given to any other means of diverting the enemy to help the blockships reach their target. No time was apparently spent in considering other ways of silencing the shore batteries. Blinkered vision set in.

Keyes firmly believed in delegating authority. A commander should, he considered, duplicate himself by his choice of subordinates. It could be a dangerous policy. Keyes had a reputation as an officer with the 'Nelson touch', one who would attack whatever the odds. To leave subordinates of the same frame of mind to carry out the preparations for the attack invited trouble. Detailed considerations disappeared in the desire for action. The suggestion that if things go wrong the people at the sharp end can simply play it 'off the cuff' is an abdication of responsibility. Of course, relatively junior officers have to make fast decisions in action but it helps if their commander has already contemplated possibilities.

One looks in vain for a realistic appraisal of the odds. German gunnery, both at sea and on land, was formidably accurate. No leap of fevered imagination was needed to guess that the shore batteries could communicate with each other. The telephone was no unknown invention. Every gun could turn its attention to a single target if necessary.

The estimate that 1000 enemy troops, in prepared defensive positions, garrisoned Zeebrugge Harbour seems to have been brushed aside as of little consequence. A roughly equal number of Royal Marines and jolly Jack Tars, imbued with fighting spirit, would easily take care of the beastly Hun. British grit, courage and enthusiasm would win through. It was totally unrealistic but Keyes would brook no argument. As one officer recalled in later years, 'questions were out of fashion in the *Vindictive*'.

It was another case of ignoring inconvenient facts. The defence could put up a very fierce fight. This was the Imperial German Navy, marines and sailors, equipped with modern weapons, not Chinese Boxer rebels

58

armed with century-old smooth-bore muskets or Fuzzy-Wuzzies flourishing spears. A realistic assessment, though, would have demanded many more troops if Keyes' spirited ideas of taking the Mole, blowing up its installations and even penetrating closer towards the lock-gates were to approach reality.

A slight flavour of what Keyes and his officers anticipated the fighting would be like can be inferred by the instructions issued, certainly, to the Marines under training:

> Officers . . . are to imbue their commands with the idea of carrying the operation through with the bayonet; rifle fire, machine-gun fire and bomb throwing are only to be resorted to when necessary to break down enemy resistance.

Rosoman somehow made time to sort out accommodation for the Royal Marine officers who would live on the ship in the period before the flotilla sailed for action. Osborne, the gunnery specialist, found a series of nooks and crannies in which to store ammunition, explosives, smoke flasks and other warlike equipment. Much of it ended back on the deck as Rosoman tried to keep working spaces clear. He wanted to stuff the same space with every bit of buoyant material he could beg, steal, scrounge or find. If *Vindictive* was holed, the longer she stayed afloat the better.

In the middle of this confusion, with every day being vital if the timetable was to be met, Wing Commander Brock's pyrotechnics arrived.

Brock was personally briefed by Keyes. The Wing Commander had worked hard to improve the illuminations on the Dover Barrage. Now Keyes wanted an even better smokescreen than already existed. It had to be, Keyes stressed, thicker and denser than anything previously achieved.

Brock got to work. Three officers and thirty-seven men arrived at Dover from the experimental station. More followed. Brock also suggested some new and exciting gadgets to be used in the attack – phosphorus flares, rockets and fearsomely lethal flame-throwers, both portable and fixed to the deck.

Brock had a price for his willing cooperation. He wanted to go to Zeebrugge himself. His argument was simple. He understood the technicalities of the apparatus he had designed. His knowledge would greatly assist the operation. Additionally, intelligence reports had drawn attention to a system of metal tubes mounted on the Mole. Brock alleged that these were probably the *Goertz* range-finding system for the shore batteries. He felt he was the very best person to examine them and bring back a report on their operation.

Keyes agreed. He would be there himself. Nobody ever doubted Keyes' physical courage and he expected it in others. It was an amazing and foolish decision. One cannot blame Brock for wanting to see action. He was a young man. He had friends in the trenches or fighting in the air. But whatever Brock personally desired, he was unquestionably a vital component of the Navy at a time when the war itself was becoming steadily more technical. To risk his capture or death was short-sighted in the extreme. It was akin to allowing Barnes Wallis to fly as a bomb-aimer on the Dams raid in the Second World War.

Brock's new and improved smokescreen, or 'artificial fog' as he preferred to call it, was ingenious. Essentially, a chemical mixture was injected directly under pressure into the hot exhausts of the motor torpedo boats and other small craft or the hot interior surface of the funnels of destroyers. The larger ships each had welded iron contraptions, in the region of ten feet in height, hastily assembled at Chatham. These were fed with solid cakes of phosphide of calcium. Dropped into a bucket-like container full of water, the resulting smoke and flames roared up a chimney and were dispersed by a windmill arrangement. It was more toxic than its predecessor. Taking in a lungful was an extremely unpleasant experience.

A snag arose. Brock's patent chemical mixture included a large amount of chloro-sulphonic acid, an essential in the manufacture of artificial sweeteners.

Keyes went to Wemyss. Wemyss spoke to Geddes. The First Lord asked the Prime Minister. Lloyd George obtained the War Cabinet's blessing to prohibit the production of saccharin. The chemical, some sixty-three tons in all, went to Brock's department. Not only diabetics grumbled about their unsweetened tea throughout March and April 1918. Sugar was already rationed although temperance organizations, ever anxious to spread their message, swiftly pointed out that there would be plenty for everyone if the brewers stopped making beer. Those with a sweet tooth took the restriction philosophically as yet another horror of modern war.

Sixty staff at Dover from Brock's experimental station worked long, tiring, tedious hours turning out vast quantities of the Wing Commander's invention. Production could not be rushed. An accident caused by indecent haste would not only slow manufacture but possibly poison people as a side effect.

Keyes vented his frustration in a letter to Scapa Flow. 'Brock means well, I believe,' he complained to Beatty, 'and has been invaluable in providing the latest trench warfare devices and special rockets and flares but I am afraid he is unreliable and he has certainly let me down in the matter of smoke.'

Roger Keyes expected all or nothing.

The arrival of Brock's various pieces of dangerous apparatus caused a new surge of activity at the dockyard. The *Vindictive* gained flame projectors. Rosoman hastily reviewed the firefighting procedures.

Mattresses arrived to protect two special shelters, one abreast the forebridge, one at the after end of the upper deck. Inside the two shelters, Brock's experts installed his terrible flame-throwers.

Improvised splinter precautions guarded the three funnels. Flames would shoot through any holes. It was spectacular to see. It added extra excitement when the flames could reach the piles of ammunition stored on deck.

Rosoman went to some lengths to screen the conning-tower below the ship's bridge. It was the alternative place from which the ship could be commanded. Sandbags were optimistically piled high all round to protect it against anything short of a direct hit.

As a final gesture, the two willowy and incongruous masts yielded to the conversion. The foremast was shortened to become a Lewis gun position. The main mast was taken out and fastened horizontally across the quarterdeck with its base embedded in concrete. The end extended some several feet beyond the ship's port side to serve as a bumpkin or fender. It should prevent the *Vindictive*'s port screw from fouling the toe of the Mole.

Lieutenant Commander Bury, the engineer, not only cared for *Vindictive*'s engines. He was also responsible for the blockships and ensuring those vessels were in prime order. Despite this, he found time to study the aerial photographs and confidential plans to make a plasticine model of the Mole. This was hidden away in a locked cabin. Selected officers, as they arrived for duty, were allowed to see the model and contemplate what the future might hold.

Riveters, welders, carpenters and every other dockyard trade thronged the *Vindictive*. Despite the secrecy and the attempts to mislead any unauthorized eyes and ears, it was extremely difficult to hide a ship of some 6000 tons. The very look of her as the modifications proceeded gave a very clear idea of the task ahead.

Rosoman and Bury had worked wonders in the short time at their disposal. 'There was never a more overworked and harassed man', a fellow member of the *Vindictive*'s wardroom recalled of the First Lieutenant, 'or one so highly gifted with the qualities of imperturbability and cheerfulness . . .'.

Even so, doubts enter the mind. The Royal Navy has an acknowledged flair for improvisation but there is a continual nagging uncertainty about the timescale of the operation. It came down to a period of five weeks in which to put together the expedition. A strong feeling of makeshift permeates the preparations and the whole affair. Most operational planners are well aware of the dangers of simply deciding that something will just have to do because there is no time to consider alternatives. Working against time may well be necessary but it can also be extremely dangerous.

It was not simply a case of making *Vindictive* ready. The blockships had to be prepared. The commanders of those and of the host of other vessels that would go to Zeebrugge had to be thoroughly briefed. One searches in vain for contingency plans. Somehow, and it is not necessarily a bad thing, there was a shining belief that nothing could or would go wrong. It was a dangerous stunt, to be sure, but boldness would see it through.

Much of this can be attributed to Keyes himself. His enthusiasm carried all before him. He appears to have been totally unaware of the dangers that his unwavering optimism created. Only a few had the temerity to question not only whether the attack was properly planned but whether circumstances still demanded it should go ahead.

The staff of Earle's Cement Works at Ellesmere Port in Cheshire received a rush order from the Admiralty. A large amount of cement was urgently required. The delivery date seemed impossibly tight so the management called in everybody they could to work day and night. It was unclear why the Admiralty needed so much cement but nudges and winks told all. It was for an operation that would come very close to winning the war.

The newspapers made much of the execution in France of Paul Marie Bolo who preferred to be known as Bolo Pasha. He had briefly been a dentist. Surviving charges of bigamy and theft, he founded banks in South America. On the strength of this, he persuaded the Khedive of Egypt to appoint him as his financial agent in Paris. The Khedive was pro-German or, more accurately, pro-Egyptian and thus anti-British. Bolo tried to buy French newspapers in order to peddle propaganda with funds supplied by way of the Deutsche Bank. A French firing squad executed him for 'assisting the act of treason'. He had his moustache curled specially for the occasion and sported white gloves when he was led out to die.

The Royal Flying Corps, soon to join with the Royal Naval Air Service to form the Royal Air Force, promptly gave the nickname of 'Bolo House' to the Air Ministry.

In Downing Street, Lloyd George tried to ignore the urgent appeals of Sir Douglas Haig for more troops. It was known, without doubt, that the German Army was preparing a massive strike against the Allies on the Western Front. More than seventy enemy divisions were ready to smash the British. Many of them came from the Eastern Front after the collapse of Russia. A high proportion of their men were pre-1914 or early war veterans. If they failed to destroy the French and British before the Americans were in the front line, Germany would lose the war. It was a gamble but one which Ludendorff and Hindenburg were prepared to take.

Lloyd George celebrated one victory over the despised generals. After much debate and discussion, the dour Field Marshal 'Wullie' Robertson was replaced as CIGS. The new man in the post was General Sir Henry Wilson, a smooth-talking, highly ambitious Anglo-Irishman. Wilson had been the British representative on the Supreme War Council, another device which Lloyd George had promoted as a way of assuring political control over his military leaders. It is a minor irony that Wilson proved to be as great an intriguer as the Prime Minister himself. More irritatingly, Wilson, thanks to a determined French governess, was bilingual. He cheerfully conspired in both French and English.

The removal of Robertson was slight compensation for the disappointing Smuts report. Haig stayed in post but Lloyd George could console himself with the knowledge that he was tightening his grip on the generals and admirals.

If Lloyd George's *War Memoirs* are to be believed, the Prime Minister feared a military takeover. The idea of Sir Douglas Haig leading several battalions down Whitehall to Downing Street in a putsch against the elected Government is bizarre. It reveals much about Lloyd George's fevered imagination. The country was running out of food. Even though the rationing imposed would have been sybaritic luxury to German civilians, Lloyd George was ready to convince himself that all was lost. If the U-boats had a killing season as the winter seas became milder, the larder would empty rapidly.

There was a glimmer of hope. The attack on Zeebrugge could not be long delayed although Wemyss seemed peculiarly reluctant to reveal any details. In fact, the First Sea Lord was well aware of the story that anything secret told in Downing Street before dinner was discussed over breakfast the following morning by Hindenburg and Ludendorff. Lloyd George liked to confide in his intimates.

It was, the Admiral believed, much better if he upheld the Navy's reputation as the Silent Service. Time enough to tell the Prime Minister when the deed was done.

CHAPTER SIX

Keyes had called for officers and men to take part in 'a secret and dangerous mission' early in February 1918. Although his plans were incomplete, time was crucial. Keyes canvassed South Coast Command and the Grand Fleet.

Admiral Sir David Beatty at Scapa Flow was enthusiastic. Famed for wearing his cap at a rakish angle, he was another officer to whom life and warfare were a great adventure. Beatty approved thoroughly of the audacious scheme. Both Wemyss and he were anxious for the Navy to retrieve its reputation for taking the war to the enemy. This had been sadly dented by the Battle of Jutland. Although the German High Seas Fleet remained bottled up at anchor, many of the general public felt as Lloyd George did. The Royal Navy was skulking in port. The sailors enjoyed an easy life while the Army fought and bled in the muddy trenches of the Western Front.

Keyes was well aware of this feeling. It coloured his attitude towards Operation ZO. A daring assault from the sea would restore the Navy's reputation for dash and resolution. More than once, when the Zeebrugge plan was questioned, Keyes asked the doubters what the Army would say if the Navy remained in port.

Beatty passed on the request for fit young sailors who should be good sportsmen, unmarried and with no family commitments to every ship under his command. He promised Keyes that the Grand Fleet would provide all the officers and men needed, including Marines. Sir Stanley Colville, the commander at Portsmouth was equally enthused. He was prepared to arrange the manning of the *Daffodil* and *Iris* while Sir Doveton Sturdee at the Nore pledged whatever was needed, be it men or materials.

Rosoman, effectively the only seaman on board the *Vindictive* was soon joined by Lieutenant Edward Hilton Young, a Volunteer Reserve officer – and, incidentally, a Member of Parliament – who had spent some time in France in command of a railway gun. Many of its crew had volunteered for the 'undertaking of real danger'. Young, whose men appreciated his imperturbable habit of smoking a cigar when under fire, decided to apply.

Two Admiralty interviews later, Lieutenant Hilton Young, MP, RNVR reported to HMS *Hindustan* at Chatham for special service. The *Hindustan,* a pre-Dreadnought battleship had been retired for some while from the 3rd Battle Fleet but she was ideal for her new role. Wemyss happily handed her to Keyes as the depot ship for the operation. The curious may still see part of this relic of the Zeebrugge Raid. When she was broken up after the war, wood from her and HMS *Impregnable* was sold off cheaply and used in building the mock-Tudor frontage of Liberty's Regent Street store in London.

Hilton Young arrived in the middle of March. He was immediately put to work to train the crews of *Vindictive*'s remaining four 6-inch guns. Their crews came, not from volunteers, but from new recruits at Chatham. Keyes felt that, as conscripts to the Army could hardly pick and choose where they went, the same should apply to ratings. Even those landing on the Mole itself should not be volunteers. Only the crews of the blockships would have the luxury of choosing whether or not they took part because they would fill posts of particular danger.

In practice, every man was a volunteer. The bluejackets who came from the Grand Fleet were mostly men who were bored with sitting on static battleships. Some had spent time in the cells for petty indiscipline. Keyes' call to arms came as a breath of fresh air. Some First Lieutenants seized upon Beatty's call to persuade their troublemakers to volunteer for the unspecified dangerous duties.

One of the first Grand Fleet officers to arrive was Lieutenant Ivan Franks. He came well-recommended. Beatty had specifically suggested him. Franks had previously commanded a submarine. He had also served with Keyes' younger brother, Lieutenant Adrian Keyes, on a Q ship – tattered-looking merchantmen which wandered the High Seas trying to tempt U-boat attacks. Once hit, a 'panic party' would evacuate the Q ship, scrambling into the boats and rowing away as hard as they could.

It was ideal for frustrated actors. One Q ship group was particularly proud of its parrot in a cage. Another had a cat which clung with grim feline determination to a sailor's shoulder as the boats were lowered.

A highly satisfied U-boat commander would then surface to sink the unlucky tramp with leisurely gunfire. At which point, the White Ensign would flutter boldly from the stern as various structures of wood and canvas fell away to reveal some severely spiteful guns manned by equally spiteful Royal Naval gunners.

66

Franks was accepted. Keyes assigned him to command the blockship *Iphigenia*. The lieutenant promptly asked for his close friend, another submariner, Lieutenant Edward Billyard-Leake as his second in command. Keyes agreed. He could never resist the requests of brave men.

Keyes delegated the initial work of preparing the *Iphigenia* and the other blockships to Franks. It was a privilege for being an early volunteer. It was crucial that, once the blockships were in position, they sank rapidly and evenly. Nothing would be more embarrassing than a waterlogged ship, bows in the air, which could be towed away by a determined tug. It was not simply a question of opening the seacocks before jumping over the side. *Iphigenia*, *Thetis*, *Intrepid*, *Sirius* and *Brilliant* must sink in a properly nautical way.

Franks did little more than agree the suggestions made by the dockyard engineers. Sometimes, they did not even consult him as they worked out where to put the rubble, thoughtfully acquired by knocking down some derelict buildings in Chatham dockyard.

Keyes had finally concluded that it was not possible for the blockships to enter the harbour, navigate their way along the dredged channel and sail along the canal to ram the lock-gates. Every previous plan of attack on Zeebrugge had regarded the lock-gates as the key. Damage them and Bruges was useless. Keyes decided that a greater hope of success lay in blocking the narrow waterway. He was to change his mind yet again.

Even if the gates were left alone, the task appeared formidable. First, the ships had to be sunk so that they could not be removed. Second, quite obviously, they had to block the canal entrance. Third, they should cause the channel to rapidly silt up.

Franks learned that there was fifteen feet between low and high tide at Zeebrugge. To be effective in obstructing shipping, the upper works needed to be within six feet of high tide level. To build up silt, the ships had to sit as squarely across the channel as possible. Once positioned, explosive charges would wreck the hull. Tons of the Earle Works' best cement would blow through the water. The experts were sure that silt would rapidly accumulate. It would, they were convinced, take months to clear the damage.

One complication was that the blockships were about 100 yards in length. They had to close off a minimum width of 340 feet. The existing silt prevented much manoeuvring if the blockships drew more than eighteen feet six inches. Engineers flourished slide rules to calculate exactly how much cement, concrete and rubble could be put into the unladen ships.

All auxiliary machinery was stripped from the ships. Copper and brass fittings – metals of which the Germans were desperately short – were removed. All the guns, except for the three foremost ones, disappeared. Barely sufficient coal for the return journey if the operation was called off with the target in sight was poured into the bunkers. Every pound of weight that came out was replaced by a pound of rubble.

Concrete surrounded the boilers and steering connections. More was packed into the bow above the waterline. To balance the ship, the stern received similar treatment. In the middle of the vessel, labourers tipped barrow load after barrow load of rubble into empty spaces. Finally, bags of cement were heaved into position in the most inconvenient spots. If the enemy tried to cut away parts of the ships, they would have to fight Earle Cement for the honour.

The five ships were fitted with extra steering positions with duplicate controls. All had defensive mats. The gun positions acquired half-inch thick steel shields. The masts vanished. Each ship gained a set of Wing Commander Brock's smoke-making machinery. Deep inside the hulls, nine explosive charges were laid. Firing keys were placed in the control positions.

To satisfy the curious, who might have wondered why *Vindictive* and her sisters were receiving such unparalleled attention, a story circulated that the ships were being readied in case Calais fell to the Germans.

It is not clear whether this tale ever reached German ears or, if it did, whether they took it seriously. Certainly, the idea of blocking Zeebrugge had been a topic of conversation in Naval wardrooms for a good while. In any event, the German defences were never going to be a pushover, forewarned or not.

As the preparations gathered pace, Keyes looked for a Staff Officer to handle the detailed administrative work. His first choice was unavailable so Keyes called upon his former navigating officer who had served with him in HMS *Venus*. Commander Alfred Francis Blakeney Carpenter was at the Admiralty. It will surprise few to learn that he was at the Plans Division who agreed to loan him to the Dover Patrol. His most recent job, by an amazing coincidence, was dealing with the proposal to attack Bruges by blocking Zeebrugge and Ostend. He was an officer who, Keyes believed, had an incredible grasp of detail and was well able to deal with the complications of the operation.

Carpenter arrived at Dover. Keyes cheerfully asked him if he knew anybody who might care to captain a blockship. He did. Lieutenant Stuart Bonham Carter took command of *Intrepid*.

The *Thetis* was still without a commander. Keyes finally filled the vacancy on the recommendation of his liaison officer at the Admiralty. Commander Ralph Sneyd took the position.

Keyes had ruled that only single officers and men could volunteer for the blockships. He believed it to be so dangerous that the chances of survival were negligible. Keyes noted in his *Memoirs*:

> It was very interesting to watch their reactions when I told them that the enterprise would be hazardous, and finally said that the best chance of escape I could offer them after it, was a German prison camp until the end of the war. With one exception only, they appeared simply delighted and most grateful for the honour I had done them in offering them such a wonderful prospect! Then I gave them an outline of the plan, and said that although I would make every endeavour to save them after they had sunk their ships, I felt that it was a very forlorn hope. They took everything for granted, asked few, if any, questions and went away apparently full of joy and gratitude.

The single exception was Commander Sneyd. With more experience than the two lieutenants, he asked questions and expected answers. Keyes recalled:

> He raised so many questions, ifs and buts, that I became impatient and said that if he did not feel enthusiastic about it I had no wish to employ him, there were scores who would give anything to be given the chance I was offering him.

Sneyd made it clear, nonetheless, that he wanted the command. He was cautious but no coward.

Keyes filled the posts for the Ostend blockships without referring to anyone. *Brilliant* went to Commander Alfred Godsal who was on *Centurion* when Keyes took command. For *Sirius*, Keyes sought out an officer from his Dardanelles days. Lieutenant Commander Henry Hardy had single-handedly stopped a rout of French colonial troops at Sedd-el-Bahr in May 1915. He was in command of four trawlers engaged in collecting wounded. Appalled by the sight of the demoralized Senegalese infantry, Hardy found a trumpeter. He rallied the frightened men whilst the trumpeter sounded the charge. Hardy led the soldiers back to their trenches, stabilized the line and handed over the position to the French military. It was an episode after Keyes' own heart.

Iris and *Daffodil* had new captains from the Grand Fleet. Keyes did not look amongst his officers from the Dover Patrol. They would have been well acquainted with the vagaries of wind and tide off the Belgian coast. Keyes, however, as the Vice Admiral in command of Operation ZO was well within his rights to pick whosoever he chose. It is nonetheless curious that none of the officers selected to command the blockships or the assault craft was acquainted with the vagaries of the shifting sands of Flanders waters.

The *Iris* went to Commander Valentine Gibbs. He first came to Keyes' notice as a young midshipman in the Far East. His non-Naval claim to fame was that he had won the 1913 Cresta Run. Keyes considered Gibbs not only brave but resourceful and cool under fire. They were qualities which the captain of the *Iris* would soon need in abundance.

Lieutenant Harold Campbell took command of *Daffodil*. Again, he was an officer who had impressed Keyes in earlier years. He was First Lieutenant of the destroyer HMS *Lurcher* in 1914 when Commodore Keyes used *Lurcher* as his command ship during the Battle of Heligoland Bight, an action which had impressed the public with the dash and spirit of the Royal Navy. The Germans lost three light cruisers and a destroyer with a casualty list which exceeded 1000. No ships were lost by the Royal Navy and the total casualties were thirty-five killed and about forty wounded.

The problem of how to attack the Mole viaduct was solved by an officer already on the staff of the Dover Patrol. Lieutenant Commander Francis Sandford was another who came to Keyes' notice during the Gallipoli campaign. Then the torpedo lieutenant on HMS *Irresistible,* he led a demolition party against the Turkish gun positions at Sedd-el-Bahr. He later volunteered for an attack on the minefields below Chanak when the civilian minesweeper crews refused to have anything more to do with an enterprise that laid them open to the vicious fire of the Turkish shore batteries.

Keyes put Sandford on his own staff but he did not stay long. He lost an eye in an abortive attempt to mine the approaches to Smyrna. Invalided home, and after many months in hospital, he was resigned to spending the rest of the war in a dingy office. Keyes sought him out. Sandford joined the Dover Patrol. Keyes' loyalty to those who had served with him nourished loyalty from them in its turn.

Keyes asked Sandford to solve the crucial problem of destroying the viaduct. If left intact, the enemy would quickly reinforce his troops on the Mole when the attack started.

Sandford experimented with rafts packed with explosives and detonated by time fuses. His theory was that these could be towed to a

70

point west of the viaduct. The current would then sweep them to the viaduct supports where they would explode in a satisfying manner.

It did not take long to prove that this was not a brilliant scheme. The rafts would have to be taken in very close to the viaduct before release. It was extremely probable that the enemy would notice the approaching tugboats with their tows. It would take an extremely cool skipper to stay on course as machine-gun bullets splattered around him. Unless they were released at a precise spot, the rafts would miss their target. Even more ruinous was the likely result if a German rifleman missed his aim and hit a raft instead.

Sandford then had the brilliant thought of pressing two old C Class submarines into service. A handful of these lived at Portsmouth. Their only use was for local defence so there was little objection when Sandford acquired two of them. His plan was to pack them with amatol, a peculiarly destructive and sensitive explosive. They would be towed across the North Sea. When close to the target, they would start engines and ram the stanchions and girders of the viaduct. One would be sufficient but Sandford liked the idea of a back-up.

Sandford 'finding a young married officer in command of *C 3* managed to effect an exchange'. Mindful of Keyes' strictures, Sandford found a single officer to take command. His younger brother, Richard, cheerfully took on the job.

Keyes did ask the elder Sandford how the crews would escape before the explosion. He was told that the submarines would be fitted with gyroscopic controls which would allow them to travel the last hundred yards or so without crew. Keyes had his suspicions which he later recorded:

> . . . I do not believe that he or his brother ever intended to make use of it, and they only installed it to save me from a subsequent charge of having condemned six men to practically certain death.

That is a statement typical of Keyes and many of his contemporaries. No matter what the trials, the main thing was to avoid being a wet blanket and rise above them. Making much of dilemmas and tribulations caused one to be branded a 'pompous ass'. The War had bred fatalism. Suicide missions were all part of it. Nevertheless, such tactics are essentially alien to Western thought. It would be totally unfair to suggest that Keyes had no concern for the lives of his men. However, his reactions suggest that he met losses with an equanimity that was denied other commanders. For Keyes, doing one's duty was sufficient. If one died doing it, that was no more than the roll of the dice.

He was, of course, absolutely entitled to delegate the detailed planning to subordinates even if some of them seem remarkably junior and inexperienced to modern eyes. Senior officers have a staff precisely because, amongst other things, attacks and offensives, campaigns and operations must be planned. Nobody expects them to sit down with a very large sheet of paper and a sharp pencil to personally write every paragraph of an operation order. The work must be delegated.

Nonetheless, a great commander pays careful attention to every aspect of his plan. He should review, and carefully review, the work done by his subordinates, questioning every aspect of his staff's effort. The corollary that a commander who pays such attention is thereby great is not, sadly, equally true. More than one staff officer has been driven close to homicidal despair when dealing with a pedestrian pedant who had no other redeeming feature save an infuriating ability to question the size of the dots on the i's and the angle of the crossbars of the t's.

Gyroscopic controls or not, the crews of the submarines would need rescuing. The arrangements smell, very slightly, of nonchalance. The elder Sandford decided he would command the rescue craft himself. A brand new picket boat was borrowed on its way to Portsmouth from Chatham. Sandford telegraphed the respective Commanders-in-Chief that it was needed for the Dover Patrol for about two weeks. 'I can think of no one I have ever met,' wrote Keyes 'who carried enterprising initiative further than that most gallant officer . . . and it was a long time before my office was free of correspondence connected with his activities.'

Keyes had his executive officers. They, in turn, chose their crews. By the middle of March, they were all assembled.

Commander Carpenter was still putting out operation orders. The big ships could not approach Zeebrugge without a host of motor launches and coastal motor boats around them. The ML and CMB crews would have a very busy time laying smoke before, during and after the attack. When they were not engaged in that useful task, there was the small matter of nipping into Zeebrugge Harbour to fire a torpedo or two at targets of opportunity.

A glance down the orders shows the variety of tasks allocated to each vessel. *CMB 24A* and *CMB 17A* were responsible for the central smoke floats. *CMB 5* and *CMB 7* were to make the torpedo attacks inside the harbour. *CMB 21B*, *CMB 25B* and *CMB 25DB* were to fire Stokes mortar bombs over the Mole parapet. *ML 558*, *ML 424*, *ML 265* and *ML 552* were to guard *Vindictive* during the crossing.

It was an immensely complicated business but Carpenter had complete faith in their commanders and crews. 'We felt,' he recorded, 'they could be relied upon to tackle any situation, however difficult or unexpected.'

Many of the ML vessels were commanded by Volunteer Reserve officers. Carpenter's praise is a graceful tribute from a professional to the wartime volunteers.

The plan had taken shape. *Vindictive*, *Iris* and *Daffodil* lacked only the landing parties. They would not be long delayed.

Keyes' concentration on Operation ZO was rudely shattered on the evening of 21 March 1918. News trickled through that General Erich Ludendorff had unleashed his mighty assault on the Western Front. Early reports were patchy and confused although it seemed clear that the BEF was being torn apart.

The immediate task of the Dover Patrol was to keep the Channel crossings protected. The supply lines between England and France were vital.

A reminder that the Imperial Navy was still active came that night. Nine German destroyers and six torpedo boats hurtled down the coast to bombard the Allied left flank. Their targets were the railway depots which supplied the British front line. Split into three groups, the German forces were under orders to attack railway traffic east and south of Dunkirk, the line at Bray-Dunes and the railheads of La Panne and Dunkirk. The bombardment was to last for an hour in which time they would dump 1100 shells on the despairing Allies.

It was just bad luck for the Kaiser's ships that Keyes' force at Dunkirk had been startled by an air raid and left harbour. The French destroyer *Oriflamme*, the British monitor HMS *Terror* and its smaller comrade *M 26* were off La Panne itself when the Germans arrived. Three more French destroyers, *Bouclier*, *Magon* and *Capitaine Mehl* together with HMS *Morris* were near Dunkirk. Their Flotilla Leader HMS *Botha*, with Captain Douglas and Lieutenant Commander Haselfoot on board, joined them after a surreptitious mission to chart the Belgian coast.

The Germans opened fire at 03.50 hours on 22 March 1918. Even before the second salvo was fired, *Botha* went hell for leather north-east to block the intruders' retreat. *Terror* pumped several hundred thousand candlesworth of star shell into the night sky and immediately opened fire with her 6-inch guns. The three French destroyers chased after *Botha*.

The Germans were obviously dismayed. Unsure of the strength of the Allied fleet but definitely shaken by their swift reaction, they hurried for Ostend. Fifteen German ships were hotly pursued by four destroyers.

It was a scenario that would have delighted Keyes and appalled his predecessor. Admiral Bacon had frequently declared that it was all too easy in night battles to confuse friend with foe. Keyes had dismissed this argument. He maintained that a simple identification light code would prevent any such errors. Even if the occasional mistake should occur, it was better to engage the enemy than skulk in port.

At 04.35 hours, *Botha* was chasing the escaping enemy with her three French consorts close behind. Five German destroyers were sighted. *Botha* opened fire. Her opponents might have been leaving with some urgency but German gunnery still possessed an enviable accuracy. A single shell hit her number two stokehold, severed a steampipe and damaged electrical circuits. *Botha* lost way even as she ran into a smoke-screen laid down by the hastily departing enemy. Once through the screen, the *Botha*'s captain realized the Germans were drawing away. He turned to port and fired two torpedoes after them. Continuing the turn, he was suddenly faced by two German torpedo boats scurrying after the bigger ships. *Botha* rammed the *A 19* before tightening her turn to dole out the same treatment to the other MTB. The second ramming failed but the enemy, raked by *Botha*'s venomous guns, started to sink.

The British ship had now turned through 180 degrees. She was back in the smoke. The German shot had done damage. The electrical circuits died. Lights flickered and went out.

The darkened *Botha* left the smoke on a course which led her directly towards the French destroyers. The Torpedo officer of the *Capitaine Mehl* had no doubts. He had seen the Flotilla Leader, lights shining, guns blazing, dash into the smokescreen. Moments later, a destroyer with silent guns and no lights appeared on a different course and at a substantially different speed.

The French torpedo hit *Botha* in her after stokehold, effectively ending her ability to proceed at any speed whatsoever. After a few moments of stunned realization, HMS *Morris* got a line aboard. *Botha* was ignominiously towed back to Dunkirk. Keyes' belief in lights had overlooked the fact that battle damage can happen in even the best-run Navy. Admiral Bacon probably considered the incident a fine example of poetic justice.

Gloomy news was followed by good tidings. On the evening of 22 March, HMS *Terror*, screened by some busy destroyers, had positioned herself 26,500 yards from Ostend harbour. Under the guidance of Captain Douglas, she fired thirty-nine rounds, each one weighing nearly a ton, at the port. She ceased firing when the Germans released a heavy smokescreen and Ostend Naval base vanished.

74

When the next day's aerial photographs were examined, they showed that all thirty-nine shells had fallen within the target area. It was a great improvement upon forty out of one hundred and eighty-five.

Vice Admiral Roger Keyes could turn his attention back to Zeebrugge. At the end of March, *Vindictive*, *Iris*, *Daffodil* and the five blockships moved out of Chatham and steamed down the Medway. They anchored out of sight of land at the mouth of the Thames Estuary. The final fitting-out was completed away from prying eyes. The *Vindictive*'s landing brows were rigged. The last touches to her role as an assault ship were completed.

There was one late arrival who joined *Vindictive* as she passed through the lock. The former commanding officer of HMS *Amazon* reported for duty. Lieutenant Ferguson was going back to sea. 'I attributed his failure,' Keyes wrote to clarify his action, 'to lack of experience rather than want of courage, and I felt so sorry that so young an officer should have his future in the Navy damned at the outset of his career that I sent for him and offered him an appointment in the *Vindictive*, which he gladly accepted.'

Another newcomer was the medical officer, Staff Surgeon James McCutcheon. Rosoman's account is stunningly simple:

> He joined with no idea of what we were playing at, and asked me if I could tell him how many casualties he was to be prepared for. I asked him if he knew anything about the show. He did not, except that he understood he had joined a Suicide Club. I thought a bit, and told him I had no authority to tell him what it was. As he was coming along and must keep quiet, I decided to tell him . . . His reply was simply ripping: 'It is not a Suicide Club at all! No, I can do a lot of good work and save many lives'.

It is almost impossible to grasp, in the light of modern-day thinking, that the casualty arrangements were quite so haphazard. The apparent lack of briefing and assessment of casualty rates is all but incredible. A moment's thought would indicate that 1000 men storming ashore into the teeth of a determined and well-protected opposition would be lucky to escape with less than forty per cent casualties. Simple arithmetic suggests rather more than 400 dead and wounded.

That the senior medical officer could be assigned with no idea of what he faced is frankly unbelievable. At the very least, he should have been well enough briefed to be aware of the hideous potential suffering. One has the uneasy feeling that, once again, nobody really believed there would be serious casualties. A few moment's discussion with a

75

regimental medical officer on the Western Front might well have produced a slightly different picture.

With all his stress on 'suicide missions', it seems odd that Keyes should ignore the medical arrangements. It was his responsibility to make very sure that the organization for treating the wounded was adequate. It was not something to be left to a single poorly-briefed medical officer of less than senior rank. The Marines brought their own doctor and attendants, interestingly from the Royal Army Medical Corps, which did rather bite into Keyes' desire for an all Naval affair.

The BEF commanders were well aware of the importance to life and morale of proper casualty evacuation. Keyes should have concerned himself with the medical arrangements just as he should have checked a myriad of other details. It is one thing to delegate, to encourage junior officers to exercise authority. It is quite another to ignore one's own responsibility. A commander must do more than just walk around in a big hat with gold braid on its peak and snap orders at deferential juniors.

The fleet anchored at the Swin, just off Clacton. The storming parties would soon arrive. The period during which time and tide would be right was 9–15 April. It was now all down to the weather.

Keyes wrote another letter to Beatty on 4 April 1918. Professing himself more than happy with the depth of training and planning, he then made an extremely significant comment:

> I only hope we get light northerly weather – otherwise we will have to do it in moonlight, can't afford to wait until May. The hour is 'written' and I feel sure when it comes it will be the best possible for the operation – anyhow I am happy and confident.

Keyes was already thinking that conditions could turn against him. Despite his repeated assertions that darkness was essential, he was considering taking a chance and attacking when the moon was full. In the last resort, it was clear that tactical considerations would take a back seat.

Operation ZO was a reality. It would be carried out, no matter what difficulties presented themselves.

CHAPTER SEVEN

Keyes had, at a very early stage, flatly rejected a suggestion that the Army should be involved. Operation ZO was a Naval affair. The Navy's own soldiers, the Royal Marines, were to hand.

Keyes did not appear to consider fighting experience necessary. It was available in abundance in the 63rd (Royal Naval) Division in France. Although recuperating from its losses in 1917, the Division could still muster the necessary numbers. Sir Douglas Haig might well have been persuaded to provide some seasoned troops to provide stiffening.

Officers with knowledge of the Western Front would probably have enquired about measures taken to silence the German batteries. Almost certainly, there would have been discussion about the means of getting men onto the quay. Bitter experience would have taught them that a mass of men arriving quickly was essential.

Even with that query satisfied, they may have wondered about the bottleneck that would inevitably occur when their heavily-burdened men were contemplating a jump of fifteen feet to the ground from the Mole parapet. Only one man at a time can use a scaling ladder. Even more to the point was how men got back on board *Vindictive* especially if there were wounded to consider. Not many of the sailors without ships who fought in the trenches retained a boyish delight in a wizard stunt to upset the dimwitted Hun. They had learned brutal lessons in a brutal school.

As it was, even though the Royal Marines had some officers and men who had fought in France, this most glaring deficiency does not appear to have been questioned. The Marines and the sailors who were to storm ashore would learn very quickly that things can go savagely wrong in a very short time. It does seem that Keyes, succumbing to a desire for secrecy, preferred not to give specific details of what was really involved until it was effectively impossible for the plan to be amended.

The 200 sailors had been recruited, in batches of fifty each, from the

1st, 2nd and 4th Battle Squadrons and the Battlecruiser Squadron, an arrangement which allowed one officer, five seamen and five stokers, from the battlecruiser HMAS *Australia* to join the mayhem and add to their countrymen's reputation for taking part in any good fight that was going.

The bluejackets started their training on 1 March 1918 under Captain Henry Halahan who had commanded the Naval siege guns in France. He had called for volunteers according to Keyes' request and forwarded their names with a covering letter. Its last paragraph was to the point:

> May I say that if the operation for which you said you might want these men is eventually undertaken, I should very much like to take part in it. I would willingly accept the same conditions, viz., that I should not expect to come back.

Halahan's request was granted. He took charge of the the Naval invasion parties.

Keyes' plan envisaged two storming operations. One, entrusted to the seamen, was an assault on the Mole batteries. The prime target was the 5.9-inch battery at the end of the Mole together with the lighter guns on the Mole extension. Their capture and destruction would let the blockships slip into the canal virtually unchallenged.

The second attack was a Marine affair. Approximately 150 yards towards the shore from the 5.9-inch battery was a fortified zone. Light artillery and machine guns were so sited that they could cover the length of the Mole as well as the harbour. After silencing the hostile gunners, the Marines would move towards the viaduct. Enemy reinforcements would be stopped in their tracks. The Marines would be assisted by the destruction of the viaduct when the submarines smashed into it.

The destruction of the viaduct would rather inhibit a triumphant advance towards the lock-gates but this part of the scheme looks to have been quietly dropped.

The storming parties, once they had achieved their objectives, would be followed by a demolition company. They were to do as much damage as possible. Keyes anticipated that the seaplane base would be destroyed together with all the other buildings on the Mole.

The sailors started gently. Their first week was devoted to route marches and swimming before training began in earnest. The Territorials of the 5th (Reserve) Battalion, Middlesex Regiment, billeted at Gillingham, took on the role of Germans.

The bluejackets learned close-quarter fighting. Using the bayonet, throwing Mills bombs, firing Lewis light machine guns and coping with poisonous gas. At the end of each day, they trooped back to the *Hindustan*.

Halahan split his men into four companies according to their Battle Squadron. Each company was divided into sections, each one of which took men from two Grand Fleet ships.

The sailors and their khaki opponents fought each other in night exercises at Raynham and Wouldham in Kent. At Wouldham, just outside Chatham, a disused chalk quarry served as the Mole. The sailors were not told their objective but there was a strong rumour that it was something to do with Calais. They cheerfully charged canvas buildings and taped outlines.

Live ammunition was used for the final practice. The Lords Commissioners of the Admiralty came, in all their glory, to watch. One Stokes mortar team miscalculated the elevation. Bemused eyes watched the shell rise, curve lazily, turn over and land at its point of origin. Two of the crew were wounded in the explosion.

They, at least, were more fortunate than the Marines. A round in one of their mortars exploded prematurely. Four marines died and four were wounded.

Strangely, there is no mention in survivors' accounts of scrambling up a narrow plank at an angle of forty-five degrees and running across a flat roof before jumping to the ground fifteen feet below during this training period. There is certainly no reference to clambering back fifteen feet, scuttling across a flat roof and sprinting down a narrow gangplank. The original thinking was that the sailors would stay on the parapet and jumping onto the quayside would be left to the Marines. Sailors knew all about gangplanks and they had no need to descend fifteen feet to the ground.

Those sailors who fondly imagined that they would storm ashore in dark blue, wearing Naval Landing Rig, were sadly disillusioned. Towards the end of their training, they spent a day at the Royal Marine Barracks at Chatham. 'We next were fitted out with khaki,' Leading Seaman William Childs remembered. 'This was very amusing for the sailors . . . invariably had yards of puttee trailing behind them.'

There was frantic sewing over the next evenings. The khaki uniforms had no badges of rank. No self-respecting rating would walk around without his proper grade being visible.

It was not until the end of March, when the sailors had technically finished their training that they learned their objective.

Able Seaman Wainwright recalled:

... came the awakening: the platoons were gathered together under their commanders who . . . fortified with models and aerial photographs, explained to us our objective – we were to block the entrance of the Bruges canal at Zeebrugge and Ostend . . .

The magnitude of the scheme overwhelmed us, the sheer audacity of tackling a place like Zeebrugge . . . where a change in the wind or tide at the critical moment would undoubtedly result in the total loss of the expedition. Viewing the whole outlook in cold daylight the large element of luck that must accompany us . . . was evident, also the knowledge that such an undertaking was impossible without a huge loss of life. . . .

Not a single man withdrew.

The bluejackets were confined to the *Hindustan* and the next few days were spent in practising landings. After a relatively lazy week with onboard sports and concerts, the four companies were dispersed. A and B Companies, from the Battlecruiser and 4th Battle Squadrons went to *Vindictive*. C Company boarded the *Daffodil* and the *Iris* became home to D Company.

It was only then that the men of the Grand Fleet learned that they had moved to make space for the traditional targets of messdeck humour, the Marines. Transfer to the *Vindictive* gave time for some last minute training. Hilton Young, who had been responsible for the gun crews noted later:

The ship's company and the landing parties mustered at the stations which they would occupy when the ship was approaching the Mole, and did for exercise all that they would have to do in the action. Our proceedings were controlled by a series of signals on the whistle. My station was at the 6-inch guns on the port or Mole side. When we were alongside and could no longer shoot at the batteries on the end of the Mole the crews of the two port guns were to mount on the landing deck over their heads and to make fast the retaining hooks that were to hold the ship to the Mole. There were two of these hooks, one fore and one aft – they were like gigantic fish-hooks about five feet long – and they were hung on wire davits with a wire hawser attached to each. We were to swing out the davits, to lower the hooks over the wall of the Mole, and we were then to make the hawsers fast.

It was all very simple. It worked wonderfully well when done without a parapet, in impeccable time, to the blasts of a whistle.

1a. Admiral Sir Reginald Bacon
commanded the Dover Patrol
until the end of 1917.

1b. Admiral Sir Roger Keyes took over
from Bacon and was the man who
planned the Zeebrugge and Ostend
Raids   *(Author's Collection)*

2. HMS *Vindictive* shortly after she joined the Fleet. *(Author's Collection)*

3. The officers of the 4th Battalion, Royal Marines. Lieutenant Colonel B. Elliot is in the front row, centre. On his immediate left is the adjutant, Captain A. Chater. The only officer captured on the Mole, Captain J. Palmer is the last man, on the extreme left, in the second row. Sixteen of the twenty-eight officers in this picture became casualties in the action. *(Royal Marines Museum)*

4. At home in the 'Pirate's Lair'. A U-boat loading torpedoes at Zeebrugge.
(Johan Ryheul Collection)

5. *UB 10* at Zeebrugge. This boat was the first command of *Kapitänleutnant* Otto Steinbrinck, the most successful U-boat ace in British waters. *(Author's Collection)*

6. The Germans were waiting. Naval infantry, in a heavily posed photograph, amidst the sand dunes. *(Author's Collection)*

7. On the Mole were the gunners. Another picture to impress the German public. *(Author's Collection)*

8. *UB 38* clears Zeebrugge Harbour. The lighthouse forms the backdrop.
(Johan Ryheul Collection)

9. *Vindictive* on her way to Zeebrugge. The landing brows are clearly visible on the right. Lieutenant Rigby, who was killed in the foretop, took the photograph.
(Royal Marines Museum)

10. Lieutenant Sandford and the submarine *C3* shortly before the Raid. *(Russell White)*

11. The captors of the ill-fated *CMB 33* inspect their booty. *(Johan Ryheul Collection)*

12. The morning after. German sailors inspect the damage on a torpedo boat.
(Johan Ryheul Collection)

13. *Iphigenia* and *Intrepid* in the canal. The photograph was taken at low tide some days after the Raid. The wooden piers have already been removed. *(Johan Ryheul Collection)*

14. A German sailor poses on board *Iphigenia*. In the background is *Intrepid*.
(Johan Ryheul Collection)

15. British dead on the Mole Parapet. The body in the foreground is possibly Lieutenant C. Hawkings. The white shirt indicates an officer and the uniform appears to be regular Naval wear. *(Copyright Alain van Geeteruyen Collection)*

16. The prisoners. Sergeant H. Wright is on the extreme right of the picture. The sergeant next to him is W. Taylor who was in charge of the signallers. The burly figure next to the Marine with his arm in a sling is Able Seaman A. Smith who enjoyed the melancholy distinction of being the only unwounded Royal Navy rating to be captured on the Mole. *(Johan Ryheul Collection)*

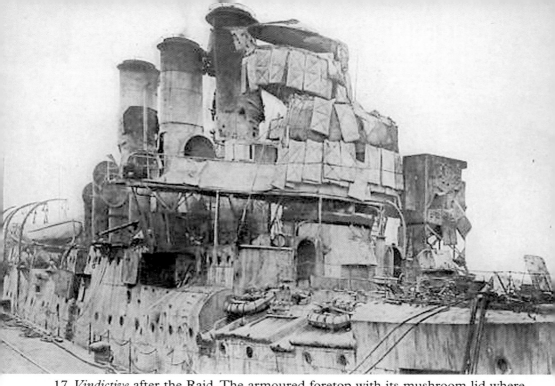

17. *Vindictive* after the Raid. The armoured foretop with its mushroom lid where Sergeant Finch won his VC can be clearly seen. *(Author's Collection)*

18. Captain A. Carpenter (with arm in sling) and surviving officers. Commander E. Osborne (holding cat) is on Carpenter's right. Lieutenant Commander Bury is on his left. *(Royal Marines Museum)*

19. A seemingly inexhaustible supply of black cats feature in the 24 April photographs. The *Pembroke* cap tally was worn by the ratings, it being the Navy's name for the Chatham depot. *(Royal Marines Museum)*

20. The survivors. A clearly posed publicity photograph on the upper deck of *Vindictive*. This photograph was taken on 24 April. At least two of the subjects are wearing Army issue greatcoats. Note the two bowler-hatted photographers on the left of the picture. *(Royal Marines Museum)*

21. Three months in the making, three minutes in the destroying. A German youth magazine cover extols the virtues and valour of the U-boat crews.

(Author's Collection)

22. *Kapitänleutnant* Schütte (3rd from right) and his officers pose with their newly awarded decorations. The officer wearing a bow tie on his immediate left is probably *Oberleutnant* Rodewald. On the left of the picture, the other officer wearing puttees is possibly *Leutnant* Zimmerman. (*Johan Ryheul Collection*)

23. Gunners of the *Tirpitz* Battery display their Iron Crosses for gallant service. The Battery played an important role against *Vindictive* on 10 May 1918. (*Johan Ryheul Collection*)

24. The point on the Mole where *Vindictive* moored. The photograph was taken shortly before development work destroyed the spot. The white rectangle on the wall is the commemorative plaque recording the event. *(Johan Ryheul Collection)*

25. The Kaiser gazes at *Iphigenia*. The original of this photograph appears to have been taken on a pocket camera. *(Royal Marines Museum)*

26. Troops on bicycles were raised in several countries, often as a cheap alternative to cavalry. British propaganda made much play with a story that a whole company of German cyclists perished on the Mole. It was untrue but the Flanders Marine Divisions did boast such a unit. Here they are seen riding, in impeccable formation, through Zeebrugge. *(Johan Ryheul Collection)*

27. *Vindictive*'s battered hulk clearly failing to block the entrance to Ostend Habour. *(Author's Collection)*

28. The graves of Commander A. Godsal, Sub Lieutenant A. Maclachlan and other crew members of *Vindictive*. The bodies were recovered from the wreck by the Germans and buried with full military honours.　　*(Johan Ryheul Collection)*

29. Albert McKenzie receives his Victoria Cross from King George V.
　　　　　　　　　　　　　　　　　　　　　　(Via Colin McKenzie)

Hilton Young observed that:

> . . . when leaving the Mole we were to recover the hooks . . . and . . .
> then stand by our guns again to engage the Mole batteries. But
> there was always something a little perfunctory about our orders
> for what we were to do when we were coming away.

Four companies formed the 4th Battalion of the Royal Marines – one
company each from Chatham, Portsmouth and Plymouth and a
machine-gun company from the Fleet – and began their training on 25
February 1918. To aid identification, officers' helmets had a white band
painted horizontally above the rim. Marines from Plymouth wore white
triangular shoulder patches. Portsmouth Company displayed a white
circle. Chatham men had a white diamond. The machine-gunners
sported a white diagonal cross, faintly reminiscent of the Vickers Gun
badge of the Machine Gun Corps.

To help them scamper ashore, an original scheme that the men
should wear gym shoes was agreed. Several hundred pairs of canvas
shoes with rubber soles were ordered but it was finally decided that
boots would be worn. After some debate, the gym wear went back to
the stores. As a compromise, the Marines wore their regular boots with
the metal heel plates removed.

The 740 officers and men were commanded by Lieutenant Colonel
Bertram Elliot. The Colonel had won a well-deserved DSO for his
exploits in Serbia in the first exciting months of the war. His experience
of the Germans was less extensive.

The Marines marched and drilled, did physical exercises and practised their bayonet fighting. They were firmly under the impression they
were going to France to capture a dried out canal used as an ammunition dump and hold it for two and a half hours. The model they saw
showed a target about two miles long which was peppered with pill-
boxes, ammunition dumps, trenches, strong-points and machine-gun
nests. Some Marines wondered why the authorities were sending 1000
men to France for a couple of hours when a million or so were already
there.

Early in March, Winston Churchill inspected the 4th Battalion.
According to one survivor, he told them that they were going on a daring
and arduous mission from which none might return. One wonders if
Keyes had told his old friend all the details. Secrecy and security are
always relative.

After this cheerful encouragement, the Marines paraded again on
7 March 1918. King George V visited the Deal Depot. The 4th marched

past with a swagger. The King took the salute. Some thoughtful Marines suspected that all the attention had a more sinister aspect.

A few days after the King's inspection, a single platoon of the Portsmouth Company were involved in what the surviving records delicately call an act of 'collective insubordination'. The word 'mutiny' was studiously avoided. Number 7 platoon refused to parade on the afternoon of Friday 17 March. The reason for this is not totally clear as the proceedings of the two Boards of Enquiry are lost to view.

It appears some Marines were unhappy about being confined to barracks. Their wives were a short distance away but they could not meet. Whatever their grievance, the system could not countenance indiscipline.

Colonel Elliot wasted no time. The platoon was arrested en masse with the exception of two men who had refused to join the protest. The culprits went under escort to Portsmouth to await proceedings. The officers and NCO ranks were similarly relieved of their duties. There had been, according to one officer, 'a very severe breakdown in command'.

The two marines who had not joined the protest were quickly reinforced by seventeen short service recruits from Deal together with ten former buglers and drummers. The ex-musicians presented a difficulty. Traditionally, bandsmen did not bear arms and had no weapons training. The volunteers made it plain they had stepped forward because they wanted to fight, not puff at bugles or bang drums. A suggestion that they could have revolvers was dismissed on the grounds that they would be of more danger to their comrades than the enemy. Finally, the pugnacious bandsmen agreed to accept the traditional cutlass.

Colonel Elliot believed that the keenness of the new arrivals would make up for any deficiency in their training and military knowledge. It was a pious hope, one which had been uttered by many an officer on the Western Front when his command received raw troops just before a major action.

Still baffled as to their exact task, the Marines practised hand to hand fighting, some of which was in gas respirators. They did a night exercise using a tape and canvas replica of the Mole. After that, they practised again with twelve mile route marches and a lot more close-quarter training. As a final gesture, there was another night exercise with a smokescreen, gas shells, star shells and other fireworks.

As with the sailors, no survivor's account mentions spending time running up a juddering, heaving, narrow plank, carrying an enormous amount of equipment, before somehow getting to the ground fifteen feet below.

However, they did know about the jump. The leap onto the quayside was represented by a piece of white tape. Allegedly, they stepped over the tape and pretended they were landing in the canal bed.

The Marines left Deal on the morning of 6 April 1918. They marched to the railway station to board a special train. At 07.00 hours it pulled out for Dover. There they embarked on *King Edward VII*, a one-time Clyde ferry steamer which one Marine recognized wistfully. Large boxes and crates, all clearly labelled 'For France' covered the upper deck. The Marines were shepherded below. Once out of sight of land, the ferry turned north to Shoeburyness. There, the passengers transhipped to *Daffodil* which took them to the Swin. They reached the *Vindictive* at 16.30 hours.

One of the new arrivals to 7 Platoon was James Feeney, an Irishman, who recorded the whole procedure in his diary:

> We had been below about three hours at sea when we were ordered up, and were transferred to another boat. This left us in a knot. We could not follow the mysterious working of the mind of the Admiralty. We went below again, and were four hours in this, when we came up to be landed on a battleship, which we got on about half-past four in the evening. Some of the old marines told me we were anchored at the mouth of the estuary of the Thames.

The next day, on board *Hindustan*, they too learned their destination:

> We are to land on the Mole and destroy all we can in the space of time that the wind and tide allow, and whilst the concrete ships are being sunk. The general opinion here at the moment is that it will be either completely successful or we shall be all wiped out.

Keyes visited the flotilla on that same date. He told everyone that they faced a hazardous task. Their chances of survival were slender. The fortunate ones might see a German prison camp. If any of them were married or had a special reason to withdraw, they could do so. They need not give any reason nor be questioned or pressed to give an explanation.

Not a solitary man asked to stand down.

Keyes was a charismatic and natural leader. His open approach and honesty about the approaching ordeal drew forth hearty cheers on each ship. Even allowing for peer pressure which would make it difficult for a single individual to withdraw, it is a remarkable testament to Keyes' vivid and powerful personality. Patriotism, a strong sense of honour, doing one's duty for King and Country are qualities derided or not understood today. To Keyes and his men, they were wholly admirable and a stark reality. Most of his audience knew that their Admiral had a copy of Kipling's *If* pinned up above his washbasin. It was not a matter of amusement but a source of pride.

Keyes' offer did inspire a number of requests which might induce incredulity in some modern readers. The blockships were to sail with full crews until they were about fifteen miles from their objective. A skeleton crew would take them on to Zeebrugge and Ostend, the surplus men transferring to the minesweeper HMS *Lingfield*.

The sailing crews applied to stay aboard so that the blockships would steam on fully manned. They were turned down. Some of the more determined applicants decided to make their own arrangements.

Before he left, Keyes presented Carpenter with a gilt horseshoe. It was a present from the admiral's wife, Eva, to bring good luck to the ship and her complement. With much cheerfulness, it was fastened to the casing of the middle funnel on the side which would face the Mole, high enough to be visible to the enemy.

Keyes originally planned to use *Vindictive* as his command post. In true Nelsonian tradition, he would command the proceedings from its very decks. It did not take too much effort to realize that this was hideously impracticable. A commander needs communications and the ability to move around to supervise all aspects of the operation. Striding the quarterdeck of the assault ship, undoubtedly romantic as it was, would render the Admiral powerless.

Keyes chose instead to fly his flag in the very new and very fast destroyer HMS *Warwick*. This created a minor problem of protocol and procedure in terms of seniority. Keyes had appointed Commander Carpenter as his Flag Captain for the operation. Carpenter's intimate knowledge of the operation and his navigational skills made him a very suitable choice to take the *Vindictive* alongside the Mole. Although Carpenter was relatively junior, there could be no complaint if he was working directly under the command of Keyes himself. The original plan called for *Vindictive* to lead the centre column of the force and Carpenter himself would be Fleet Guide.

Keyes' decision to use the *Warwick* altered matters considerably. A junior commander would now be in control of possibly the most important ship in the flotilla. Even if Carpenter should magically be promoted by Keyes himself, this would be a local, acting, unpaid rank. Captain Halahan, with substantive rank and seniority would automatically outrank Carpenter.

Keyes' first reaction was to follow the rulebook. Halahan would command *Vindictive*. Carpenter, bitterly disappointed, agreed that there was no choice. There matters would have rested except that Halahan himself learned of the problem. He immediately offered to waive his seniority. Keyes was able to effect a compromise outside the strict interpretation of King's Regulations which served the purpose. Carpenter would sail the ship and lay her alongside the Mole. He would have no command over the boarding parties or the assault crews. If Captain Halahan made any requests in respect of matters of time or position, Carpenter would do his best to abide by them. In essence, Carpenter had become an old-time sailing-master.

As a final flourish, Keyes told Carpenter to put up an extra ring and published the promotion to Acting Captain in local orders.

On the Western Front, Ludendorff's mighty advance was steadily crunching its way towards Amiens and the Channel ports. Calais, Dunkirk, Boulogne looked as if they might fall to the enemy. Belatedly British troops, held back in England at Lloyd George's behest, were hastily shipped across the Channel.

On 9 April 1918, four German divisions smashed into that part of the front line held by a reluctant ally. The illiterate, neglected, uncomprehending Portuguese conscripts, shivering in the cold of a northern spring, had little enough idea why their country was fighting Germany. Most of them had no inkling of where, what or why Germany was. The Portuguese 2nd Division withered away under the might of the 1st and 8th Bavarian Reserve Divisions, the 35th and 42nd Divisions of von Quast's Sixth Army

The Swin anchorage contained some highly impatient men. The first possible date for the operation, 9 April 1918, was a day of high winds and rough seas. There was no possibility of the armada sailing. The next day was the same.

Keyes fretted. The First Sea Lord and Geddes visited the ships. They were encouraging and cheerful. Everything would go well as soon as the weather cooperated.

On 11 April the meteorological reports were promising. That same day Sir Douglas Haig issued his sombre Order Of The Day to emphasize the desperate situation in the Second Battle of the Somme. Its last paragraph was blunt and brutal:

There is no other course open to us but to fight it out. Every position must be held to the last man; there must be no retirement. With our backs to the wall, and believing in the justice of our cause,

85

each one of us must fight on to the end. The safety of our homes and the freedom of mankind alike depend on the conduct of each one of us at this critical moment.

The field marshal might have felt that his Army still showed remarkable morale when these stirring words were greeted by an interested query from an Australian private – 'Where's the bastard wall then?'

Keyes issued the preparatory signal.

The first vessels away, in advance of the main group, were HMS *Erebus* and HMS *Terror*. With them went Captain Douglas to guide them to their position off the Dutch coast. From there they would hurl shells at the Zeebrugge batteries. Haselfoot joined a rather smaller monitor. Screened by some hungry-looking destroyers, the monitor would lay light buoys – another invention from the resourceful Brock – at twenty-mile intervals to guide the principal force. These were identified by letters – A, B, C, and D. There was one more buoy, G, which marked the start of the British-laid Belgian coast minefield through which an entrance had been carefully cleared.

Vindictive had only to lead her followers from buoy to buoy at a given speed. At each buoy, the time would be checked and speed increased or lessened to arrive at the following marker at the correct time. The final buoy was about sixteen miles north of Ostend and the same distance north-west of Zeebrugge. At this point, the flotilla would split into two. The main force would head straight for Zeebrugge. The smaller group would turn south for Ostend where they would come under the charge of Commodore Hubert Lynes who commanded the Dunkirk segment of the Dover Patrol. The distance was short enough to allow for a dead reckoning course to be accurate enough even though the cross-tide could play havoc with the most careful arithmetic.

At Dover, Commodore Boyle, the Chief of Staff, sailed in the early afternoon. HMS *Attentive*, a light cruiser with four destroyers led by HMS *Scott* set out for 'C' buoy. One destroyer anchored there. Two more dropped off at 'D' buoy.

Attentive went on to 'G' buoy. Boyle's task was to note the wind force and direction. The bare details would be sent by Aldis lamp to the ships at 'D' who would silently transmit them to the vessel at 'C'. No replies would be made in case the enemy saw the flickering lights.

There was strict wireless silence. Only *Warwick* would transmit, and only single code words at that, on Keyes' personal order.

At 16.00 hours on the afternoon of 11 April 1918, *Vindictive*, the five blockships and the two Mersey ferries weighed anchor and sailed to join the armada from Dover. They met at a point seven miles east of Ramsgate. At 19.30 hours the entire squadron set sail for the Belgian coast.

Leading Seaman William Childs, sailing on the *Vindictive* recalled that not everything went perfectly to plan:

Misfortune seemed to dog us on this trip, for no sooner had we left the Swin, than a fire was discovered in the gunner's store, a bale of waste having caught fire. Needless to say, we got windy for in this store were stowed 3000 Mills bombs and a goodly collection of Stokes Mortar shells all ready for use . . . all hands soon made short work of transporting the bombs and shells to another stowage, and we all breathed freely once again.

As night crept across the water, hopes were high. The sea was calm and a gentle wind blew towards Belgium. It was exactly the breeze that was needed to make the smoke really effective. Nerves tightened imperceptibly as the hours crept by. In later years, Keyes was to write of this moment:

My thoughts turned constantly to the assault on Santa Cruz in the Island of Tenerife in July, 1797, when Nelson's impatient ardour impelled him to undertake a hazard, fore-doomed by the state of the weather. All went well for a time, such wind as there was blew gently towards the Belgian coast, and I prayed that it would continue to do so – at any rate until we got to grips with the enemy – and that if it did not, that I would have the moral courage to break off the operation and await a more favourable opportunity.

Everything was, however, on schedule. At 23.00 hours, the *Warwick*'s wireless stuttered out a few staccato dots and dashes. The operation was to continue.

The first Handley Page 0/400 bomber of 215 Squadron had bumped across the uneven grass of its Dunkirk airfield at 22.40 hours. Its twin Rolls Royce Eagle VIII engines dragged its 13,000 pounds weight into the air. The pilot, a twenty-two year old Canadian, Captain John Allan, headed for Flushing. His task was to engage in desultory bombing. This would attract the Zeebrugge searchlights, drawing their attention inland, away from the sea.

The Handley Page was not a fast aeroplane. Its maximum speed was less than 100 miles an hour. Allan and his crew arrived over Zeebrugge at about 23.40 hours. For the next hour, trundling gently along at a modest 4000 feet, they dropped 112-pound bombs at decent intervals.

Spectators on the ships saw probing searchlights and the 'flaming onions' of the German anti-aircraft batteries chasing the Handley Page. In the far distance, what looked like sheet lightning was the artillery on the Western Front. The BEF was still fighting for its life.

The fleet reached the final light buoy. At this point, the five block-ships discharged their surplus crew. Each ship had thirty extra stokers who transferred to a minelayer for the journey back to Dover. The Ostend blockships and their escorts steamed south.

At 00.30 hours, the wind dropped. A few moments later, men on deck felt it on their cheeks. It was blowing to the north, away from the coast. Smoke drifted with the wind. If the breeze did not change, the attack would have no cover. With a garrison on edge after the bombing raid, approaching without smoke would be a desperate business.

Keyes was faced with a decision of peculiar difficulty. His ships were less than ninety minutes from their target. Every officer, every man was ready for battle. Keyes could not be sure that there would be a second chance. There was every possibility that the whole scheme was known, if only in outline, to the enemy. To turn round and go home might mean the total collapse of Operation ZO. Keyes recalled later:

I went through a pretty difficult time during the next few moments. I knew that every man in the expedition felt as I did, keyed up for the ordeal. How they would hate to be called off and then asked to undertake it all over again. Or perhaps, worse still . . . if the Admiralty thought for a moment that the expedition would no longer be a surprise, they would be absolutely certain to declare it off. What would our feelings be if the weather proved favourable after turning back? It would be so much easier to go on and trust to the God of Battles. . . .

Keyes decided.

The *Warwick*'s wireless stuttered again. The operation was called off.

It was dark. Not a single vessel showed navigation lights. Keyes' decision required seventy-five vessels to turn about onto a reciprocal course. It could have been a disaster of epic proportions but the Royal Navy has always counted very fine seamen in its numbers.

HMS *Warwick* stopped her engines. She waited south of the main force. Matters were complicated because both *Daffodil* and *Iris* had proved to be bad sailers in the waters of the North Sea. It had been decided to tow them behind *Vindictive*. To save fuel, the two submarines, packed with amatol, were also under tow. The picket boat which was to rescue the submariners was similarly fastened to a big sister as were the CMBs. Every large ship towed something.

The CMBs rumbled into life, their commanders keeping the tow ropes taut as they turned. One failed. She was cut down during the manoeuvre and sank although the crew was rescued. None of the smaller craft had wireless. They had been instructed by lamp. By good fortune and no little skill, the blinking lights were unseen by the enemy. A few salvoes into the middle of the fleet as it turned would have been catastrophic.

Warwick started her engines. She made way just as four heavy shells screamed out of the darkness. The Germans were awake. What is more, they had remarkably accurate sound or wireless range-finders. The shells splashed into the water only 200 yards from the destroyer with her enormous ensign.

Above Zeebrugge, Allan did not know the operation was cancelled. At 00.40 hours, he turned towards the sea, ready to drop flares to guide *Vindictive* and assist the landing parties. One of the water-cooled engines went on strike. The 0/400 lost height. Allan turned towards Nieuwpoort on the Belgian coast. Low cloud blanketed the area. In a short while, Allan was lost. The crew fired distress signals as the aircraft got lower and lower. The Handley Page crashed into the sea, seven miles off Ostend.

The observer, Captain Bewsher, and the gun layer, Lieutenant Purvis, were rescued by a coastal motor boat which saw the flares. Allan was never seen again.

Bad weather had set in over the Belgian coast. Six Handley Pages from 214 and 215 Squadrons were scheduled to bomb the coastal batteries and the guns on the Mole. Only three found their way through the rain and mist to drop their bombs. One aircraft had to land in the Netherlands. The crew were courteously interned. A grateful *Nederlandseluchtmacht* added another aircraft to their eclectic collection of strays.

On the way home, *Vindictive* suffered the second fatality of Operation ZO as Childs recollected:

> Leading Seaman Pearce, in charge of A Company's Lewis Gun, was accidentally shot through the thigh, the bullet cutting his main artery, causing his death within two days through loss of blood. This was rotten luck as he had gone through the Siege of Ladysmith and the Boer War.

As a result, Childs found himself in charge of the A Company Lewis gun team.

Commodore Lynes gathered the sixty or so vessels of the Ostend force together for their return. The monitors, which had been bombarding Zeebrugge, fired a few final shells and the force retreated. There was one absentee.

CMB 33 had gone missing. Nobody knew where she was or what had happened to her. Except her crew. And the Germans. She had grounded on shoals near the Ostend canal mouth. Her crew were hardly able to resist the polite officer of the Imperial Navy who requested their surrender. It was unfortunate that *CMB 33*'s commander had disobeyed his instructions quite so comprehensively and taken his secret orders with him. They described the plan of attack on Ostend in some detail. They referred to Operation ZO. Even the dullest intelligence officer in the German Navy would have guessed that Zeebrugge was also under threat.

Korvettenkapitän Eric Schülze, the senior intelligence officer on the staff of Admiral von Schröder who commanded the Marine Divisions in Flanders was far from a dullard. He wrote in 1927:

> In this boat we found a map giving us first hand information concerning the plan of the expedition: it was the English naval chart Nr 125 'Ostend Roads': written in black ink was the inscription 'No 33 Boat Chart April 9th 1918.' This map indicated the course to be steered, with full explanations such as 'Line of Blockships approach'. It was not difficult for us to draw the necessary conclusion for Zeebrugge. We were thus warned of the imminent danger. The date also could be approximately guessed, for it had to be on a night on which tide, moon, wind and the state of the sea all concurred to render the attack possible. This was the case on the evening of April 22nd and all the troops as well as all the coastal batteries had been specially alarmed. The only thing we did not know was the plan for landing on the mole and for the destruction of the viaduct.

Schülze was, at the very least, a touch ingenuous. He had concluded only that Operation ZO implied Zeebrugge was also a possible target for a blocking operation. The diversionary landing or the attack on the viaduct still held the chance of surprise. Clearly, the captain also felt that a full moon was no hindrance to a blockship operation. This was not unreasonable if no landing was contemplated.

What is clear, and other evidence supports it, is that the defences were brought to a state of heightened alert. They may not have known exactly what was afoot but they knew enough to be especially vigilant.

The commander of *CMB 33* had a lot to answer for.

Keyes cannot be criticized for his brave decision to call off the attack. Many others in the same position would have carried on. So much effort, so many resources had been expended. It would have been very tempting to assume that everything would somehow work out. To turn round and tamely sail away took considerable nerve.

The next morning, 12 April 1918, Keyes visited the ships and explained why he had called off the assault:

It was not a pleasant atmosphere. I was feeling very unhappy . . . and I felt they were looking sideways at me, and wondering if I really meant business. I told them that we were going to have a great success, not a heroic disaster, and I swore before heaven that I would take them alongside the enemy; but they must trust me and wait until I considered that we could undertake the business with a fair prospect of success. Their shout of approval . . . lifted the awful cloud of depression and I think we all felt happier. At any rate I know I did.

Feeney's diary entry is interesting confirmation:

Admiral Keyes came on board . . . and explained the reason that we retired last night without firing a shot. He said without a smoke-screen that would be effective we would not have a dog's chance, and last night the wind changed and the smokescreen would be useless; hence his order to return. It takes a very self-reliant man to give an order like that in the last few minutes.

Keyes may have looked and sounded confident – and there can be no doubt that his officers and men were solidly behind him – but he knew that time was pressing. The April dark period was coming to a close.

On the morning of 13 April the wind was within limits. Keyes went through the reports of the aborted mission and then sent the preparatory signal to all units.

The Swin Force got under way. The rest of the Dover flotilla prepared for sea. At Dunkirk, Lynes issued his orders. The Naval and Marine gunners looked forward to an evening of hard work.

The wind freshened. Within an hour, it was strengthening to gale force. Keyes sent the cancellation signal.

Keyes was aware that his mentors, Wemyss and Geddes were becoming restless. There was apparently no longer any chance of a successful surprise attack. Even though the misdemeanours of

CMB 33's captain were not known in all their hideous detail, it was inconceivable that the enemy was not ready and waiting.

Keyes, naturally, wanted to continue to fight to the end.

The Admiralty finally decided that the operation must be cancelled, the Marine battalion disbanded and the sailors sent back to the Grand Fleet. Even though Keyes anticipated the Admiralty's decision, the arrival of Sir Rosslyn at Dover could only herald the worst.

Wemyss was his usual urbane self. He felt for Keyes as his words made clear. He assured him that his decision to withdraw had been absolutely correct. Then he cited the loss of the surprise factor, that the men's morale would inevitably droop, that it was impossible to keep the assault troops cooped up on the ships. 'It will be,' he said, 'at least three weeks before the next dark period.' Keyes, desperate to keep his plan in being, interrupted, 'Why wait three weeks? I want to try again in nine or ten days!'

The First Sea Lord was patient. 'But it will be full moon then, and you have always stipulated a dark night with no moon.'

Keyes was adamant. 'No, no! I always wanted a full moon but I couldn't wait for one. Please go back and tell the Board that you approve of my carrying out the attack in the next period when high tide occurs about midnight!'

Wemyss, it is recorded, after a brief silence, laughed. 'Roger,' he rejoined, 'what a damned liar you are!'

We know that Keyes had already decided that his assessment that the operation had to be at a dark period could be thrown out of the window. Even allowing for an effective smokescreen, the full moon could fall on a night of no cloud. Certainly, Keyes could assume the enemy would find it hard to believe that anyone would be foolish enough to launch an attack under such conditions. Schülze, however, had already decided otherwise. The defenders of Zeebrugge and Ostend had been brought to a state of preparedness.

Curiously neither Wemyss nor Keyes referred to the *raison d'être* for the whole enterprise – the denial to the enemy of Ostend and Zeebrugge as naval bases. If the operation was to be cancelled without any more discussion, presumably the need to bottle up the U-boats was substantially less than it had been just four months earlier. At that time, it had been so vital that Jellicoe and Bacon had been replaced. It is true that if the Germans took the Channel ports, attacks on Zeebrugge and Ostend would be pointless. The war would effectively be at an end. However, desperate though the situation was, defeatism did not roam through Admiralty Arch. The Allies would hold. The North Sea harbours would remain in enemy hands.

It can be argued that some in the Admiralty already suspected that the U-boat threat had peaked. Certainly Hall's Intelligence department knew that German submarine commanders were now advised not to try to pass through the Straits of Dover. The new measures were taking their toll. Service in the Flanders Flotilla was fast becoming a route to a short life.

Similarly, the Admiralty knew that shipping losses were only about a third of the terrible month of April 1917. British Intelligence was also aware that U-boat crews were no longer all volunteers. Experienced engineers and petty officers were at a premium. Most significant of all, there was a growing tendency for U-boat crews to surrender rather than fight. Operation ZO had, apparently, become an end in itself.

Nonetheless, Wemyss went back to London to persuade the Admiralty board to accept the new dates. Wemyss, it is accepted, liked to get on with everybody but the spectacle of a First Sea Lord deciding to try and countermand Admiralty board orders at the whim of a Vice Admiral is slightly unusual.

Keyes received new orders.

The attack was to be launched on the first promising afternoon after 22 April, just one week away. Keyes had won. Next time, there would be no turning back, no matter what the weather.

CHAPTER EIGHT

Seven dreary days to wait.

The Marines and sailors who had sailed on *Vindictive*, *Iris* and *Daffodil* moved out of their congested ships to return to the *Hindustan*. Conditions were cramped. Another depot ship arrived to ease the congestion. HMS *Dominion* joined the fleet.

A minor disaster was averted only by swift action. The depot ships ran out of cigarettes. Twenty-five thousand were rushed from Dover. An influx of cooks and stores improved the food but tedium ran through the steel hulls. After high anticipation, anticlimax crept through the messdecks.

Some cautious souls worked at providing extra protection for the more exposed positions. First aid dressings were piled around the decks of the three assault ships. Owners of Crown and Anchor boards made every effort to become millionaires.

Gambling on Crown and Anchor was prohibited, although not actively discouraged, in both the Army and the Royal Navy. On the *Hindustan* and *Dominion*, the regulations were tacitly ignored. The players were, after all, just as likely not to return.

Crown and Anchor needed a dice and a cloth with six squares marked with the four card suits, a crown (the 'sergeant major') and an anchor (the 'mud-hook'). The punters put their stakes on the squares. The banker used one variation or another of the following patter – which some soldiers and sailors of 1914–1918 could remember fifty years later:

> Lay it down, my lucky lads. The more you put down, the more you pick up. You come here on bicycles, you go away in motor-cars. The old firm, all the way from Pompey. What about the lucky old mud-hook? The old mud-hook's badly backed. Any more for any more before we turn 'em up. Lay it down, my lucky lads, thick and heavy. Have you all finished, have you all done? Right, up she comes. Two jam tarts and the lucky old sergeant-major.

Keyes was back in Dover. There was the usual paperwork. Nothing could be done by sitting on his flagship for a week. Others waited with him. Brock, Osborne the gunnery officer, and a handful of others.

The plans were perused yet again. Some minor tinkering took place. The gap in the Belgian coast minefield was surreptitiously widened. Its entrance was marked by two Aga buoys, another invention of Brock's, with their flashing lights.

Keyes made one crucial alteration. Arrival at the buoys would mark zero hour. Come what may, the mission would go on from that point.

Time ticked by. A few men went sick. Then Keyes was faced with a major casualty. Lieutenant Ivan Franks collapsed on board *Iphigenia* with acute appendicitis. Just before he was evacuated to Chatham hospital, he scribbled a note to Keyes. In it, he begged the Admiral to appoint his deputy Lieutenant Billyard-Leake in his place.

Keyes had already once yielded to Franks' pleas that his fellow submariner should join the expedition. Billyard-Leake was a lieutenant of only one year's seniority. Giving him command of a vital component of the blocking operation might be too hazardous.

As Keyes pondered the problem, another piece of paper arrived. It was signed by every member of the *Iphigenia*'s crew. It asked that Billyard-Leake should be appointed captain.

The admiral admitted defeat. The lieutenant took command of one of His Majesty's ships at the advanced age of twenty-two.

Sub Lieutenant Maurice Lloyd joined the *Iphigenia* from HMS *Dominion*. Lloyd already held a Distinguished Service Cross, a remarkable achievement for a very young officer.

On board *Sirius*, one officer was accidentally gassed when tinkering with one of the smoke cylinders. Brock's chloro-sulphuric gas did not encourage clumsiness. His place was taken by Sub Lieutenant Alfred Knight who also came from *Dominion*.

In the week of waiting, twenty-two posts became vacant. There was fierce competition to fill them. Although not all of the details were necessarily known to everybody, there was intense competition to get on board any of the ships that were to sail against the enemy.

Grudgingly, slowly, the days passed. The first possible high tide date was 22 April. That morning promised little. The northerly wind, so essential for a successful smokescreen, was erratic. The skies were clear. Visibility off the Belgian coast was very good. It was a less than favourable situation on a night of full moon. Nevertheless, Keyes was certain that the time had come.

He either did not know, or believe it mattered, that the high water mark at Zeebrugge would be nearly four foot less than on the previous attempts. It was another shading of the odds against the attackers.

There is no doubt at all that Keyes was determined that the armada would sail unless everything was totally against him. The orders that went to every vessel in the expedition listed the signals and the action to be taken. 'NURSLING' was the cancellation but there was a significant meaning to the letters 'ZB'. It would be made during the crossing if the wind was favourable but the seas too high for the small craft. On receipt, all the smoke-layers would turn back. The only small craft remaining would be *ML 110* and *ML 128* which had the job of mooring calcium buoys off the Mole and the canal. Once they had done that, they were to rescue the blockship crews. *ML 282* and *ML 526* would also remain to help with rescue. *CMB 29A* and *CMB 34A* served the Ostend blockships.

Everything else – the smoke-floats, smokescreens, the buoys, the torpedo attacks on vessels anchored in the harbour – would go by the board. The bigger ships would have to make do with their own resources. The directions show a very determined mind.

Keyes issued the preparatory orders. At 10.45 on 22 April 1918, signal flags fluttered in the breeze. 'NASCENT'. It was the codeword to all ships to weigh anchor and proceed.

Wing Commander Brock joined the *Vindictive*. Dressed in khaki, he had two holstered pistols and carried a cutlass, rather like the Pirate King in Gilbert and Sullivan. He was not the only member of the party to wield the Navy's favourite edged weapon. Although there must be some question as to the purpose cutlasses would serve in the face of machine-gun fire, it is essential to remember that Keyes' plan envisaged a swift, close-quarter action amidst the guns at the end of the Mole.

Thirty-four of Brock's experts from the Admiralty experimental station at Stratford were on *Vindictive, Iris* and *Daffodil*. Under the command of Lieutenant Graham Hewett of the RNVR they were to operate the fixed and portable flame-throwers and phosphorus bombs. Strangely, for an all-Naval operation, Hewett's deputy was a Royal Engineer, Lieutenant Eastlake.

In the early afternoon, Vice Admiral Roger John Brownlow Keyes walked down to Dover harbour to keep his date with history. His wife was by his side to see him off. Often quoted is her remark to him. 'Tomorrow is St George's Day. It is sure to be the best day for our enterprise. St George can be trusted to bring good fortune to England.'

The 'our enterprise' makes one wonder how much she knew.

At 17.00 hours, the armada set sail. As dusk fell, *Warwick* blinked a signal to *Vindictive*:

Saint George for England!

There was a pause as the bridge signaller relayed the message. *Vindictive*'s lamp flickered rapidly. Carpenter's reply was short and optimistic: 'May we give the dragon's tail a damned good twist!'

The force headed eastward in three columns. In the lead, in the centre, *Vindictive* had *Iris* and *Daffodil* in tow. Behind her came the five blockships with a paddle minesweeper, HMS *Lingfield* and five motor launches fussing along behind them to take off the extra crews.

HMS *Warwick*, easily distinguished by her enormous ensign, was well in the lead of the starboard column. The destroyers *Phoebe* and *North Star* followed. Their prime task was to guard *Vindictive* from attack once she was alongside the Mole. Astern, HMS *Mansfield* towed the submarine *C 1* in company with HMS *Trident* who pulled *C 3* behind her. HMS *Tempest* was to escort the two Ostend blockships.

The port column was led by *Whirlwind*, followed by *Myngs* and *Moorsom* who were to patrol north of Zeebrugge. In the same column was *Tetrarch* who would join *Tempest* on the journey to Ostend. Each one towed one or more coastal motor boats. Between the columns buzzed gaggles of motor launches. More than sixty of them, sounding like demented wasps, kept station as best they could.

Eighteen miles out from Dover, Lieutenant E. E. Hill, commanding *CMB 35A* suffered a captain's nightmare. His boat fouled her propellers and steadily dropped behind the column. Hill was a determined officer. He persuaded, or possibly threatened, the captain of a passing drifter to tow him to Dover. On arrival there, he cajoled an assorted group of dockyard staff to work like maniacs to free his jammed propellers and repair some other minor damage.

At 21.40 hours, Hill manoeuvred the *CMB 35A* out of Dover, demanded full speed, directed the nose of his vessel towards Zeebrugge and went like an arrow to rejoin the fleet.

The 61st Wing and Dover squadrons of the Royal Air Force scouted ahead of the column, looking for stray German aircraft. There was nothing to be seen. The attacking force sailed on, unmolested, as dusk fell.

Moonlight silvered the North Sea. For a short while, clouds had drifted across the sky but these had soon vanished to leave a cold clear night.

Captain Wilfred Tomkinson, nominally Keyes' Destroyer Fleet Captain, stood beside him on the bridge. Every vessel was sharp and clearly defined in the shining night. Keyes had sudden doubts. His decision to attack at a time of full moon was looking, to put it mildly, more than foolhardy. Tomkinson's comment scarcely reassured him:

> But there's one thing about it. Even if the enemy does expect us, they will never think we could be such fools as to try and pull it off on a night like this.

The clouds trickled back, slowly, reluctantly. A mist crept across the water. Visibility shrank to less than a mile. For those of a supernatural or religious turn of mind, Saint George was clearly doing his best for England. For the purely superstitious, the horseshoe on *Vindictive*'s funnel served the same purpose.

Rosoman breathed a gentle sigh of relief:

> The wetness caused by the . . . Scotch mist pleased me, because I was somewhat afraid of fire, owing to the large amount of wood in the ship – assembling platforms, ramps, brows, etc., which I had drenched in some anti-fire mixture supplied by the RNAS, but of the value of which I knew nothing.

The aircrews of 214 and 215 Squadrons looked at the weather. It had been consistently bad for flying all month. This was another night when bombing was impossible. The Navy would have to manage without them. The mechanics folded the big 100-feet wings on the Handley Pages and resignedly pushed the bombers back into their hangars.

On board the attacking force, some men kept busy. Ammunition was heaved out of storerooms and stacked ready for use. The handful of sick berth attendants heaped field dressings in convenient places. Candle lamps were placed near electric lights. Imperceptibly, tensions increased.

At 22.00 hours, the columns arrived at 'D' buoy, sixteen miles from Zeebrugge. This was the point at which the surplus stokers and extra crews were to be transferred to the *Lingfield* and her attendant launches.

Not everything went quite to plan.

On *Iphigenia*, twelve stokers simply vanished when the time came for them to disembark. When the launch that was to take them back to England had left, they reappeared, grimy, dishevelled and full of fight.

Intrepid had thirty-four extra crewmen. Their launch broke down

98

before they disembarked. *Intrepid* set off for Zeebrugge with eighty-seven souls on board. It was an admirable spirit which just happened to make the task of the rescue launches fractionally more difficult.

Chicken soup was served. Mugs of cocoa appeared. The rum ration went round. The night was silent. The thin rain got heavier. The keen-eared could hear the sullen rumble, far-away thunder, of artillery on the Somme.

The convoy moved towards 'G' buoy. They reached the gap in the minefield where *Attentive* stood guard exactly on time. 22.30. 'X' hour. Zeebrugge was fifteen miles, ninety minutes steaming time away.

The tows were slipped. *Iris* and *Daffodil* were set free to cover the last miles under their own steam. There was no turning back.

The Ostend force moved off. *Sirius* and *Brilliant* and their patient shepherding destroyers and motor launches headed for their target.

Keyes led *Warwick*, *Phoebe*, *North Star*, *Whirlwind* and *Myngs* ahead of the main force to drive off any enemy ships which might appear. Nobody knew if a counterattack was festering in the darkness.

North Star and *Phoebe* were to shepherd the assault ships the last miles to the Mole. After that, they would become the outer guard for the blockships which were scheduled to enter the harbour twenty minutes after *Vindictive* began her diversionary attack.

Keyes decided to move *Warwick* so that she could drive off any torpedo attacks from the seaward side of the Mole. If German destroyers or even submarines lurked in the open sea, the assault craft would be in a truly perilous position. Anchored to the Mole, totally defenceless, three torpedoes would put paid to the whole assault force.

It cannot be that this thought came to Keyes only during the last ninety minutes before the attack. One has to assume that it was in his mind at an early stage and was not particularly specified in the main operations order.

At 23.10 hours, the first units of the assault force went onto their final leg. *CMBs 24A*, *17A* and *15A* surged forward to drop smoke across the entire front of the attacking force. Ten minutes later, *CMB 16A* tore south to lay smoke-floats off Blankenberg harbour.

A few minutes after midnight German time, 23.07 hours British time, *Artillerie-Maat* Richard Policke, a Petty Officer Gunner with the Mole End battery, described the scene:

A hazy, clammy night. About 2000 metres visibility. Shortly after midnight, the look-out post reported engine noises out to sea. The alarm bells rattled through the shelters. The crews jumped to their guns and hurled star shells into the mist. Shot after shot! Nothing to be seen. The garrison grabbed their gas masks and took up their battle stations as calmly as if they were on exercise. The ammunition hoists creaked as shells were hauled into position.

Keyes fretted as *Warwick* approached the target area with forty minutes to go. There was no bombardment of Zeebrugge and Ostend. It was obvious that an air attack was out of the question but the monitors should have put to sea.

Tactical air support of ground operations was not the essential in 1918 that it is today. It is true that the infantry on the Western Front were learning the lesson that air superiority or, preferably, supremacy is the key to victory on the ground. German soldiers were becoming increasingly demoralized as constant ground strafing by the Royal Air Force took its toll. Keyes, though, clearly did not believe that the planned diversion from the air was an important part of his plan. He was probably right. It certainly would not have perturbed the enemy who were well accustomed to British air raids on Zeebrugge and Bruges. These usually killed more Belgian civilians than they did German sailors and marines. The gunners sat tight in their bunkers until the bombing stopped. After which, metaphorically, they dusted the furniture, replaced the ornaments and manned their guns.

The first monitor shell was fired moments later at 23.20 hours. Captain Douglas had been hampered by the low visibility. Only when he picked up the Oost Gat light which marked Dutch territorial waters, which he had almost entered, was he able to start the bombardment.

At Zeebrugge beach, *Vizefeuerwerker* Schröder, the equivalent of a Petty Officer Ordnance Technician, had just finished his inspection of the *Friedrichsort* position:

Just as I returned to my dugout, there were several explosions in the immediate vicinity. My first thought was that it was an air raid but that was quickly shown to be wrong. Several minutes later, there was the familiar whine and howl of heavy-calibre shells and the muffled sound of discharges from the sea. In the meadowland behind the Battery, the bursts created great fountains of earth. In the dug-outs on the right side of the battery, the crews were tipped out of bed by an explosion. The shells were hitting for the most part near the 5-cm battery and fifty to two hundred metres behind the guard-room, east of the battery. Without waiting for the alarm signal, the crews went to action stations. If a general coast alarm

100

sounded, the Battery was already prepared. Meanwhile, the small neighbouring batteries sent up starshell.

Keyes would probably have continued the attack even if the monitors had not started firing. His determination to carry on was so great that he would probably have ignored the setback.

The monitors, *Erebus* and *Terror*, escorted by *Termagant*, *Truculent* and *Manly* began their bombardment. Once again, the Belgian civilians went wearily into their cellars until the noise and tumult ended.

Monitors were at Ostend too. *Marshal Soult*, *General Crauford*, *Prince Eugene* and *Lord Clive* with the smaller monitors *M 21*, *M 24* and *M 26* were to bombard the German batteries. Guarded by HMS *Mentor*, *Lightfoot* and the well-known *Zubian* and the French destroyers *Capitaine Mehl*, *Francis Garnier*, *Roux* and *Bouclier*, their shells dropped into the area of Ostend harbour.

To add to the general confusion, the Royal Marine and Royal Naval siege guns in France joined in the clamour. The aim of the exercise was not only to persuade the enemy to stay under cover. It was to make this night just the same as many others which had preceded it. The Germans would, it was argued, be totally surprised when *Vindictive* and the block-ships arrived.

This was little more than a pious hope. The defences were ready. The alert had spread like fire down a fuse all along the coast. An *Alarmbereitschaft* had brought all units to readiness. A rumour had also spread that the British intended a major landing with 20,000 men. This was not, as it happens, too far removed from Admiral Bayly's plan of 1916. Every gun crew, every machine-gun post was waiting for the invasion.

A *Tagesbefehl* or Daily Order from von Schröder's headquarters had added further to the anticipation of the defenders. Battery personnel were expected to fight and die by their guns if need be. No matter what later claims were made, it is evident that the Germans were not taken by surprise. The men of the three divisions and the air units of *Marinekorps Flandern* were ready for trouble.

The Debusschere family – mother, daughter Maria and sons Gustaaf and Roger – of Torhoutsesteenweg 448 in Ostend took shelter under their stairs. The eleven-year old Roger recalled that his mother firmly believed that it was the safest part of the house. Bombardments were not all bad either. Sometimes a horse was killed. The quick-witted and agile were able to get to the carcass before the Germans hauled it off for their own rations.

101

The German coastal batteries reacted quickly. The heavy guns of the *Tirpitz*, *Eylau*, *Friedrich* and *Hindenburg* positions rattled the doors and windows of Torhoutsesteenweg.

Keyes was keen to note in his official dispatches that the German guns failed to do any material damage to the bombarding force. He failed to state that the monitor and siege gun bombardment had an equally small effect on the defence.

As the first shells from *Erebus* and *Terror* whistled into Zeebrugge, *CMB 28A* headed inshore to lay smoke inside the Mole. Nine motor launches followed her like a gaggle of ducklings, ready to copy whatever mother did.

At 23.30 hours, *Warwick* was ten minutes ahead of the assault ships. She passed a light buoy five miles north-west of Zeebrugge just as the resourceful Lieutenant Hill cleared the last minefield in his rush to join in the battle. He took up his smoke-float patrol and, for his trouble, became an object of great interest to one of the Blankenberg batteries.

The destroyer screen divided to deal with any threat that might arise. *CMB 22B* and *CMB 23B* rushed forward to lay smoke to blind the Mole guns and any observers in the lighthouse. *CMB 5* and *CMB 7* took a wide arc which would place them inside the curve of the Mole to torpedo any destroyers at anchor. Their sister craft, *CMB 21B* and *CMB 26B* went in the opposite direction. From the far side of the Mole, near the viaduct, they would use Stokes mortars to lob bombs over the parapet.

The smoke thickened. Thick acrid artificial fog wrapped itself round *Vindictive* and her companions. Another fifteen minutes. That was all it would take to reach the target.

Interestingly, Keyes timed the first German reaction at 23.30 hours, some ten minutes earlier than the estimates of the other participants. The first star shells had gone unnoticed. The invaders were too far away. Now, more flowered in the dark sky. Without warning, the night became noon. Searchlights on shore probed questing fingers of light towards the open sea. Whatever the exact time, every survivor agreed that the defences were challenging the incursion some fifteen minutes before the assault ships arrived.

Policke was in no doubt:

> . . . a dark thick cloud of artificial fog through which a fine rain formed an impenetrable mass. The roaring of the approaching motorboats was constant. The first enemy fire cracked out at the

battery. Our coloured flares gave the alarm that the harbour was threatened.

Concise orders came from the fire control centre. Range. Distance. 'Fire!'

Able Seaman Albert McKenzie, with one of the seaman assault parties, had his own theory about who disturbed the defenders:

Well we got within fifteen minutes run of the Mole when some marines got excited and fired their rifles. Up went four big star shells and they spotted us.

This alertness from the Zeebrugge garrison simply confirms that the defenders were well aware that Tommy was up to something.

British accounts consistently maintain that complete surprise was achieved. A later interesting embellishment claimed that all the officers had gone to a party that very evening, leaving their men to cope as best they could. *Kapitänleutnant* Robert Schütte, the Battery Commander on the Mole, was emphatically present by his guns. So was *Oberleutnant* Adolf Rodewald of the 1st *Marine-Artillerie* Regiment. *Leutnant* Zimmerman was also on duty. The trio would make life rather difficult for the attackers.

The defence could see nothing as the coastal motor boats belched out more smoke. The German heavy batteries lobbed shells which roared over well beyond the attacking flotilla.

Vindictive, *Iris* and *Daffodil*, protected by the smoke, sailed confidently towards the Mole. Lieutenant Arthur Welman, the Flotilla Commander for the coastal motor boats, on board *CMB 23B* was close enough to the Mole extension to hear the gun crews shouting. A machine gun rattled into action. Small-arms fire spattered the water.

The drizzle continued. The wind had died. All ranks were at action stations except for the senior officers in charge of the assault teams. They had ignored orders. Colonel Elliot of the Marines and Major Cordner, his deputy, stood side-by-side on the bridge of the *Vindictive*, peering like eager trippers into the murk. Captain Halahan, accompanied by his second-in-command, Commander Edwards was on the upper gangway deck.

At 23.56 hours St George, the patron saint of England, changed sides.

Vindictive was 300 yards from the lighthouse when an errant puff of wind blew away the smokescreen. Star shell and searchlights lit the

103

cruiser from end to end. It took several seconds, most witnesses agree, before the Germans opened fire.

There were two schools of thought. One was that even the German naval gunners could not believe their eyes. The second was simpler. They believed *Vindictive* was a blockship and would turn into the harbour. *Kapitän* Schülze had warned both Zeebrugge and Ostend of an impending attack but, by his own admission, knew nothing of the diversion.

This is confirmed by Policke. The defenders decided that the captain of the cruiser was mad as the ship moved at high speed towards the Mole. They did not anticipate an attempt to put troops ashore.

The incredulity did not last.

What some thought must be every gun in the entire universe aimed at *Vindictive*. The Mole extension guns fired at what was, in gunners' terms, point-blank range. At 200 yards, there was not an artilleryman in the world who could have missed. It took the *Vindictive* three minutes to move into the cover of the Mole. By the time she reached it, she was just fifty yards from the muzzle of the end gun on the Mole extension. Amazingly, incredibly, *Vindictive* escaped being holed below the water-line. If that had happened, Keyes' great adventure would have turned into instant disaster.

Operation ZO lacked what United States planners call the OS Factor or 'Oh, Sugar!' when all goes wrong. The British, more politely, refer to Plan B. In both cases, this is often the option of beating a hasty retreat. Even if there had been a Plan B, however, it is equally clear that the Royal Navy and Royal Marines would have ignored it.

Carpenter was conning the ship from the forward *Flammenwerfer* hut. He had lined up *Vindictive*, at the right angle and speed, to arrive along-side the Mole in the correct position. One can hardly blame him for taking an instant decision to increase speed and close the Mole at a different angle. The *Vindictive* swung to port, all of her own guns battering away in an attempt to reduce the German onslaught. In the hut with him, a fascinated spectator, was the hapless Lieutenant Eastlake of the Royal Engineers who was to operate the flame-thrower when the exact moment arrived.

Rosoman, the First Lieutenant, was in the protected bridge below. Every minute he coolly enquired, as pre-arranged, if his captain was all right. If ever there was no reply, Rosoman would take command.

As Carpenter put his ship on to her new course, she became an increasingly large target. Already her funnels were lacerated, flame and sparks shooting up from them like a bizarre Bonfire Night display. Two shells hit the forecastle. The forward howitzer crew died. A relief crew, from the port 6-inch battery who took their places were scythed down immediately.

'Every man was serving the guns,' Policke wrote for the benefit of the readers of *An Flanderns Küste*, the magazine for the Marine Divisions who guarded the Belgian coast, 'dripping with sweat, covered in powder marks, everybody from the Battery Commander to the youngest sailor, worked to keep every gun firing as rapidly as possible. There were no ranks, no commanders.'

Two more shells slammed into *Vindictive*'s hull just below the bridge. The first exploded on impact. The second went in and wrecked everything in the area. The upper and false decks took severe punishment. Rosoman's mattresses protecting the bridge were shredded. Stokes mortar and Lewis gun teams were caught by flying splinters.

The *Friedrichsort* battery was also in action as Schröder relates:

At one o'clock *Leutnant* Zimmerman reported from the *Friedrichsort* battery observation post that an enemy cruiser, about five hundred metres distant, was approaching the Mole. Immediately, three salvoes were fired at a range of 3500 metres. Unfortunately, the firing then had to stop to avoid damage to the Mole installations.

Disaster beckoned with a bony finger. Some landing brows were already matchwood. Worse, Colonel Elliot and Major Cordner had been killed instantly when the first salvo screamed across from the Mole.

Captain Halahan, on the false deck below them, was also dead. His deputy, Commander Edwards, was severely wounded in both legs. Two of his men took him below despite his urgent orders that he should be carried to a gangway so that he could land on the Mole. Within seconds, both Marine and bluejacket storming parties lost their senior officers.

The carnage on *Vindictive* was fearful. Sergeant Harry Wright's 10 Platoon of the Marine contingent had won the draw to lead the 4th Battalion on to the Mole:

. . . in the darkness we stood ready to land. We were packed tight in five ranks, Lieutenant Stanton in front of me, as Platoon Sergt in the rear. The two rear ranks were standing directly underneath one of the *Vindictive*'s Cutters.

It is usual, of course, when boats are hoisted inboard for the plug to be removed for the water to drain. This had not been done and the Cutter was half full of rain water.

The first shell inboard, fired from the Battery at the sea end of the Mole exploded directly overhead and some 30 members of my Platoon were killed. Those of us standing under the Cutter escaped unhurt, the water breaking the force of the fragments of the shell.

Lying mortally wounded on the deck of the *Vindictive* was my young officer, Lieutenant Stanton. As I knelt beside him he had just enough time to whisper, 'Carry on, Wright' before he died.

Another Marine in 10 Platoon escaped more or less unharmed:

... the first shell that hit the *Vindictive* ... killed dozens and set them all aflame, all the lads around me were blown to bits and I was flung between her funnels, my tin hat was shattered and so was my rifle but I soon found some more. ...

It was Marine Ernie Clist's first time in action:

We were packed like sardines. When the Germans got on target, they gave us hell, the row was deafening ... there must have been 30 or 40 of our chaps laid out on the deck, killed or wounded.

The only unwounded officer for the naval storming parties was Lieutenant Commander Bryan Adams. Lieutenant Commander Harrison who should have taken over was unconscious with a shattered jaw. Others lay dead or wounded. There had been a rush by both officers and men from under cover to the upper deck as soon as the firing began. Inexperience, excitement, enthusiasm had been poor protection against bullets and shell splinters.

It will come as no surprise to discover that the suddenly hard-pressed Surgeon McCutcheon and his assistants could not keep pace with the steady stream of bloodstained men. About half the seamen and Marines in the landing parties were killed or wounded before the *Vindictive* reached the Mole.

The aged cruiser took terrible punishment for three minutes. One motor launch alone saw her peril. She 'dashed forward', Hilton Young remembered, 'leaping – almost flying – across the waves with furious haste, pouring out smoke as she came. She swung across us, right between us and the batteries and under the very muzzles of their guns, and vanished into her own smoke unharmed. It was a gallant act, and glorious to see.' Midshipman David Morris, gazetted just six weeks earlier, was on board the launch. 'When we arrived outside Zeebrugge' he wrote in a letter home on 28 April 1918, '15 inch shells were flying about and we got it pretty hot. We sighted the *Vindictive* and as she was

106

getting badly hit, and no smoke screen to shield her, we decided to get our screens going. We then went between her and the Mole which is 160 yards away.'

The orders to the smoke launches contained no instructions to check the wind. Keeping the assault ships screened at all times, no matter what the cost was an obvious requirement. *Vindictive* should have had at least two dedicated motor launches with the sole function of keeping her approach obscured.

Carpenter's decision to increase speed assuredly saved his ship and its men from even worse carnage and, quite probably, total destruction. As it was, he put her alongside the Mole some 400 yards beyond her planned position. Four hundred yards, in fact, from the chief objective of the storming parties.

The guns at the end of the Mole were as safe as if they had been on the moon. The men who were expected to rush ashore were without most of their officers. They would land in an unfamiliar area. Their objective was far away and protected by barbed wire and machine guns.

It has to be remembered, however, that even in these catastrophic circumstances, Operation ZO was still very much alive. The landing on the Mole was the diversion. The blockships, still twenty-five minutes away, were what really mattered.

The situation would rapidly worsen for *Vindictive* and her incredibly gallant men. They had, as one observer recalled, ' a singular contempt for death'.

Legends and myths were to sprout about the next sixty minutes in which some of the bravest acts in the history of the Royal Navy and Royal Marines were performed.

CHAPTER NINE

Vindictive bumped against the Zeebrugge Mole at 00.01 hours on 23 April 1918. St George's Day.

Well out of position, she bobbed like a cork in a weir. Her increased speed had trapped a huge surge of water between the ship and the side of the Mole. She rose. She fell. She rolled – all in a violent swell of her own making. Time after time, she smacked against the Mole. The landing brows, some already smashed by hostile fire, were splintered some more by unyielding concrete.

Carpenter's orders had been precise. He was to place *Vindictive* 'exactly 500 yards from the Mole lighthouse and to secure the ship alongside the Mole so that her stern is 200 feet from the eastern end of the broad part of the Mole. When the ship is secured, the Mole will be stormed.'

The 'exactly' was another way of asking for the impossible if total surprise was not achieved.

Carpenter did his best to regain his correct station. The engines went astern. Water frothed as *Vindictive*'s screws thrashed violently. To add to his problems, a three knot tide-race added to the surging torrent.

It was time for an immediate decision. The starboard anchor chain rattled in a crescendo. Carpenter held his ship steady by alternately reversing his engines until the anchor gripped. It did not. *Vindictive* continued to behave like a frisky mare.

More German shells and machine-gun bullets punished the cruiser. Partially protected by the Mole, her upperworks were clearly visible in the dazzling light of the pirouetting star shells. Red-hot splinters skittled across the deck. Marines and sailors dropped with depressing regularity.

In the foretop, the Marines manning the pom-poms and Lewis guns targeted anything that looked dangerous. Their fire lanced across two destroyers and two torpedo-boats moored in the harbour. They took a devastating return fire which increased as the harbour crews on the moored ships reached their action stations. Machine-gunners and battery commanders focused on the armour-plated mushroom. Marines died.

On the exposed quarterdeck, Lieutenant Reginald Dallas Brooks of the Royal Marines brought the 11-inch howitzer into action. Throughout the whole affair, Brooks maintained a steady and disconcerting fire in the general direction of the enemy.

Carpenter did not know whether his orders had reached the cable party by the anchor. He asked Rosoman to investigate. He had hardly spoken when Lieutenant Eastlake with his fearsome flame-thrower decided to enter the fight. As he gave the order to switch on, a piece of shrapnel spun into the hut and neatly severed the nozzle. The undirected flame would have incinerated everybody in the area but St George had switched sides again. The fuel lines had already been cut by German fire. Brock's terrible weapon was a piece of useless metal.

The cable deck reported. The starboard anchor was jammed. Neither brute force nor colourful curses could move it. The port anchor chain rattled out. Carpenter ordered engines astern. *Vindictive*'s stern swung away from the Mole as the port anchor bit. With the helm to starboard, Carpenter put his ship in towards the Mole again.

The men trying to get the grapnels to hold the ship close to the Mole had no success. What had been so simple to the blast of a whistle in a secluded anchorage became a very different proposition when machine-gun fire and shrapnel raked the reeling deck. In any event, the crews detailed for the task were mostly dead or wounded. Hilton Young, the officer in charge, had become a casualty with a smashed shoulder as the *Vindictive* approached the Mole. The grapnels swung out, clawed feebly at the concrete and slid back towards the *Vindictive*.

Carpenter tried again, this time with the helm amidships. Too far out. Helm hard to port. She swung far out again. For a moment, the bow mole anchor caught. Hope plummeted as the ship rolled, taking the anchor with it.

The cruiser crunched against the concrete. Another try, then another, to get the grapnels to hold. Failure. Some marines and sailors, like Wainwright, swore that the anchors 'had continually been thrown back from the wall by a few Germans whose bravery was eclipsed by none, until they were driven off by rifle-fire'.

These courageous enemy were probably duty men from the fire control centre of the *Friedrichsort* shore battery. *Vindictive* had docked just yards from the observation post.

What was ideal on paper at Chatham was disastrously inadequate in

109

practice. It is a powerful condemnation of the planning that there was no rehearsal using a real ship with a real grapnel on a real quayside. A desire for secrecy is admirable but this failure jeopardized the whole operation. What worked for British infantry scaling the uneven stonework of Napoleonic fortresses was one thing. Very romantic and very boys' adventure tale. It was starkly different on a rolling ship under heavy fire.

It can be argued, as some later did, that experienced naval officers had no need to practice such a manoeuvre. It is doubtful if they had ever tried to clasp a bucking cruiser to a smooth concrete quayside under hostile gunnery with nothing more than a pair of huge and unwieldy hooks.

The operator at the *Batterie Mole* answered an urgently jangling telephone. 'Enemy troops attempting to land!' Schütte gave quiet orders. *Oberleutnant* Adolf Rodewald began to round up spare men in accordance with a well-rehearsed plan.

Daffodil and *Iris* arrived three minutes after *Vindictive*. Lieutenant Harold Campbell, commanding *Daffodil*, half blinded, blood streaming from his head where a German shell had smashed onto the bridge, put the ferry's blunt nose against the side of the big cruiser. The engine room telegraph rang urgently for full power. *Daffodil* pushed and pushed. Three hundred and forty-two feet of ship weighing 6000 tons was thrust with agonizing slowness against the Mole. *Daffodil*'s engineers prayed to whatever deity they could think of. The ship normally raised a modest eighty pounds head of steam. Much more was needed to pin *Vindictive* in position. The stokers worked furiously, shovelling best naval coal into the furnace. The gauge needles trembled upwards, creeping towards 160 pounds of pressure, passing the danger mark slowly but surely. Every rivet in the rugged little Tyneside ship shivered with the effort of keeping the *Vindictive* hard against the Mole.

Already five or more minutes had passed without a single man landing on the Mole. Surprise, if there had ever been any, was now out of the question. Every sixty seconds that passed gave the enemy a full minute to prepare. Operation ZO was crumbling fast.

Keyes' official dispatch of 9 May 1918 states clearly that the landing brows were down and the first men were ashore before *Daffodil* arrived. Survivors' accounts are, quite understandably, confused but the majority clearly believed that it was the ferry boat alone that enabled them to get ashore. Keyes admits that the mole anchors failed to hook, an admission that really only emphasizes the lack of preparation. However, he glosses over just exactly how long it took to get the landing parties on to the quayside. And rightly so. The inadequate planning was having crucifying results.

It is, of course, easy to be wise in hindsight. The Board of Admiralty, it will be remembered, had picked on this very difficulty. The essential factor, the be-all-and-end-all, the vital need to get troops on to firm ground quickly and in quantity had not been achieved. There is only one person to blame.

Daffodil had replaced the two motor launches suggested by Admiral Sir Herbert Heath, the Second Sea Lord. The little ferry was doing a magnificent job but, as we shall see, at a price.

Only two of the landing ramps still worked. The German batteries had shattered the gangways which received even more damage as the ship rolled against the Mole. Frantic efforts by the crew eventually got two more into operation but the necessary flood of troops was doomed to be no more than a trickle.

The two remaining brows hit the parapet. *Vindictive* rose and fell. The gangplanks juddered, rising several feet with the ship. The end on the quay sawed backwards and forwards, backwards and forwards, close to sliding off entirely. To the Marines and sailors who were to go ashore, twenty-seven inches suddenly became the width of a piece of string.

The men went forward without hesitation. They were led by junior officers. With one exception, every designated commander was dead or badly wounded. Thus Lieutenant Commander Bryan Adams gained imperishable glory by being the first man on to the Mole. He was followed by a scratch squad from the remnants of A and B companies. Many of the men in the assault teams were already dead, dying or wounded. Getting there 'fastest with the mostest' was no longer an option.

It took nearly fifteen catastrophic minutes to put the first landing parties on to the shore. *Vizefeuerwerker* Schröder recorded the details:

From the Battery, we could clearly see the masts and funnels of a ship on the seaward side of the Mole. At 0115 hours came the last report from the Mole. Troops were landing in the area of the *Friedrichsort* bunker.

Leutnant Zimmerman, with his surviving duty crew, ran to the fortified zone to join Rodewald's informal assault detachment. His *Sturmabteilung* was reinforced by sailors who had doubled to the defences from the ships at the quayside. As the troops from *Vindictive* tried to get ladders in position, fell wounded or dead from gangways or parapet, *Gruppe Rodewald* formed into fighting sections. There were

111

twenty-three men and two officers.

Keyes' estimate of 1000 German defenders on the Mole was wildly inaccurate. Apart from the seventy men who formed the *Hafencompagnie* responsible for manning the machine guns, a further 200 men were at the seaplane station. Not even the most ardent advocate of air power ever claims that aviation groundcrew make formidable infantry. These, nonetheless, were ready to join the fight.

At the Mole end, Schütte, known to his gun crews as 'The Pope' was in full control. 'Gun teams to landing defence. Infantry to positions.'

The first steel-helmeted defenders moved forward. Three NCOs, ten men. They grabbed their Mauser '98 rifles and stuffed *Stielhandgranaten* through their leather belts.

They joined the machine-gunners, wiping beaded moisture from the sinister barrels of the '08 Maxims, one on either flank. The machine-gun crews checked the ammunition belts, each one containing 250 rounds. The Maxim fired 500 shots a minute but no gunner worth his arm badge wasted a belt in thirty seconds of continuous fire. Short sharp killing bursts of two or three seconds each. The breaks in firing often encouraged an incautious enemy to run for it.

Soft sinister clicks confirmed bayonets were fixed. Safety catches flicked off. Oiled bolts eased forward, pushing cartridges into rifle chambers. The remaining ten men stood ready. More hand grenades. More ammunition. *Gruppe Rodewald* was open for business.

In his subsequent report, Schütte rather grandiloquently and not quite accurately referred to them as assault troops or *Stosstruppen*. They may not have done the official course for such units but they were trained Marines and seamen. Like their British equivalents, they were formidable fighting men.

The landing parties were, as Leading Seaman Childs recalled, greatly hampered by the weight of their equipment. Childs and Able Seaman Albert McKenzie were the only upright survivors of their gun team. McKenzie carried the Lewis gun with eight 47-round magazines, a revolver with 100 rounds, spare parts for the Lewis gun, gas mask and steel helmet. Childs staggered under the weight of sixteen drums of ammunition for the Lewis gun, a rifle, two bandoliers, each holding fifty rounds, two Mills bombs, an electric torch, wire cutters and the obligatory gas mask and helmet. Neither had a cutlass.

Some of the first men ashore tried to fasten the Mole anchors. Bathed in the blinding light of German star shells, crouching on the parapet, laced by machine-gun fire, they struggled desperately to fasten the grapnels. Rosoman climbed a derrick but the grappling-anchors were desperately heavy. The end came when the forward davit smashed against the Mole. The steel prongs fell into the sea.

There was only one solution. *Daffodil* would have to keep the big cruiser rammed against the Mole. Aside from the chance that her boilers might explode, this meant her own anxious Marines could land only by scrambling over her prow to reach *Vindictive*. A handful of men from the demolition party managed the hazardous journey on to the swaying, heaving ship. For all the good the rest did, despite their efforts to reach the Mole, they might just as well have stayed at the Swin playing Crown and Anchor.

Daffodil spent fifty minutes holding *Vindictive* close to the Mole, a quite remarkable feat as her engine room had already been hit by two German shells. Water trickled ominously into two compartments. The engine room crew spent anxious minutes stopping the North Sea from reaching the boilers.

Lieutenant Commander Adams led his depleted party on to the Mole parapet. They were gratified to find it apparently deserted, a consequence of the fierce fire from *Vindictive*'s foretop. Lieutenant Charles Rigby and his determined Marines were using the pom-poms and Lewis guns with considerable skill and no small valour. *Vindictive* was being hit consistently. The butcher's bill was edging remorselessly upwards.

Adams turned left towards the lighthouse on the end of the Mole. His original task was to silence the guns on the end of the Mole extension before the blockships arrived. He was determined to carry out his duty even though it meant a 250 yard advance against entrenched defences.

Snug behind their concrete emplacements, the Germans waited with interest. A single comment brought nervous laughter. 'Here come the footballers!'

The British press had made much of the 8th East Surreys kicking footballs towards the enemy lines on the opening day of the 1916 Somme battle. Captain W. Nevill had bought them for the four platoons in his company. He was a young officer who spent part of each evening standing on the fire-step of his trench to shout insults at the Germans.

Nevill himself kicked the first ball towards the German lines when his company climbed out of its trench at 07.30 hours on 1 July 1916.

The German papers had picked up the story from their English counterparts. Not surprisingly, they did not consider it a fine example of British pluck and humour. It became a symbol of the amateur Tommy who believed that war was a sporting contest and that a football could overcome savage shellfire and malignant machine guns.

Adams and his men were joined by Wing Commander Brock. He had dashed onto the Mole before most of the landing parties. Rather than wait until the area was secure, he got into the front ranks.

The sailors had gone about forty yards when some Germans, sheltering close to the parapet, made a dash towards a moored destroyer. They had eighty yards to run. McKenzie described it thus:

> I turned to my left and advanced about fifty yards then lay down. There was a spiral staircase which led down into the Mole and Commander Brock fired his revolver down and threw a Mills bomb. You ought to have seen them nip out and try to get across to the destroyer tied up against the Mole, but this little chicken met them half way with the box of tricks, and I ticked about a dozen off.

The sailors continued onward. They reached a concrete observation post. On top of the squat building was what looked like a range-finder. A courteous seaman tossed a Mills bomb inside. Brock, satisfied the hut was empty, went inside.

This building was almost certainly the one vacated by Zimmerman and his team. Brock had found his range-finding equipment.

An iron ladder close by led down to the Mole. Adams posted three of his men at the bottom to guard against an enemy counterattack. He then led his group, including the redoubtable McKenzie and Childs, forward for another forty yards. Survivors' accounts are understandably confused but this is probably the point at which Adams and his men came under bitter small-arms fire.

A small group of Germans emerged from a bunker to make a sharp counterattack before falling back to the protection of the concrete emplacements. *Gruppe Rodewald* was growing in numbers.

Adams' party, becoming smaller every minute, took what shelter they could. Pinned down by the German fire, their chances of survival were clearly very slim.

This was about the moment that the enemy batteries finally disposed of most of *Vindictive*'s gallant foretop. Two heavy rounds smacked into its armour. Rigby and all of his men, save one, were killed or disabled. The survivor was RMA/12150 Sergeant Norman Augustus Finch. Despite severe wounds, the sergeant continued to fire the pom-pom. Its staccato sound gave enormous encouragement to the men below but where German shells had hit once, they could hit again.

The planned order of landing on the Mole by the 4th Battalion was in total disarray. Their tasks were now far more difficult. The original first objective was the fortified zone some 150 yards from the lighthouse.

114

In theory, they would have secured that from the rear before moving towards the viaduct. If *Vindictive* had reached her intended position, this would, on paper, have been a simple operation, albeit it overlooked the presence of *Oberleutnant* Rodewald and his resolute ad hoc stormtroopers. Keyes' plan hinged on speed. Any delay was deadly. And the *Kaiserliche Marine* would have done their damndest to stop the assault.

There were, after the Raid, suggestions that Carpenter had put the plan in peril by failing to put *Vindictive* in her proper station. The idea that the whole affair stood or fell on the precise positioning of the ship is more a condemnation of the planning than anything else. There was no back-up. There was no alternative thinking. There had never been an attempt to cover the almost inevitable possibility that events might go wrong. Marines and sailors, men and officers alike, had to muddle through.

It is a justifiable criticism of Keyes and the operation that it needed no great skill of prophecy to foresee that *Vindictive* might not hit the exact spot specified. It is reasonable to query whether Keyes was correct in hazarding so many lives if success depended absolutely on positioning a ship at night-time with extreme accuracy on a curving mole one and a half miles in length. Keyes may only have got low-grade passes as a midshipman but he did know that ships have no brakes. It was very likely that the *Vindictive* would be under fire as she approached the quay. To expect any captain to position the vessel with hair's breadth accuracy is absurd.

The position Carpenter reached did, in fact, protect the ship from the Mole batteries. If *Vindictive* had berthed at the very spot Keyes demanded, there was still a parapet. The grapnels would still have failed. The gangways would still have been smashed to pieces. Disembarkation would still have been slow and difficult.

The only difference would have been that some very determined German Marines and Naval Infantry would have counterattacked with grenades, machine guns and other assorted ordnance before the landing had even started. The smoke blowing away from *Vindictive* as she approached her target was perhaps a blessing in disguise.

Major Bernard Weller, the senior surviving officer of Marines and Captain Arthur Chater, the adjutant, rapidly improvised. Chater went ashore with Lieutenant Theodore Cooke and 5 Platoon. He instructed them to move westward along the parapet pathway towards the shoreline. They were to stop German troops storming towards *Vindictive*. The Marines, under a hail of bullets, reached a point some 200 yards from

115

the *Vindictive*'s bows. There was a fierce engagement with a handful of enemy riflemen who caused havoc with an accurate, deadly fire.

Chater returned to the ship. There were no obvious steps down to the Mole. Chater told Battalion Sergeant Major Charles Thatcher to get ropes and ladders ashore. Scaling ladders were to be maintained in position so that the men could get back.

These should have been the first items to be carried onto the Mole. In truth, the casualties were so heavy that such an obvious task had fallen by the wayside as men died, as ratings tried to get anchors to hold, as Marines fell wounded and officers and petty officers and sergeants tried valiantly to prevent confusion becoming chaos.

Cooke's sadly under-strength platoon gave covering fire as 9 and 10 Platoons landed. They each had two ladders and two knotted ropes. Sergeant Wright reached the parapet:

> . . . continually swept by machine gun fire from the sea end of the Mole, hence the heavy casualties amongst the Naval Officers and ratings trying to fix the grappling irons . . . From the ship to the rail was simply a 'Death' walk with that devilish machine gun in action. Nevertheless, for some unaccountable reason, maybe the gun was jambed (*sic*) or the gunner was changing a belt, this gun was certainly out of action as I lead (*sic*) the remnants of my Platoon on shore. We just had time to place our ladders and ropes in position before the machine gun opened up again, and we reached the lower part of the Mole in safety, killing two German sailors as we did so.

It is a truism of warfare that very few plans survive the first contact with the enemy. The orders for the Royal Marines betray a certain quaintness along with an apparent lack of comprehension as to what might await them. Even so, it has to be remembered that their author believed they would land at the Mole end. Ashore, they would themselves be protected by the Germans' own concrete defences.

In part, they read as follows:

> The Battalion Quartermaster will establish an ammunition and bomb dump on the Mole, abreast of the ship; demands for ammunition and bombs should be sent to Battalion Headquarters or to this dump.
>
> Battalion Headquarters will be established in a favourable position on the Mole abreast of the ship. Reports should be sent to this position which will be indicated by a white flag.

116

German reactions to a group of clearly unfriendly troops raising a white flag and busily processing demands for ammunition would have been interesting. But, of course, it never arose. There was no chance at all of ammunition dumps or headquarters being set up in the teeth of unremitting hostile fire.

Wright and his platoon were at last on the Mole. Chater was swiftly joined by Major Bernard Weller, whose runner, Ernie Clist followed diligently wherever he went.

Lieutenant Charles Lamplough, commanding the survivors of 9 Platoon, joined up with Sergeant Wright and his men. They dashed across the Mole to establish a strongpoint at the western end of No 3 Shed. Any Germans approaching from the landward end of the Mole would face an extremely irritated group of Marines. In front of them was the rapidly expiring remnant of Cooke's platoon. Cooke's men, desperately exposed, faced fierce and unrelenting fire. Cooke was wounded. Once and then again. His soldier servant, Private Press, was himself wounded but he carried his officer back to the relative safety of *Vindictive*.

Lamplough's determined detachment was reinforced by the men of 7 Platoon. With them came Captain Edward Bamford. Private Feeney, that last-minute replacement, recalled that:

. . . Plymouth section went over before us. The sailors were going over individually before that. Sergeant Braby gave us the order to go up and over. The fire-main had been perforated by shrapnel and we had to pass under it. We got something to keep us cool; down my back I got a shower. The sergeant stood very near it. He was trying to hide the bodies of three of the pom-pom's crew from us . . . The battalion sergeant-major and the adjutant were superintending the getting over of the ladders.

Well it was not like anything I ever saw on parade, except these two were just as cool. I offered to give a hand with the ladders when I was passing up the gangway, but [the] sergeant-major told me to go over . . . I walked up very carefully, and in the anxiety to keep my balance on the see-saw of the gangway, I forgot about the rain of lead, and I really felt comfortable when I put my foot on the concrete.

The sea-face of it stands about twenty-five feet over high water, the outer face, for about four feet deep, is three feet higher than the inside. When I got off the outer face, and stepped down on the promenade portion, I thought it was the Mole proper; but when

we moved over to a three-foot railing and looked down, we could
see what appeared to be a very wide street about twenty feet below.
Then I knew what the ladders were for. We had some trouble here.
I was ten minutes before I got a ladder to go down by.

. . . There was a group of bodies at the foot of the ladders – all
Germans – who tried to knock the ladders, and amongst them,
three men in white ducks. The light during the landing was
wonderful. . . . The German star shells . . . light (*sic*) up the sea and
land for miles.

In the foretop, Sergeant Finch finally collapsed by his gun. Another
badly wounded Marine, Gunner Sutton took over. A few rounds later,
the German gunners finally demolished the position. Finch and Sutton
no longer had a single working weapon. Both wounded yet again, the
pair crumpled by the battered pom-pom.

Whilst the men of *Vindictive* struggled, those on board *Iris* were also
enduring a most trying time. She had run alongside the Mole some 200
yards nearer the shoreline than *Vindictive*. Her captain, too, was well
out of position. She had even outrun the spot where the Marines fought
to maintain a perimeter. The swell badly affected the sturdy Geordie-
built ferry boat which bobbed and swayed like a punch-drunk boxer.
Although the enemy had hardly hit her, most of her scaling ladders were
smashed as she bumped against the Mole. Not that it made much difference. The easily dismissed four-feet difference in the high-water mark
meant that her ladders did not reach the parapet.

In addition, as with *Vindictive*, the crew of *Iris* had the greatest difficulty in getting her Mole anchors to hold. Smooth concrete offered no
purchase to the claws of the grapnel. In an attempt to berth the ferry,
outstanding gallantry was the order of the day. As *Iris* lurched and
swayed in the swell, Lieutenant Claude Hawkings clambered up a
scaling ladder held upright by his men. As the ship rolled towards the
quayside, Hawkings jumped to land on the parapet top. He made it and
turned to try and fasten the ladder. He died, firing his revolver at the
Germans who advanced towards him.

Lieutenant Commander George Bradford clambered to the top of a
mole-anchor derrick. Thirteen valuable minutes had already slipped by.
Under fire, he reached the Mole, somehow lugging the anchor with him.
He hooked it into position. A German machine-gunner neatly stitched
a seam of 7.9mm rounds into the naval officer. Lifted by the bullets,
just thirteen minutes and a few seconds into his thirty-first birthday,
Bradford fell between the quay and the ship's side. The anchor dropped

from the parapet as *Iris* rolled in the swell. Petty Officer Michael Hallihan jumped into the water to save an already dead man. His leap was accompanied by a hail of machine-gun fire and the *Iris* rolling back against the quay. So perished a twenty-eight year old Irishman from County Cork.

The crew of *Iris* tried again and again to get the anchors to hold. Each time there was a surge of determined hope. Each time the grapnels fell back uselessly.

Adams' sailors, advancing along the parapet roadway, approached the fortified zone. They were lit not merely by German star shells but by Brock's own illuminations. One of his specialists fired rockets from the *Vindictive*'s stern portholes in an attempt to guide the blockships. The result showed the sailors in sharp relief, black silhouettes against the glare. Rodewald's men opened a rapid fire augmented by assorted weaponry from the enemy craft at the dockside.

The sailors found what cover they could. Adams doubled back to the concrete lookout post. There he found Petty Officer George Antell and a handful of men. Antell was wounded even before he landed. Adams took a brief look at the damage to his hand and arm and instructed him to rejoin *Vindictive*. The other men were ordered up towards the rapidly diminishing force facing the Mole barricade.

As they moved off, Lieutenant Commander Arthur Harrison joined the group. He had been knocked unconscious in the run-in. Nursing a fractured jaw and head wounds, he nevertheless joined the men on the Mole. He sent Adams for reinforcements before leading the rest forward. Gathering up any sailor he saw upright, Harrison led a rush to join Able Seaman McKenzie and the other men facing the entrenched Germans.

Adams reported to Major Weller, still with the faithful Clist by his side. Weller organized the survivors of 11 and 12 Platoons to support the hard-pressed bluejackets whilst Adams doubled back to join his men.

The sailors certainly needed help.

Harrison decided to charge the German positions. He and his men had to cover more than 100 yards, devoid of any cover, along the parapet. Harrison drew his cutlass, waved it in the air and pointed it towards the German position. With a cheer, the sailors began to run forward.

One machine gun stopped firing. Its crew muttered as they freed the jam. The second ceased a few seconds later as the ammunition belt came to its end.

The sailors charged on, still shouting. Eighty yards, then fifty. The machine-gunners, ready once more for action, stayed passive, at a word of command. Forty yards. The temporary *Sturmabteilung* waited. The British sailors continued, the cheering getting hoarser by the second. Twenty yards to go.

A flurry of stick grenades sailed from the defenders. The 'potato-masher' was a deadly weapon. Harrison, shouting wildly, was the first to die. His cutlass skittered across the concrete as he crashed to the ground.

As the attack faltered, a German NCO gave a single crisp command, '*Los!*'

The defenders spilled out from behind their barricade. They went in hard and close. A British sailor had no time to appreciate that play-acting bayonet fighting with a Territorial Army recruit was of little use when facing a brutally efficient enemy. The bluejacket's lunge was contemptuously brushed aside. A rifle butt thumped into his chest. As he fell, his opponent reversed his rifle. The long bayonet of the Mauser pierced the sailor's stomach. The recoil of a single shot jerked the 18-inch steel blade clear.

Childs recalled that:

> . . . the Germans scored a direct hit on our Lewis Gun, blowing it out of our hands. This was bad luck, as at the time it was doing glorious work. McKenzie was severely wounded again. The Lewis Gun ammunition now being of no use without the gun, we threw the trays into the sea, thereby relieving us of some of the weight and we reverted to secondary armament. McKenzie his revolver, myself my rifle.

Despite his wounds, McKenzie was full of fight:

> My Lewis gun was shot spinning out of my hands and all I had left was the stock and pistol grip which I kindly took a bloke's photo with it, who looked too business-like for me, with a rifle and bayonet. It half stunned him and gave me time to get my pistol out and finish him off.

The sailors displayed that incredible gallantry which had already been seen so many times on the battlefields of France, of Flanders, and of Gallipoli. Human bodies, however, cannot brush away bullets and bayonets. It was a glorious, valiant effort, doomed before it began.

The British retreated. The Germans advanced.

Harrison's attempt to storm the German position left every man in his group dead or wounded. Able Seaman Eves, himself a casualty, tried desperately to bring back Harrison's body. He failed as he was hit again. He collapsed. His fellow Marines decided he must be dead. Eves regained consciousness in a German hospital.

Policke, writing for his comrades, allowed a note almost of pity to creep into his account. It should be remembered that the Germans believed at the time that the landings were entirely carried out by Royal Marines:

> The machine-gunners fired their provocative tak-tak-tak along the wall. From below, the stern-chaser of a torpedo boat, manned by the commander himself and a single crewman, opened up against the landing area.
>
> This was too much for His British Majesty's Royal Marines. Those who were not dead or wounded jumped with despairing leaps over the parapet. It was the last action they ever made.

Even allowing for an understandable sense of triumph, and knowing that some of Harrison's party finally made it back to *Vindictive*, Policke leaves the reader in no doubt that the attackers had taken a severe drubbing. The commander was *Kapitänleutnant* Albert Brennecke and his gunlayer *Fähnrich* Klintzsch on board *V 69*. Optimistically, they later euphorically claimed that their firing persuaded *Vindictive* to leave in a hurry.

A new, more urgent sound joined the cacophony that was the Mole. A group of Germans, possibly seaplane mechanics, reached that something nasty on the concrete – a Hotchkiss *Kaliber 3.7cm Revolverkanone des Flakzuges*. Designed for anti-aircraft work, this was a grown-up Gatling gun with unbridled ambition. Its 'flaming onions', so detested by the pilots who regularly bombed Zeebrugge, roared towards the unfortunate *Vindictive* in a ferocious display of dislike.

As McKenzie, Childs and their fellow survivors fell back, they were caught up in another desperate fracas. Some bluejackets had tried to attack a moored torpedo boat. Savage hand to hand fighting erupted on the quayside as the German sailors responded with a fierce determination.

Rodewald's men joined the mêlée. Rifles, bayonets, knives, cutlasses, coshes, boots, fists. Anything was acceptable as a weapon.

Torpedo-Obermatrose Hermann Künne of *Torpedoboot S 53* attacked a British officer armed with a revolver and a cutlass. Künne also had a cutlass. He slashed his opponent across the neck and grabbed the revolver. The British officer, desperately wounded, stabbed Künne as he fell. They both died on the quayside within feet of each other.

German accounts persistently claim that the British officer was Harrison but this does not tie in with the stories of any British witness. The survivors of Harrison's party are adamant that he died at the head of the charge against the Mole battery.

There is a nagging possibility that the officer could have been Brock. He wore almost identical rank badges to Harrison. He had certainly been in the area shortly beforehand. Künne and his unnamed opponent died close to the fire control bunker for the *Friedrichsort* battery.

McKenzie recalled:

> I found a rifle and bayonet . . . All I remember was pushing kicking and kneeing every German who got in the way. When I was finished I couldn't climb the ladder so a mate of mine [Childs] lifted me up and carried me up the ladder and then I crawled on my hands and knees inboard.

Elsewhere, small defending parties, mostly off-duty crewmen from the moored vessels, erupted at intervals from ships or darkened doorways to attack the intruders. Behind their barricades, more of Rodewald's men sniped at figures in the distinctive British steel helmet.

The demolition crew had followed the Naval storming parties ashore. Lieutenant Cecil Dickinson commanded, in theory, fifty ratings and twenty-two men of the Royal Marine Light Infantry to carry the explosives. However, it was a much depleted group that finally got onto the Mole. The majority of the men were trapped on board *Daffodil*.

In Keyes' original assessment, this party would have blown up every shed it could find, wrecked the seaplane base and generally caused havoc. This did not happen.

As with the other shore parties, the lack of ladders caused a crowd on the parapet. Dickinson's men finally reached the lower part of the Mole and moved towards their first objective, No. 3 Shed. Heavy fire from one of the vessels anchored alongside the Mole stopped their advance.

Dickinson attempted to put a charge alongside the destroyers but the little group was driven back by concentrated fire. They threw a few bombs on the deck of the nearest ship, an action which encouraged a sharp reply from the enemy.

The RN experimental station had produced volunteers to work the portable flame-throwers and phosphorus grenades which Brock believed would cow the enemy. Among them was an RNAS air mechanic, whose original platoon of forty was down to ten men. The group attacked a virulently aggressive destroyer. The wide eighty yards stretch of concrete to reach it was a very long distance to cover. Their attack failed. The air mechanic claimed that he 'roasted about forty Germans'. This is undoubtedly exaggerated.

A Marine, identifiable only as 'Bill', wrote in a letter home:

> . . .one fired point-blank with his revolver at one of our lads, but he paid dearly for it, for our Captain crowned him with his loaded stick. We then tried to board a destroyer which was laying alongside the quay but she sent out oil fumes at us and we replyed [sic] with liquid fire. . . .

Nobody had specific orders to tackle the ships at the quayside. Even if every single assault troop had landed in the intended spot; even if the Mole batteries were destroyed; even if the machine-gunners were overwhelmed so that the invaders could advance along the Mole as planned, they would have faced a withering fire from the moored vessels. As it was, the ships' crews, with overlapping fields of fire, took the sailors and Marines in flank.

Nonetheless, all of the four moored ships took some damage. It was mostly superficial. None were sunk. All were on the Order of Battle the following month.

Lamplough felt his platoon had achieved little:

> During the period we were on the Mole we did what we could to harass a destroyer alongside with such weapons as we had available and also dealt with a few Germans who came down the Mole close to the sea wall as if in an attempt to interfere with our scaling ladders.

In the inferno on the Mole, the Marines at the end of No 3 Shed faced the shore. There were ominous signs that a thoroughly aroused enemy was preparing an assault.

The surviving sailors at the other side of the perimeter were pinned down by a consistent fire from *Gruppe Rodewald*. *Kapitänleutnant* Schütte controlled the defence of his batteries with a calm and clinical detachment

No objective observer could doubt that the initiative was, twenty-five minutes after *Vindictive* reached the Mole, firmly with the German defenders.

Then five tons of amatol exploded into the night sky. Sandford and *C 3* had arrived.

CHAPTER TEN

His Majesty's Submarine *C 3* slipped from her tug, the destroyer HMS *Trident* at 23.26 hours. The submarine's crew of six found themselves alone on the dark sea. There was no sign of the picket boat which was to pick them up once the viaduct had been rammed. No sign either of her sister vessel *C 1*.

Both the picket boat and *C 1* had earlier lost their tows. The picket boat had displayed dismal sailing qualities when pulled at a respectable speed in the prevailing wind and sea. Twice on her beam ends, and extremely difficult to steer out of trouble, she was saved from capsizing only by the cable parting. After that experience, she made for Zeebrugge under her own power.

C 1 also reverted to her own resources when the line to HMS *Mansfield* parted. By the time her captain, Lieutenant Aubrey Newbold brought her back on course, *C 3* had vanished in the night.

Both vessels were ten or more minutes behind *C 3* which headed towards Zeebrugge at a respectable eight and a half knots. Her petrol engines were far from new but had been tuned half a dozen times in the previous weeks.

At midnight, as *Vindictive* steamed at speed for the Mole, *C 3* was one and a half miles from the viaduct. A change of course brought her in at right angles to the viaduct piers with their web of iron spars. Speed crept up to nine knots. A random star shell hung idly, bathing *C 3* in its light. The briefest of pauses ticked by before a shore battery opened fire.

Sandford dismissed the moment. 'The firing from the shore was a bit severe at 200 yards, and only the fact that the sea was a bit rough and we were up and down a good deal saved us.'

The firing stopped after a few rounds. *C 3* continued towards the viaduct. Another flare curled upwards, etching the target in sharp relief. *C 3* trembled as she reached nine knots. Searchlights stabbed the darkness, first from one end of the viaduct, then from the other. A third on

124

the shore swung an investigating beam across the dark water before turning away. The enemy still held their fire.

It was more than possible that the Germans believed the diminutive submarine was trying to slip into the harbour and would be trapped in the viaduct cross-braces. So held, she could be captured intact. Whatever the reason, she was not challenged.

The lattice work of the viaduct was starkly outlined against the light of the star shells and flares bursting over Zeebrugge harbour. By their light, with just 100 yards to run, Sandford ordered the tiniest change of course to ensure that *C 3* hit in the best possible position. Sandford had decided against using the automatic gyro steering. The only way to make sure that the viaduct was blown was to steer the submarine manually to the point of impact. The three searchlights glared unwaveringly at the approaching submarine. Still the guns were silent.

The whole crew clambered on deck. Lieutenant Richard Sandford, Lieutenant John Howell-Price, Petty Officer Walter Harmer, Engine Room Artificer Allan Roxburgh, Leading Seaman William Cleaver, Stoker Henry Bindall. The six men stared silently towards the black, unforgiving, relentless bulk of the Mole.

Stoker Bindall gave a concise account of the final minutes of the attack:

> . . . with her engines running smoothly the submarine glided into the shoal waters of Zeebrugge at midnight, the whole crew of six being on deck. The Mole, looming up black in the darkness and the Viaduct joining it to the shore were clearly seen.
>
> It was a silent and nervy business. She was going at full tilt when we hit the Viaduct. It was a good jolt but you can stand a lot when you hang on tight. We ran right into the middle of the Viaduct and stuck there as intended. I do not think anybody said a word except 'We're here all right'.

Bindall makes no mention of any opposition from the viaduct before *C 3* smacked her nose precisely between two rows of piers at a flat-out nine and a half knots. Later accounts of the Raid alleged that at least two hundred Germans were standing on the viaduct, jeering and shouting at the submarine's crew as they scrambled to leave their tiny craft.

The six men of *C 3* were ready. Sandford set the fuses. Only as they began to row away was there any reaction. The searchlights came back on. Twin beams pinned them in their light. At least one machine-gun nest on the shore stammered heavily to stop the intruders. A handful of riflemen at the western end of the viaduct started shooting. Bindall recalled:

> We lowered the skiff and stood by while the commander touched off the fuse. Then we tumbled into the skiff and pushed off. We had rather a bit of bad luck. The propeller fouled the exhaust pipe and left us with only a couple of oars and two minutes to get away.
>
> The lights were on us now and the machine-guns going from the shore. Before we had made 200 yards the submarine went up. We had no doubt about that. There was a tremendous flash, bang, crash and lots of concrete from the Mole fell all round us into the water. It was lucky we were not struck. Coxswain Harmer and I took the oars first, till I was knocked out. Then Cleaver grabbed the oar and carried on till the coxswain was hit. I was hit again, and Lieutenant Price, lifting me and Harmer into the bows , took the oar and was afterwards relieved by Roxburgh when Lieutenant Sandford was hit.

The explosion destroyed power and telephone cables. The searchlights at each end of the viaduct flickered out. Contact between the Mole gunners and the shore was extinguished. The firing from the viaduct died away as the skiff, hardly visible on the black, heaving water, vanished into the welcoming darkness.

Minutes later, the picket boat under the command of Sandford's elder brother found the leaking skiff. The grateful crew of *C 3*, four of them wounded, were rapidly taken aboard. Soon afterwards, the picket boat, herself leaking at the bow, transferred her rescued cargo to HMS *Phoebe*. For Sandford and his men, it had been a very long night.

A seaman on the blockship *Iphigenia* claimed he saw masses of German soldiers on bicycles ride into the newly blown gap and drown. They were pedalling so furiously to join the fight that they omitted to notice a 100 feet column of flame or hear and feel the ferocious blast. The seaman appears to be the only witness to the event. German casualty figures fail to support the claim. In the excitement, in the adrenaline rush, one man on a heavy service bicycle could easily become a whole company of *Marine-Radfahrerstosstruppen*.

The anecdote has been repeated many times. As Herr Professor Göbbels so eloquently claimed, repetition of a lie eventually makes it truth. The story has passed into the realm of instant acceptance. There has to be some doubt as to whether the seaman on *Iphigenia*'s bridge could actually have witnessed the event given the relative positions of the ship and the viaduct at the time.

126

The legend has to claim, to account for the singular lack of corpses, that every soldier was dragged to the bottom of the harbour and trapped in the silt. Neither bodies or equipment were ever seen again.

For anyone, wearing battle kit with rifle, who has ridden a bicycle of 1918 design, the idea that such enormous speed can be built up that it becomes virtually impossible to stop, is risible.

If these tales of drowning cyclists and exploded Germans are true, *C 3* and her crew accounted for at least 300 German troops. It was a worthy number to later put beside the British losses.

A cyclist unit did exist in the *Marinekorps Flandern* but one seeks in vain for any suggestion of casualties on 23 April. The unit was safely ensconced in barracks some distance from Zeebrugge. Its records show no casualties. It has to be said that the story is almost certainly an invention.

Such optimistic and not quite credible accounts can be traced almost directly to contemporary propaganda. The Ministry of Information much preferred their output to bear the imprint of reputable publishers. Both sides gained. The Ministry paid all the costs of publication. The publisher kept all the income and scooped up a guaranteed profit. The Ministry spread its message through apparently untainted sources.

The Glory of Zeebrugge by 'Keble Howard', revealed, curiously, as 'J Keble Bell, 2nd Lieut R.A.F' on the title page, was one such book. It appeared, certainly, in British, American and French editions. Any doubts of its provenance and dubious veracity are dispelled by a glance at the *Schedule of Wellington House Literature*. Only one copy of this remarkable document apparently exists. It is a list of the propaganda documents produced by the British between 1914–1918. *The Glory of Zeebrugge* is number 997.

Its accuracy can be judged by the fact that Captain Chater was incensed by the sentiments and actions attributed to him. He had been interviewed but recognized little in the book as his words. He wrote to Keyes, asking that some action be taken to prevent fresh publication. A curiously evasive reply came from the Admiral. In essence, truth must not obstruct propaganda.

Submarine *C 1* was still some way from the viaduct when her captain saw the enormous flash of the explosion. By a quirk of acoustics, there was no sound. Lieutenant Newbold decided that the most sensible course of action was to wait patiently in case his destructive vessel might still be needed.

Carpenter, too, saw the explosion but heard nothing. An old sailor standing next to him asked, presumably with some disappointment, 'Was that it, sir?' as a column of flame shot high into the air.

Carpenter had glimpsed the first blockship enter the harbour. The diversion had clearly worked. With the viaduct blown and no danger of reinforcements from the shore storming *Vindictive*, Carpenter made a rapid tour of his command:

> Every available space on the mess deck was occupied by casualties. Those who could do so were sitting on the mess stools, awaiting their turn for medical attention. Many were stretched at full length on the deck, the majority being severely wounded. Some had already collapsed and were in a state of coma. I fear many had already passed away. It was a sad spectacle, indeed. Somehow, amidst all the crashing and smashing on deck, one had not realised the sacrifice that was taking place.
>
> A return to the lower bridge showed little apparent change in the situation. Shell was still hitting us every few seconds and many casualties were being caused by flying splinters. Large pieces of the funnels and ventilators were being torn out and hurled in all directions – one wondered how much more of this battering the ship could stand.

The entry of *Thetis*, *Iphigenia* and *Intrepid* into Zeebrugge had minimal effect on the punishment being doled out to *Vindictive*. At least one of the destroyers moored by the dock was markedly active with her quick-firing pom-poms. The shore batteries were also being a considerable nuisance.

On the Mole itself, the landing parties endured with grim determination. Chater recalled that he:

> . . . met Captain Bamford, B Company commander, whose totally unperturbed manner had the most reassuring effect on all who came into contact with him. Our battalion plan had been based on the assumption that *Vindictive* would be put alongside some four hundred yards from the end of the Mole. All those men who belonged to units which were to have attacked the fortified zone, therefore, now found themselves at No 3 Shed. No attack on the fortified zone had yet been made. As this was our principal objective, we decided to organize an attack . . . This entailed attacking a prepared position across some two hundred yards of flat pavement devoid of any form of cover. Led by Captain Bamford, the units started to move forward.

It would, almost without doubt, have been another killing ground for the defenders. The '08 Maxim guns were still waiting; Rodewald's temporary storm troopers had already tasted blood. Two hundred yards is a very long way in the face of enemy fire.

The men on board *Iris* were suffering. Some German marines and sailors had got close enough to open fire on the ferry. The scaling-ladders were mostly broken. Those that had survived were too short. Gibbs decided to move his ship alongside *Vindictive*. The assault groups could scramble across two sets of deck rails and get to the Mole by way of the cruiser's ladders. Closing on *Vindictive* required Gibbs to take his ship in a wide circle. It was no easy task.

Iris was delayed in her attempt to get alongside the bigger ship. *Vindictive*'s crew were all preoccupied. Minutes passed before there was any help. The marines and sailors on *Iris* made ready to storm ashore. Their comrades desperately needed them.

Carpenter, however, decided to recall the fighters on the Mole. Enough was enough. Men were dying for no good purpose. It was all down to the blockships. Commander Gibbs on *Iris* was instructed to cast off and take his ship home to Dover.

Carpenter ordered the withdrawal thirty minutes earlier than sched-uled. This posed some minor difficulties. Originally, *Vindictive*'s searchlight was to give twenty minutes notice of withdrawal. Not surprisingly, the heavy punishment she had taken had destroyed her searchlight.

After this period, the letter 'K' – perhaps a graceful tribute to the raid's guiding hand – would be sounded in Morse code on the ship's siren. Dash-dot-dash. Dash-dot-dash. Dash-dot-dash. It was an un-necessary complication. The recall could as easily have been a series of long blasts. Unfortunately, *Vindictive*'s siren was also out of commis-sion, a German shell splinter having neatly severed the steam pipe.

A message was passed to *Daffodil*. Her hooter spluttered into action in a series of dots and dashes which to the signallers on the Mole bore little resemblance to the withdrawal letter. Chater, on the Mole and preparing for the death or glory dash towards Rodewald's bellicose defenders, was not convinced that the sound he heard was the recall:

I returned to the ship and went to the conning tower, where I found Captain Carpenter, and asked him if we were to withdraw. Having been told that the recall was ordered, I returned to the sea wall and passed the order to all those whom I could reach by voice or signal. Units returned steadily to the ship, bringing wounded men with them. Several men who passed me thought I was wounded and wanted to carry me aboard. The enemy were still shelling the sea wall, and those who had to cross the Mole and climb the ladders had the most hazardous time. Fortunately, some of the ladders remained intact to the end.

Sergeant Harry Wright, with the meagre remains of his platoon, was at the landward end of the Mole. The men in front of him retired through his position but Wright had been a signaller. He knew Morse. The strange noises coming from *Daffodil* were not the distinctive dash-dot-dash of the signal to retreat. Wright decided it was a signal about which he had not been briefed. His men held firm.

The recall, unnecessarily complicated, was another example of thoughtlessness causing confusion. Men in action need clear, unambiguous indicators.

The unscathed *Iris* began her escape. After forty-five minutes of frustration alongside the quay, Gibbs at last turned her northwards. The blunt nose of *Iris* butted into the chilly North Sea as she left the protection of the Mole and came under the sights of the *Friedrichsort* battery. The gunners needed no second chance. *Iris* was hit fourteen times by its 15-centimetre shells. Another battery, possibly *Groden*, put two hefty 30-centimetre rounds into the ferry boat. One demolished the bridge. The other burst on the main deck.

A huge explosion and a sheet of flame enveloped the little ship. The port end of the bridge was tangled wood and metal. Fire licked eagerly at the conning position, reaching out to bombs and ammunition stored on the open deck, ready for the landing.

The captain, Commander Valentine Gibbs and Major Charles Eagles of the Marines were already dying when a volunteer fire party under the command of Lieutenant Oscar Henderson arrived. Lieutenant George Spencer, the Navigating Officer, severely wounded, stubbornly clung on to consciousness and conned the ship. The coxswain, Petty Officer David Smith, grasped the wheel grimly. He steered with one hand, lighting the compass with a torch held in the other.

Iris was hit again and again. She staggered under the impact. *Kapitänleutnant* Schütte's gunners on the Mole End joined in as *Iris* wandered into their vision. The savage onslaught wreaked havoc in the crowded ship.

On the bridge, Spencer whispered the course to steer. Smith swung the wheel. *Iris* heeled over, still miraculously answering her helm, and put her stubby bows northwards once more.

Iris was naked in front of the German guns. On fire, her speed dropping, she was a very lame duck. Her smoke canisters were out of action. The shore batteries had her firmly in their sights when *ML 558* appeared out of nowhere. Lieutenant Commander Lionel Chappell roared through the enemy fire to blanket the *Iris* in smoke.

He was just in time although *Iris* was working out her own salvation. Acting Artificer Engineer William Edgar of the Royal Australian Navy clambered up to the upper deck with an assistant and went to work. The smoke canisters suddenly belched black fumes as *ML 558* prepared for another run. Unable to see their target, the Germans sent a parting salvo, firing blind. The shells smacked through her decks but *Iris* was resilient, built to last. She continued sailing.

The fire under the bridge sneaked closer to the ammunition. Spencer, getting closer to death with every minute that went by, worked out the course for Dover. His scribbled notes are still preserved.

Henderson went back to his volunteer firemen. Only one survived. The Lieutenant found Able Seaman Ferdinand Lake energetically throwing buckets of sand on the blaze. The two men brought the flames under control. Lake then busied himself sorting out live bombs from the rubble.

They were very hot. Lake ignored his blistered hands, working on, pitching the lethal cargo overboard into the welcoming cold waters.

Iris crept homeward. Deep sea sailors know that ships have souls. The spirit creeps into them on the slipway as they are built. They absorb the values, the courage, the beliefs of the men who construct them. *Iris* was a Tynesider. She had all the same dogged courage and bloody-mindedness of the Geordie battalions in France. She carried on despite her wounds.

Henderson returned to the bridge to take command of the ship. Signalman Tom Bryant had dragged himself there. Both his legs were shattered. He was in desperate pain for there was no morphia available. The German guns had obliterated the sick bay. Bryant was the only surviving signalman. Somebody had to transmit messages.

Henderson's first call was stark and simple. 'For God's sake, send some doctors, I have a shipload of dead and dying.' He did indeed. Nobody had time to count the casualties. That had to wait until *Iris* reached Dover.

It took a long time for help to arrive. After several hours, the monitor *Erebus* intercepted *Iris*. Her doctor swung on board to help Captain Frank Pocock of the RAMC. All of Pocock's staff were casualties. A handful of men who knew some first-aid did what they could. Pocock managed without drugs and with a poor selection of instruments. He

131

worked non-stop for nearly fourteen hours. *Iris* finally reached Dover with her dead and dying at 14.45 hours that day.

The lack of medical arrangements has already been commented upon. The accusing finger has to point at Keyes.

Private Feeney's diary is graphic about the return to *Vindictive*:

> When I climbed over the railing at the top I nearly fell back as my rifle was slipping off my shoulder. The gangways were heaving up and down now, and the hail of shell was awful. Then we saw the cost of our landing, one thing was evident – it cost a great deal of blood. I shall never forget the sight of the mess-decks; dead and dying lying on the decks where, but a few hours before, we ate, drank and played cards.

Lieutenant Lamplough confirmed the horror:

> The ship was a shambles both on the upper deck and below, with doctors and every available individual doing their best to help the wounded.

Like Celtic warriors, the survivors carried their dead and wounded to *Vindictive*. They wanted everyone, officers, men, sailors and marines to return to their own land. Some men made the journey more than once to retrieve the bodies of their mates. Amongst those who braved the continuing German fire was the Reverend Charles Peshall, the Church of England padre who had contrived to sail with the ship. Like Brock and Harrison, he was a rugby player. Like them, he believed in teamwork. His devotion to his calling was total. Nobody ever knew how many he personally rescued that night.

Major Weller sent his runner, Private Clist to round up stragglers. The Marine found Captain John Palmer standing on the Mole, gazing at the devastation. He refused to go back to *Vindictive* until all of his men were accounted for. Clist reported this to the Major. It was a gallant sentiment.

More than sixty years later, Clist claimed that Palmer was drunk. He also mentioned that on his way back to *Vindictive* he gathered up a Marine who was marching up and down as if on Depot Sentry Duty, oblivious to the bullets sweeping the glistening, wet quayside. Clist himself collected some shrapnel in his chest as he led his bewildered comrade to safety. It was there until the day he died.

Slowly the Mole emptied. The German gunners fired with continuing determination. Carpenter narrowly avoided one nasty end when a shell set fire to a box of fused mortar bombs. Petty Officer Edwin

Youlton, disregarding any niceties of rank, ordered the deck to be cleared. Smashing open the boxes, he stamped on the flames. His service-issue boots smouldered and burned. So did his feet. Storing ammunition on open decks had distinct drawbacks.

Fifteen minutes into the retreat, Carpenter was wounded together with Rosoman and Youlton as they stood outside the conning-tower. A shell burst behind them. Rosoman collapsed with shrapnel through both legs. Youlton's arm was smashed. Carpenter took a deep wound in the left shoulder. All three were remarkably lucky.

Leading Seaman Childs' work was not done when he finally reached *Vindictive*. Having dumped his equipment below deck, he returned to the shambles that was the ship's main deck:

> . . . the next thing to do was to attend to the more severely wounded. With the assistance of AB Day . . . we went along to the sick bay to obtain some field dressings. When we got there we found a disastrous state of affairs. A shell had come through the ship's side and burst in the sick bay, wrecking it. We searched amidst the wreckage and finally found some dressings. We then went along the battery and found an old Marine Bugler with his leg smashed, and only hanging by the sinew. We could do practically nothing, except put a tourniquet on above the knee and cut his leg off with a knife. It was rather an unpleasant job . . . We . . . next proceeded to where Lieutenant Commander Bramble was directing the port after gun (6 inch). He eventually collapsed but would not be attended to until someone relieved him. We got a Captain of Marines . . . Bramble was badly wounded in the calf so we bandaged him up . . .
>
> The next thing we did was to assist Commander Osborne in getting down Sergeant Finch of the Royal Marines out of the Fore Top.

The German gunners had an undoubted genius for destroying sick-bays.

A grimly determined handful of men, the remains of 9 Platoon, held a tiny border around *Vindictive*. Other marines, prone on the parapet, supported them with rifle and Lewis gun fire. It took a long fifteen minutes to get the shore parties back on *Vindictive*.

Carpenter, told that no more life could be seen on the Mole, went to look for himself. Nothing moved. Bullets and shrapnel skittered wildly across the Mole but it looked deserted except from some ominously still bodies.

The battery commanders on shore changed tactics. The high explosive rounds that hammered down onto the three ships were augmented by gas shells.

Childs was one of the unlucky ones:

> I caught a section of it, though not a great deal, sufficient to keep me continually coughing. I fancied a drink so I went down below to get one but received a rude shock, as the fresh water tanks had been hit by shell and the water had run to waste, the only water remaining being 100 water bottles which had been filled before the action. These were given to the wounded, and very shortly there was no water at all, not even for the remaining wounded. Someone . . . suggested serving out rum. This was done, even the wounded having as much as they could get. . . .

The last group of Marines scrambled back. The anonymous 'Bill' had his own adventure as his group struggled to rejoin the cruiser:

> . . . a shrapnel shell came and scattered us, some got blown back on the Mole and some in the water. I went in the water myself, but manage (*sic*) to get on board by a rope which was flung to me, she then pushed off leaving the rest behind, I think I was the last man aboard. It seems so strange in the room here now, only five of us left out of 23, and only me + the cpl without a scratch.

Carpenter gave the order to cast off. *Daffodil* went into reverse. *Vindictive*'s bows swung away from the Mole. A line was passed from the cruiser. *Daffodil* tugged. The cable snapped but it had lasted long enough. *Vindictive* pointed towards the open water. Carpenter slipped the anchor cable and requested full speed ahead.

Flame shot from the shredded funnels as the engine room responded. Even as the Germans tried to finish the old cruiser with a final shot, her smoke apparatus burst into life. Thick black clouds of Brock's special invention rolled over the ship.

Twenty minutes after leaving the Mole, a dark, sinister shape approached *Vindictive* which looked as if she was on fire as sparks and flame wreathed her funnels. The new arrival was HMS *Moorsom*.

Somebody found a torch and blinked a signal to the destroyer. Help was needed to find the way to Dover. Compass and instruments were smashed beyond repair. *Moorsom* took up station to guide the old ship. HMS *Vindictive* was going home.

Sergeant Wright and his platoon watched, disbelieving, as *Vindictive* steamed away. They returned to the ladders, reached the parapet and waited. Wright hoped that a motor launch would arrive to take them off. A difficult jump into the sea was better than being taken prisoner.

They played dead as enemy troops advanced cautiously down the Mole but it could not last. After two hours, Wright recalled:

> . . . about 50 Germans . . . were seen approaching along the walk . . . some of the men wanted to fight it out . . . The German Officer, however, could speak English and gave his word of honour that we would not be hurt if we surrendered quietly.
>
> . . . We were captured at exactly 3 A.M., a long long two hours wait, waiting, waiting for the unknown. We were marched into a large shed and told to take everything out of our pockets and lay them on a table in front of us. The Officer told me I could put my gold pocket watch back in my pocket.
>
> . . . At that moment a senior German Officer brought in Captain Palmer, DSC and I called the men to attention and gave him a smart military salute. He returned my salute and said, 'Stand the men at ease, Sergeant, and let them carry on with whatever they are doing.' Captain Palmer, if I may say so, had been my friend as well as my superior for some years before this. Without further ado he left his Officer escort and approached me and I quote the very words he said. 'So they have collared you too, Wright, have they and don't look so bloody miserable. Here,' he continued, 'have a drink of this, it will buck you up'. He produced a small flask of whiskey from his tunic pocket and I had a drink.

With the capture of Captain Palmer, Sergeant Wright and his men, the diversionary attack on the Mole had ended.

The only question now was whether the blockships had closed the canal.

CHAPTER ELEVEN

Thetis, Intrepid, and *Iphigenia* were under strict orders. To gain the greatest advantage from the diversionary attacks, they were not to approach the lighthouse until twenty minutes after *Vindictive* arrived at the Mole.

Keyes had changed his mind once more. *Thetis* would be the first into the harbour. She was to ram the lock-gates and be scuttled in the lock entrance. *Intrepid* and *Iphigenia* would follow. Their captains were to sink their commands in the narrowest part of the channel between the lock and the sea.

Keyes personally briefed the blockship captains on 21 April. He stressed that they must not deviate from his orders. He believed that if *Thetis* failed in her task and sank short of the gates, she would be no obstruction. Her two consorts sinking between the piers would, however, cause great inconvenience to the Germans. No alternative was allowed. Once again, Keyes overlooked the obvious.

The three blockships had an exciting time avoiding a wide protective barrage, some half a mile deep, three miles outside the Mole. The arrival of *Vindictive* and her assault parties persuaded the Germans that a large-scale landing was planned. The *Württemberg* and *Friedrichsort* heavy batteries, with the enthusiastic assistance of some smaller units, plastered the sea with salvo after salvo to deter any new arrivals.

The ships reached the security of the smokescreen laid by the motor launches. As *Thetis* moved closer to the harbour, her captain, Commander Ralph Sneyd, anticipated getting his bearings from calcium buoys laid by *ML 110*. There were none. The launch, tasked with lighting the entrances to both harbour and canal, had not got very far. Approaching the harbour, she was hit by three shells. Half the crew became instant casualties, including her captain, Lieutenant Commander Dawbarn Young. His last order was to abandon ship.

Thetis was given a course correction by *ML 558*, who later blanketed the *Iris* with smoke as she left the Mole. At 00.20 hours the smoke thinned. Lit by the rockets fired from *Vindictive*, the Mole and the lighthouse went into fierce silhouette against a wall of flame as *C 3* exploded.

Sneyd ordered the helm hard over. *Thetis* increased speed and surged into the harbour. *Iphigenia* and *Intrepid* followed their leader as closely as they dared.

Ahead was the barge boom, a string of barges fastened together. Sneyd steered *Thetis* towards the barge at the southern end, opening fire first at the lighthouse and then at the barge. This was hit and started to sink. Sneyd could see a gap between the last flatboat in the line and the buoys which supported the net boom on the left.

So far, so good. Except that *Kapitänleutnant* Schütte on the Mole was nobody's fool. He knew a blockship when he saw one. The barrels of the Mole guns swung round to cover the new target. On the shore, battery commanders snapped crisp orders to deal with the intruder.

Thetis was less than 100 yards from the guns on the Mole end when they opened fire. Holes sprouted along her starboard. Hungry water poured in, racing through the hull in a frenzy of destruction.

Vizefeuerwerker Schröder's crews were not idle either:

Suddenly, illuminated in the light of star-shells from the Mole, a vessel, apparently a blockship, came out of the fog. It came from the pierhead at a brisk rate. The guns immediately had the ship in their sights. In order not to hit the Mole Batteries, the Battery waited until the ship had got further into the harbour before opening rapid fire. The first salvoes straddled the target. We then clearly observed direct hits.

Sneyd's ship started to die. She swung to the left, caught by the fast tide flowing towards the shore. The wheel was spun hard over in a frantic attempt to get her back on course. It failed. *Thetis* charged into the nets. She went on, pulling the nets behind her as she struggled to reach the canal entrance.

The Mole end batteries fired on. Guns on shore added their weight to the inferno. Machine-gun bullets sprayed the deck. The destroyers and torpedo-boats alongside the Mole joined the fray as Sneyd desperately tried to get his ship back on course. The canal piers were just 300 yards away when the trailing wire of the nets, which had been industriously wrapping itself round the screws, stalled the engines. The long trail of battered metal behind the ship slowed her relentlessly. She moved towards the shore. Her screws stopped, the engines no longer able to drive them round against the dragging metal strands. Battered,

137

bruised, *Thetis* listed to her right. Steam, smoke, flame escaped in a roar of sound. She grounded on the left hand side of the channel.

Schröder recorded the incident. 'Suddenly a huge column of smoke and steam rose from the ship and absolutely enveloped it. Soon afterwards, we heard the hiss of escaping vapour.'

The German gunners continued to hammer the cruiser. *Thetis* replied with her three 6-inch guns. It was gallant. It was brave. It was fearsomely uneven.

Sneyd had lost voice communication with the engine room. He sent a runner. Engineer Lieutenant Commander Ronald Boddie responded and did the impossible. He started the starboard engine. *Thetis* strained forward. The bows swivelled slowly round to the right into the dredged channel.

She could do no more and go no further. Sneyd ordered his crew to leave. Black smoke enveloped the ship as the smoke canisters were switched on. The charges were blown. *Thetis* settled heavily in the silt.

Both Sneyd and his deputy, Lieutenant Francis Lambert, were wounded. Acting Lieutenant George Belben took over. Only one boat, the cutter, was still vaguely seaworthy. Belben and a handful of men fought to get it into the water. The sea rushed in through two or three holes. The cutter sank lower but the crew made it to Lieutenant Hugh Littleton and *ML 526* which waited close by.

Lieutenant Bonham Carter and the *Intrepid* had a much easier time. Thanks to her leader destroying the net boom and the attention lavished by the German gunners on Commander Sneyd, *Intrepid* was almost ignored. She edged past *Thetis*, her task made much easier by the sunken ship's green starboard light which still shone brightly. *Intrepid* reached the canal entrance with no more than minor shrapnel damage.

The lock-gates were just one half-mile away. All Bonham Carter had to do was to steam towards them. Four minutes sailing time. The link between Bruges and the sea would be ruptured with very little chance of swift repair. Keyes himself had declared that the object of Operation ZO was 'to cut Zeebrugge off from the docks, submarine shelters and repair shops several miles inland, on which the enemy were dependent . . .'.

But Keyes' instructions had been especially precise. It was not Bonham Carter's job to damage the gates even though *Thetis* had not reached the canal. It seems quite incredible that Keyes did not demand that the first ship into the canal, irrespective of identity, smashed the gates.

138

Captain Grant made this point to Keyes after the Raid. Although he detested Keyes, his report of the conversation sounds accurate enough. It contains echoes of Keyes' own letter to Beatty concerning Brock's shortcomings. In his unpublished manuscript, *The Folly Of Zeebrugge*, Grant records the following exchange between Keyes and himself. The admiral promptly denigrated his own choice of blockship captains:

Bonham Carter ought to have used his common sense; he is as brave as a lion but has no brains. I ought to have had Billyard-Leake in the *Intrepid*.

Grant made the obvious response.

Well, did the orders say that the first ship in the canal was to ram the lock gate? The officers said that they had been told verbally on the 21st that *Thetis* was to ram the canal lock gate and the other two to sink in a V at the canal entrance.

Keyes reply was revealing: 'I am not going to give every order in writing, they ought to use commonsense.'

Failing to put orders in writing can be a blessing to a commander. He is able to dodge responsibility by alleging that his subordinates failed to use their initiative. In this case, Keyes' clearly emphatic instructions left no room for independent action. They also negated the whole purpose of Operation ZO.

Bonham Carter obeyed his orders to the last full stop. The glittering opportunity was tossed aside.

Intrepid reached the coastline, still unscathed. Bonham Carter ordered full speed ahead on the starboard engine and full astern on the port. With the helm hard to starboard, *Intrepid* attempted a stomach-lurching spin. She swung only ten degrees – she was a hundred yards long and the channel was only a fraction wider – when she hit silt on both sides.

Bonham Carter tried again. Brock's patent smoke was belching from every canister. It not only blinded the enemy. It stopped Bonham Carter seeing either the Germans or the canal banks. He ordered all of his crew, except those in the engine room, into the boats while he tried to improve *Intrepid*'s position. The engines throbbed as her captain backed and filled as best he could like an inexperienced driver trying to get into a very small parking space. When he could swing no more, Bonham Carter sounded the alarms to clear the ship.

Iphigenia came through the smoke, crunched into *Intrepid*'s port bow and pushed her off the silt. Bonham Carter just had enough time to blow

139

the charges before his ship slid stern-first completely out of her hard-won parking slot. The engine room crew, still below, were somewhat perturbed as the ship settled under them. Without appearing to hurry, and led by Engineer Sub Lieutenant Edgar Meikle, they were swiftly in a cutter with others of the crew, pulling towards *Thetis* and heading for the open sea. As they moved towards the canal entrance, they were greeted by *ML 526* which had picked up the crew of *Thetis*.

Sub Lieutenant Meikle and his companions were rather more fortunate than the first cutter to leave *Intrepid*. Designed to carry twenty-two men, it had left with half as many again. The extra stoking crew, it will be remembered, had contrived to remain aboard the ship. The cutter, water lapping close to her freeboard, splashed her way out of the canal, across the harbour and into the North Sea. They enjoyed a grandstand view of the German batteries battering the *Vindictive* as they passed. Amazingly, nobody saw them. Neither the Germans nor the rescue launches noticed the wallowing boat as it crept across the water.

They were faced with rowing 120 miles across the North Sea to reach England in a boat that was close to capsizing. They were already some miles north-east of Zeebrugge when HMS *Whirlwind* came to take a look.

Meanwhile, Billyard-Leake in *Iphigenia* prepared to sink his ship. Smacking smartly into his companion had simply been the latest incident in his entry into Zeebrugge Harbour.

Everything had gone well until he had tried to pass *Thetis*. As with *Intrepid*, the glowing green lamp had been invaluable. As *Iphigenia* sidled past, two shells banged into her. Probably the intended target was *Thetis* but the shells were not particular. A severed steampipe covered the front of the ship in white vapour. As this cleared, *Iphigenia* ran into a smokescreen. Billyard-Leake could see nothing ahead. When he could, he found the western pier looming up in front of him.

Both engines slammed into reverse. The helm went hard over. *Iphigenia* scraped along the western bank going between a moored dredger and a barge. She cut the hawser which joined the pair. The barge did not behave. It stayed entangled with the bows and Billyard-Leake pushed it up the canal. The barge reluctantly slipped clear in time for Billyard-Leake to run into the smoke pouring from *Intrepid*.

The Germans, unable to see *Intrepid*, turned their attention to *Iphigenia*. Shrapnel and small-arms fire hissed across the deck. Billyard-Leake rapidly closed the distance on his sister ship. *Intrepid* had grounded on the western bank, leaving a gap of about forty yards between her bows and the eastern bank.

Reasonably enough, Billyard-Leake conned his ship to fill the gap. He made a minor misjudgement. The speed failed to decay quickly enough. Experience helps judgement and Billyard-Leake was not very experienced. *Iphigenia* collided with *Intrepid*'s port bow. Engines astern. *Iphigenia* backed slowly. When she had space, Billyard-Leake took her forward, finally reversing the port engine. With the starboard engine full ahead and the rudder right over, the cruiser grounded on the eastern bank.

The crew abandoned ship. The charges exploded. *Iphigenia* settled in the channel. The high tide lapped curiously at the deck as Billyard-Leake, in leather coat and steel helmet, strode across the planking to climb into the sole surviving cutter.

On board *Intrepid* Bonham Carter, two officers and sixteen men prepared to evacuate their ship. They had a single skiff, designed to take ten men. Bonham Carter crammed the sixteen ratings into the skiff. It pulled out past the stern of *Iphigenia*. There sat *ML 282* under the command of Lieutenant Percy Dean. The skiff reached her starboard bow. The men started to clamber aboard only to be joined on the other side by *Iphigenia*'s overcrowded cutter. Lieutenant Dean was well aware that the four original motor launches detailed to rescue blockship crews had been reduced by half. *ML 526*, already full with survivors from *Thetis* and Sub Lieutenant Meikle's men, was the only other launch on station.

ML 282 got lower in the water. It was meant to carry between forty and fifty men. Something like a hundred survivors were actually on board. Dean decided that some would have to travel in the cutter. A deckhand fastened it, somewhat unconventionally, to the bow. Dean reversed out at full speed.

A bright, dazzling light suddenly illuminated *ML 282*. Bonham Carter with his officers and petty officers had used a Carley float to escape from *Intrepid*. Grimly determined they paddled an erratic course to the harbour. It was unfortunate that a large foot pressed the plunger which lit the flares. Designed for the location of survivors at night in a heavy sea, the Holmes Light behaved precisely as the maker intended.

Every gunner in the area swivelled to bear on this new attraction. Bonham Carter and his men hastily took to the water as bullets riddled the float. Dean did not hesitate. As soon as he saw the men in the water he took his overburdened launch back into the canal. Two officers and four petty officers were unceremoniously dragged aboard. In the confusion, nobody noticed Bonham Carter steadily swimming towards the launch. Dean went into reverse once more. The Lieutenant just managed to grab a rope as *ML 282* gathered speed.

A deckhand noticed the body grimly hanging on to the line. After some minor confusion as to whether the potential boarder was British or German, the sailor vanished to inform his captain. Before he reached him, Bonham Carter's shoulder joints surrendered. *ML 282*, relieved of her burden, sped faster towards the harbour entrance.

The deckhand reached Dean at almost the same moment that another mighty star shell burst overhead. Dean saw the black shape of Bonham Carter's head as the Lieutenant swam doggedly towards the shore. *ML 282* went back once more into the canal mouth. The star shell lit the scene with exquisite perfection for the German machine-gunners. Bullets hosed the launch as Bonham Carter finally dragged himself into its doubtful safety.

Sub Lieutenant Maurice Lloyd, who went to *Iphigenia* when Lieutenant Franks was invalided ashore with appendicitis, had saved the Ensign when he abandoned ship. He clutched it to him, its white field slowly turning red. He was bleeding, with agonizing slowness, to death.

Among a score of dead was one of Dean's own crew. Leading Deckhand George McKruly was a fisherman in more peaceful times. His wife Isabella would soon receive a telegram at her home in South Shields.

Still in reverse, Dean took his command into the harbour. As he cleared the canal entrance, the steering gear broke down. The crush on board had fouled the steering cable. Dean controlled his vessel by juggling with his two engines. He stayed close to the Mole itself so that the heavier guns could not depress their barrels to aim at him. Even so, accurate small-arms fire rattled into the launch with insistent regularity.

Black fumes partially gassed some of his passengers when a bullet hit a smoke canister. A fire was swiftly extinguished. By the time Dean reached the Mole entrance all of his crew, except those working the engines, were casualties. His passengers took over their duties. Dean cleared the harbour, holding a course which masked him from the heavy guns. Slowly, carefully, the overcrowded boat moved into the North Sea and the concealing night. A deckhand cut free the cutter. *ML 282* – her steering working again – pointed her nose at Dover.

They had gone only a short way when *Warwick* appeared out of the gloom. She had stayed close to the Mole until *Vindictive, Iris* and *Daffodil* were safely on their way. Keyes' personal bravery cannot be questioned. *Warwick* had moved in tightly to the action, making smoke and exchanging fire with the defending guns.

Once the assault ships had left, Keyes stayed in the area to help any stragglers. They found *ML 282*. It took more than thirty minutes to transfer the blockship survivors, the dead, the dying, the wounded and the unscathed to the flagship.

Sea-going casualties had been remarkably light. When the three assault ships finally left the Mole only two motor launches had been destroyed. *ML 110*, already mentioned, was one of them. Lieutenant George Bowen had taken command. The dead and wounded were lowered into the dinghy while Bowen went below, smashed a hole in the bottom with an axe and made doubly sure by firing two drums of Lewis gun ammunition into the hull. He then rejoined the survivors in the dinghy. *ML 110* sank just as *ML 308* came alongside to pick them up.

A similar service was provided by *ML 128* when *ML 424* was picked off by the Zeebrugge gunners as she ran out of the smokescreen. The captain and two deckhands were killed, another wounded. Lieutenant John Robinson and the remainder of the crew set fire to the engine room and made good their escape.

A greater loss was to come. HMS *North Star* lost her bearings in a smokescreen. Her captain, Lieutenant Commander Kenneth Helyar, came out of it to make the interesting discovery that there were houses close on his port bow. The next landmark was a collection of masts and funnels which belonged to *Thetis*. The destroyer was well inside Zeebrugge harbour.

Schröder, still on duty with the *Friedrichsort* battery, described events:

> The searchlights of a canal battery lit up a big destroyer on a west-erly course, about five hundred metres from the beach. One could clearly read *F 53* on her bow. Unfortunately, we could not open fire because of the short range – all of our shots would have landed in the sand-dunes. The destroyer raked the beach road and batteries with machine-gun and pom-pom fire. A searchlight clamped on her.

An anchored German destroyer was horribly vigilant. Shells splashed around *North Star*. A pom-pom found the range. Helyar turned his ship around, fired a torpedo at his attacker and made for the exit.

143

The guns on the Mole and on shore opened fire. The assault ships may have left but a British destroyer was just as good. Helyar fired more torpedoes at the ships moored alongside the quay. *North Star* swerved to avoid the barge boom and hurried for safety.

A surviving crew member summarised the excursion tersely:

> When we ran into the harbour, we ran out of darkness into light brighter than daylight. They got searchlights all focused on us and at point-blank range they poured stuff into us and all over us from guns big and little. Our port side was riddled from end to end, our aft funnel went, our wireless room was put out of action, and then they smashed our bow.

As she came to the lighthouse and freedom, the Mole gunners thumped high explosive into her boiler- and engine rooms. The *Friedrichsort* battery gunners waited impatiently to join in. Schröder described *North Star*'s determined struggle to escape: 'The Mole batteries took the destroyer under heavy fire. Their excellent shooting was clearly seen from the Battery. She went out to sea on a northerly course . . .'.

The boilers exploded. The engines seized. *North Star* floundered to a halt a mere 400 yards north of the Mole. Another searchlight froze on the crippled ship. More shells crashed into the destroyer. It was 01.25 hours.

HMS *Phoebe*, the saviour of the crew of *C 3* had spent most of the night steaming back and forth on a beat north of the Mole. When *North Star* scooted out of the harbour, under heavy fire, Lieutenant Commander Hubert Gore-Langton rushed to the rescue, his starboard guns snapping a peremptory reply at the Mole batteries.

Phoebe spun an opaque circle of thick black smoke round the stricken *North Star*. Gore-Langton went in close in an attempt to pass a line. The wind puffed at the smoke. *North Star* pulled away. The tow parted.

Phoebe made more smoke but matters were perilous. Cold searchlight fingers spread across the sea to hold the two ships in a fearsome light. A star shell burst. The Mole batteries and the guns on the shore concentrated for a kill.

Idiotically, a shower of shell splinters chopped *Phoebe*'s siren lanyard. The shriek rose high above the battle sounds. The rolling smoke lost its purpose. The German gunners simply aimed in the direction of the banshee howl. Gore-Langton did not give up. *Phoebe* came alongside.

Wires were passed. The two ships would escape like a pair of Siamese twins.

Schröder's four guns continued firing:

> In the light of a starshell, we a saw a second destroyer arrive which went alongside, stern first, and appeared to take off the crew. By the light of a second starshell, it was possible to see the second destroyer.
>
> The guns had immediately got the range, targeted the flank, and fired the first full salvo. After an interval of six to eight seconds, another six of the best followed, of which three hit the target. There was a direct hit on the fo'c'sle.

A shell ploughed between the two deckrails. Wires sprung apart. *North Star*'s capstan disappeared in the explosion.

Phoebe raced round, making smoke as hard as she could. Helyar ordered the boats to be lowered. Carley floats dropped into the water. *North Star*'s motor dinghy capsized, its occupants being thrown into the chilly dark sea. Somehow, Lieutenant Leslie Smith and four crew members survived long enough to be collected by the Germans. They joined Sergeant Harry Wright and his companions in Bruges' convict cells.

Phoebe lowered her whaler to assist before circling *North Star* one more time, acrid smoke pouring from her canisters.

For minutes, the German fire slackened. Gore-Langton went alongside Helyar again. Bracing wires passed between the two ships. They were made fast in time for more German shells to arrive on *North Star*'s decks. The wires were cut again. *North Star* adopted a fierce list to starboard. She was clearly doomed.

Helyar and his crew abandoned ship, jumping across the gap to *Phoebe*. One last sailor, whose name will never be known, was running forward to make his bid for safety when a German shell exploded by his side in a corona of flame. The horrified spectators saw him outlined for a split moment. He never landed on *Phoebe*'s deck. He was one of thirty-five casualties.

Gore-Langton cleared the cripple. He intended to ensure she sank by putting a torpedo into her but the Germans finished the job they had begun. Another salvo burst close to *North Star*. When the spray cleared, there was not a sign of her.

Phoebe made for Dover. It was 02.25 hours. Her escapade had taken a little more than an hour. Her adventures had not quite ended. At

04.00 hours, she found *Iris* plodding doggedly, stubbornly and gallantly homewards.

Phoebe had no luck with her tows that night. Three times she passed a line. Three times they parted in the six-foot swell. The destroyer finally left *Iris* alone on the heaving sea.

So ended the Zeebrugge phase of the operation. The blockships had got in. The morning would reveal whether they had sealed the canal.

The blocking of Ostend was a very different matter.

CHAPTER TWELVE

If Zeebrugge was high drama and tragedy, the attempt to block Ostend that night was almost the stuff of farce.

It began well enough. The plan called for a convoy of vessels to leave Dunkirk, under the overall command of Commodore Hubert Lynes to steam towards Ostend. They left on time. At 23.20, the four monitors *Marshal Soult*, *General Craufurd*, *Prince Eugene* and *Lord Clive*, together with two smaller companions *M 24* and *M 26* opened fire at Ostend. Simultaneously, the siege guns of the Royal Marine Artillery in Flanders added their broadsides.

Commodore Lynes later reported that their efforts inhibited return fire by the shore batteries. This may well be so. Later reconnaissance showed that none of the attackers apparently hit any enemy installations although there were some new craters in their vicinity.

The monitors were guarded by the British destroyers *Mentor*, *Lightfoot* and the indefatigable *Zubian*. The French supplied *Lestin*, *Capitaine Mehl*, *Francis Garnier*, *Roux* and *Bouclier*. The two small monitors enjoyed the exclusive attention of four French motor launches.

A further eighteen British launches were responsible for laying a smokescreen, rescuing the blockship crews and generally creating problems for the defence. Six coastal motor boats had the job of putting down light buoys to light the way to the harbour and smoke-floats to hide the intruders.

The attack on Ostend was subject to one specific discipline. Extremely accurate navigation was needed to find the entrance to the harbour and canal. The duo of Captain Douglas and Commander Haselfoot had carefully plotted the positions of two extremely important marker buoys. One was the Stroombank buoy. The other was a Bell Whistle buoy just off Ostend Beach. The two navigators calculated speeds and courses which would make very sure that the blockships would go from the Stroombank to the Bell and into the mouth of the Bruges-Ostend canal.

After the abortive attempt of 11 April, when *CMB 33* was captured, the Germans, too, knew the details. It did not take much Teutonic ingenuity to politely place the Stroombank buoy one and a half miles to the east nor to remove the Bell buoy entirely.

It is disputable whether the fault was with Keyes or with Lynes. The Commodore certainly made a great point that checking the position of the buoy – which the RAF did the day after the attack – was a highly skilled business. Locating buoys from the air was difficult even in favourable weather. April's rain and low clouds greatly handicapped the pilots who patrolled the Belgian coast. The alteration of the Stroombank buoy escaped the airmen's notice.

This does not excuse the Navy. Both sides enjoyed moving their own buoys to confuse the enemy. Sometimes, they would reposition the other side's in a general attempt to improve the war effort. Whether from the air or from the sea, which is where a Dover Patrol navigator would have earned his pay, the Stroombank buoy should have been confirmed in its position. Failure to do that was a piece of carelessness which cost lives and ships.

The first vessels to run into problems were the coastal motor boats. Cooperating with the motor launches they were to lay a double line of smoke on each side of the canal entrance. This line was a mere five miles long. After this minor task, another double line would be laid between the Stroombank buoy to the Bell buoy. Between this wall of smoke, the blockships would steam directly into the canal.

It can be argued that the plan was already in the realm of make-believe at this point. No account was taken of the wind. Given that smoke – even that pioneered by Brock – disperses easily, it was asking a great deal of the small boat crews to produce such an exact pattern over such a distance.

The first to reach the repositioned Stroombank buoy was *CMB 19* under the command of Lieutenant Francis Harrison. He was also the Flotilla Commander. He concluded that his navigation was faulty and so duly placed a calcium light before proceeding to find the Bell buoy. When it did not appear, Harrison decided that it must have drifted away. He thus positioned a second flare where he thought the buoy should be. He did not think, for a moment, for an instant, that something might be wrong.

This task completed, Harrison steered due south to find the canal entrance. The Ostend defences were very alert indeed. *CMB 19* was held in a series of fierce searchlight beams. Harrison twisted. Harrison turned. Eventually, he found the canal entrance but his erratic manoeuvres prevented him from checking his bearings. His life was made more difficult when heavy machine-gun fire crunched into his vessel. His chief mechanic was severely wounded. Harrison retreated to the Stroombank buoy to wait for the midnight arrival of the blockships.

In the meantime, the motor launches were making the best job they could of laying smoke. It was, of course, in the wrong place. Any doubts that the Ostend defences were well aware of what was happening are dispelled by the knowledge that they put down a heavy barrage in the area. Star shell lit the night. Pom-poms chattered angrily. The heavier salvos sent torrents of water into the air. All in all, the enemy had the upper hand. The motor launches were under the overall command of Captain Ion Hamilton Benn. He was, like Hilton Young approaching Zeebrugge on the *Vindictive* at that very moment, a Member of Parliament. Not all politicians occupied comfortable armchairs and pontificated on how to win the war.

Hamilton Benn, in *ML 532* retired discreetly from the calcium flare which masqueraded as the Bell buoy to the repositioned Stroombank buoy. The German gunners knew exactly where the Bell Buoy should be and guessed that a target or two would be there.

Brilliant and *Sirius* were quite probably in their correct positions at midnight. As with the Zeebrugge attack, though, St George was fickle. The wind changed. The smokescreen, already precarious, created complete confusion.

Commander Alfred Godsal already had the vague impression that he was too far north when the Ostend flotilla parted company from the Zeebrugge fleet. This faint idea allowed him to conclude that the failure of the Stroombank buoy to appear on time simply meant that he still had some way to go.

He reached the northern line of smoke. Edging through it, he discovered the empty box defined by the black fumes. No Stroombank buoy. Godsal, another import from the Grand Fleet who had no experience of the ducks-and-drakes activities with buoys in the North Sea coastal waters, turned to the east as if he had indeed seen Stroombank. This was the right thing to do but, at this point, the malicious wind led to his downfall.

The smoke in the south should have cleared enough for him to see the shore while still blinding the German gunners. At that stage, with the canal entrance visible to his right, it was a matter of running the gauntlet of the shore batteries to reach the target.

As it was, the smoke drifted over *Brilliant*. Supplementary banks rolled in from the shore. Not only the Royal Navy knew how to make smoke. Godsal, already disorientated, saw two clearly visible CMBs out to sea. To the north-east was the unmistakeable Stroombank buoy and Hamilton Benn's motor launch.

Brilliant promptly turned left, followed by the faithful *Sirius*. Godsal swung round the falsely placed buoy and took up the predetermined course for the entrance to Ostend.

Three motor launches, *ML 532*, *ML 276* and *ML 283* together with *CMB 19* escorted the two cruisers. The defenders were extremely active. There is little doubt that the gunners were firing on predetermined settings. The days since *CMB 33* had been busy ones for the *Matrosen- und Marineartllierie*. Now they were reaping the reward for their hard work.

The wind had blown the smoke offshore. Every vessel in the tiny fleet was illuminated by powerful searchlights. Hamilton Benn swung away to the left to lay more smoke in the hope that it would obscure the ships from the guns to the east. It would also hide the waterfront from *Sirius* and *Brilliant*. Neither Captain nor Commander hesitated to drive towards the target. There is no compromise once action is joined. As long as the ship steers, the tank crunches forward on its tracks, the aircraft continues to fly, prudence is relegated to a back seat.

Both cruisers were hit. The small craft led charmed lives but every salvo sent up huge splashes which could easily have swamped them.

Sub Lieutenant Edward Berthon, busy conning the ship, recorded the scene in his diary on 28 April:

The entire heavens were flooded with light. Starshells were bursting slap above us and to seaward. Blue devils, eight blue shells tied together with wire came hurtling through the air making an infernal noise and heavy stuff hit us on the focsle. One round hit the water on the Starboard side of the Bridge and [the] burst covered us with bits and with water, no-one was hurt but we all had to spit a lot to get rid of the taste. . .

. . . We were being hit hard and regularly and the machine guns were firing the blazes at us. The whole world was filled with light, one heavy shell hit us on the port quarter and started a fire, another shell hit us starboard side of the focsle and a fire began in the Sick Bay. . . .

. . . Hell had been let loose, every machine gun, every big gun was firing at us two. . . . One shell took off the top third of of the foremost funnel.

The end approached. On his right, Godsal heard the unmistakeable sound of waves breaking. *Brilliant*, full of concrete, damaged by German shells, was slow in answering the rudder. She touched. She nearly went clear for one brief moment of hope. Then her bows wedged deep into Belgian sand. Godsal called for both engines full astern. Before they responded, *Sirius* thumped into Godsal's ship on the port quarter. *Brilliant* was driven harder into the treacherous sandbank.

Godsal had no more choices. He ordered the crew to evacuate the ship, switched on the smoke canisters and fired the charges in the hull. When the crew were clear, he and his second in command, Lieutenant Victor Crutchley, stepped over the stern, slid down the ropes and into *ML 276*. Its commander, Lieutenant Roland Bourke, came alongside under fire four times to take off the survivors. Stopping for more than a few seconds was an extremely hazardous proceeding. When *Brilliant*'s captain was finally aboard, Bourke made for the Stroombank buoy.

Brilliant had been hit by a ship that was already doomed. At least two dozen shells had hit *Sirius*. She was also the target of some particularly quarrelsome machine-gunners. Lieutenant Commander Henry Hardy had closed up on his leader as the smoke billowed across them both. When *Brilliant* grounded, Hardy put his helm hard over and engines full astern. It had no effect. *Sirius* was already sinking. Water was pouring into the hull, adding its weight to the concrete and rubble. The ship carried straight on into *Brilliant*.

Sirius settled on the sand. Hardy blew out her bottom. The two ships were firmly aground 2400 yards from the canal entrance. They were only 1000 yards away from a cluster of German batteries – *Grossherzog*, *Preussen*, *Ludendorff*, *Hindenburg*, *Irene*, *Friedrich* and *Eylau*. Just two miles distant were the 38-centimetre guns of the mighty *Deutschland* or *Jacobynessen* battery. For the next hour, they continued to pound the stranded cruisers.

Hardy, Lieutenant Edward Berthon and the crew were taken off by Lieutenant Commander Keith Hoare in *ML 283*. The launch had already collected sixteen men from *Brilliant* who had abandoned ship in a whaler. This had been stitched neatly by a machine gun. Only fifty yards away from their ship it became clear that the whaler had all the buoyancy of a garden sieve. By the time the complement of *Sirius* had embarked, *ML 283* had seventy-five rescued souls on board.

Hoare set a course for the Stroombank buoy. While the launch escaped from the danger zone, Hardy and Berthon counted heads. They came to the conclusion that Engineer Lieutenant William McLaren and

151

his stokers were not on board. It was probable that they had stayed on the ship.

Hoare hailed Sub Lieutenant Peter Clarke in *CMB 10*. Hardy and Berthon joined her. Clarke called for full power. The motor boat went like an arrow for *Sirius*.

The two blockships were still being pounded by German shells. *Brilliant* was blazing. There was no reply from *Sirius*. Neither did a voice from *Brilliant* reply to repeated shouts. Clarke and his boat came under heavy fire. He weaved frantically around, dodging shrapnel and bullets, until it was clear that nothing could be done. *CMB 10* turned back for the open sea.

The stokers and their officer had already left their ship. With the cold certainty of the men who worked the boilers, they had lowered the whaler and started to row to England. They were already thirteen miles into the North Sea when the inquisitive destroyer *Attentive* found them pulling strongly for Dover. Men who heaved coal into hungry boilers had developed muscles designed to last. Many ambitious young seamen who picked a fight with the furnace crews when the pubs closed discovered that to their cost.

Hamilton Benn suffered the last embarrassment of the night. After laying his eastern smokescreen, he went to help rescue the crew of *Brilliant*. A German shell punched *ML 526* smartly on the nose at the precise moment she put her bows alongside the blockship. For some while, Benn blamed his own bad seamanship for the wrecked bows and splintered exhaust pipes. Useless as a rescue launch, *ML 526* backed away. To his great embarrassment, Benn later had to ask for a tow back to Dunkirk. Lieutenant Bourke and *ML 276* obliged.

By whatever standards it is judged, the blocking of Ostend was an abysmal failure. There can be no excuses about the position of the Stroombank buoy. It was a legitimate ploy by the enemy.

The Ostend attack depended completely on accurate navigation. A specialist in that arcane skill, especially one who knew the quirks of the coast, would have been worth his berth. There were plenty of them in the Dover Patrol but the operation appears to have been restricted to officers from the Grand Fleet.

Bravery and cool gallantry were not enough.

Ostend was still clear.

Another assault would be folly in most people's eyes. But they did not know Roger Keyes.

CHAPTER THIRTEEN

Weary grey light crept slowly, like an exhausted warrior, across the North Sea as dawn broke on the morning of St George's Day. The huge armada was split into a myriad of craft which made their way home to Dunkirk and Dover on a gently swelling sea.

At Zeebrugge, daylight picked out a few sodden bodies in the pewter-grey water on each side of the Mole. The Germans prepared a military funeral for each one. Away from the turmoil of the Western Front, it was possible to bury gallant foes with the dignity they deserved. Both sides prided themselves that they treated their dead enemies with professional respect. Between the two Navies there was the knowledge that they also fought a common foe. The ocean was jealous, unpredictable. It behoved every sailor to be humble in its presence.

The clean-up was filmed by *Leutnant* Franz Seldte and a team of German Army cameramen. Woken by the sound of the barrage, Seldte's men drove their Benz, headlights blazing, the twenty miles from Fourth Army Headquarters at Tielt to Bruges at breakneck speed. The *Leutnant* and his detachment had been busy filming Ludendorff's great offensive but a British naval attack was a great opportunity. At Bruges, the Imperial Navy supplied a guide to the harbour. Film crews might be important people but no sailor on sentry-go would give Army cameramen free right to roam.

Seldte was no back-area warrior but an old hand, a genuine *Grabenschwein*, a 'trench pig', the dismissive name that the front line German infantry called themselves with pride. With a useless left arm, a legacy of the Western Front, he had turned to capturing the war on film. He did it very well. The Kaiser himself admired his work. Seldte was overcome by a feeling of melancholy as he surveyed the scene:

Wasn't it . . . idiotic that we should be trying to smash in each other's skulls and tear out each other's throats and entrails? . . . If we fought not against one another, but side by side, couldn't we together smash the whole world, or rule and lead in co-operation?

One unexplained incident remains to be recorded. *Kapitänleutnant* Schütte stated his battery sank a motorboat at 06.30 that morning. His claim – and the account by the faithful *Artillerie-Maat* Policke – contains full details. The boat was sighted, motionless, in the early dawn. After the first salvo, the crew held up their hands. The Mole battery ceased firing. Two German torpedo boats went to bring in the intruder. At which point, the motor launch engines started with a roar and the boat tried to escape. The *Württemburg* and *Mole* batteries fired again with deadly accuracy. The launch was destroyed. German observation posts confirmed the kill.

Every Allied vessel which went to Zeebrugge and Ostend was accounted for so there is some mystery about this unknown target. Schütte's claim has been denigrated either as an attempt to gain personal glory or as part of a sinister German conspiracy to downgrade the Zeebrugge Raid. Such comments overlook the fact that the claim was duly witnessed as regulations prescribed. In fact, Schütte was ambivalent about the intruder's identity. He does not state that the vessel was British. It could have been French, Belgian or even an insane Dutchman on a sightseeing trip.

Vizefeuerwerker Schröder finished his watch. He counted more than 100 craters in the field behind his battery which had escaped unscathed from the British bombardment. If the Tommies came again, they would get an even hotter reception, he decided.

For most of the Royal Navy crews on the larger ships, it had not been a stirring time. They were mildly frustrated because the *Kaiserliche Marine* failed to intervene with a mass of irascible destroyers or a horde of aggressive U-boats. *Mansfield* had actually opened fire on a submarine just as *Vindictive* approached the Mole. Luckily, it was soon recognized as her errant tow, *C 1* which had vanished earlier.

Lieutenant Aubrey Newbold and his crew had suffered some stimulating moments after the tow broke on the way to Zeebrugge. When the hawser parted, Newbold started his engines and carried on. He quickly realized that *C 1* was much handicapped in her progress by a length of recalcitrant cable fouling her bows. The First Lieutenant scrambled across the slippery hull, released the cable, fell overboard and clambered back, wet but triumphant.

Close to midnight *C 1* met *Mansfield* and *Trident* patrolling northwest of Zeebrugge. They were no wiser than Newbold as to what was

154

happening at the Mole. Newbold decided to wait. At 00.20 hours, the large flash from the viaduct could have meant that *C 3* had done her job but there was no noise. Newbold, acutely aware that he had five tons of temperamental amatol in the hull, moved delicately eastward towards Zeebrugge. At 00.50 hours, he decided that the area would probably be clear enough for him to make his own approach. The volatile explosive on board *C 1* would provide an interesting punctuation mark if he collided with another vessel. Newbold was just 2500 yards from the viaduct when he saw the unmistakeable shape of *Vindictive* retiring rapidly. Her premature departure convinced Newbold that the operation had failed, a decision made more credible by the feel of the wind in his face. If the breeze was coming from the land, the smoke had no doubt been dispersed. In turn, that suggested the blockships had also turned back to wait for another chance. Newbold decided to return to Dover.

He arrived at 12.25 hours after an eleven-hour voyage. He quickly learned what had really happened and promptly volunteered himself and his crew for some other act of destruction on the enemy shore.

Leutnant Seldte's musings were interrupted at 06.55 hours by a de Havilland DH-4 of 202 Squadron. Heavy mist and thick clouds shrouded the harbour but Lieutenant Robert Coulthard and Lieutenant J. D. Fysh decided to try their luck.

They found a break in the clouds over Zeebrugge, dropped down to fifty feet and roared across the harbour. Fysh fired 300 rounds at a group of stupefied workmen before Coulthard escaped back into the blanketing cloud.

By 11.00 hours, the weather was clear enough for eight 213 Squadron Sopwith Camels and DH-4s of 217 Squadron to add their few penceworth. The Camels dropped eight 112-pound bombs and four 20-pound bombs. Ten 230-pound bombs left the de Havillands. They did little damage although the men on the ground prudently withdrew to the shelters.

The anti-aircraft gunners continued to be busy when 213 Squadron returned in the afternoon and dropped another seven 112-pound bombs.

Lieutenant Gerald Smith of 213 Squadron sounded singularly unimpressed by the events of the previous night:

> . . . cloudy and misty . . . went on a bomb raid to Zee Mole at 1.35 . . . I did not hit it, close to it. We have been bombing all day also with No 17 Squadron.

> The Fleet attacked Mole & Ostend last night & landed on Mole,
> did damage, we were bombing to stop them repairing it.

Vindictive arrived back at Dover a few minutes after 08.00 hours. Loud cheering from an excited crowd greeted her. The word was already out that the operation had been a great success. The cheering faltered, then died away as the first ambulances arrived. More than 200 of the men who had sailed so enthusiastically to Zeebrugge on *Vindictive* were wounded. They went by ambulance to hospital and to the station where a special train waited. There were no ambulances for the dead. They travelled inside closed motor lorries to the police mortuary in Dover for more leisurely identification.

Clearing *Vindictive* was a long, grim process. As Engineer Lieutenant Commander Bury remembered:

> We had no time to separate the dead from the living, so thickly were they packed . . . the upper deck was a dreadful sight; truncated remains, sand bags, blackened corpses, represented the howitzer and Stokes gun crews.

The Marines disembarked and went to Deal. A hospital train waited for their wounded. Marines prefer to look after their own. Private Philip Hodgson of 12 Platoon:

> . . . eventually a train of old small carriages suitable for running through the Dover tunnels was shunted alongside for us and there at the door window of one of the compartments was Sir Roger, he called for us to gather round, which we did and then he told us that the raid had been successful, he had already seen aerial photos and the Zeebrugge canal was blocked and that he did not wish us to hear from other people, he had to tell us personally how sorry he was that we had lost so many of our pals and that we had been sent to Zeebrugge to attract the gunfire to let the blockships get in safely to block the canal.

Five hours later, *Trident* arrived with *Daffodil* in tow. If it had not been for her, nobody would have got ashore but that was cold comfort for her disappointed crew and passengers.

Iris made port at 14.45 hours. For a short thirty minutes she had been towed by *Termagant*; as usual on that day, the tow parted. *Iris* limped on escorted, aptly enough, by the destroyer HMS *Attentive*. Despite the fire under the bridge, the flooded compartments and an engine room sloshing with water, she returned, still ready for anything.

The ebullient crowd hushed.

The medical orderlies worked as fast as they dared, bringing ashore the wounded, the dying and the dead. *Iris* went to Belgium with thirty-five crew, 210 Marines, sixty-seven sailors, six RAMC medical orderlies, six RNAS men from Brock's experimental station and one cat and one dog on board. The two ship's mascots were unharmed. Seventy-seven men were dead. 105 were wounded. Sixteen were missing. High explosive leaves little behind over which the relatives can mourn. All told, the mad hour on the Mole claimed 206 dead, 412 wounded and missing and nineteen prisoners. In simpler terms, seven men became casualties every minute.

If the losses on board *Iris* are deducted, the casualties on *Vindictive* estimated at forty per cent and allowance made for the *North Star*'s victims, probably between 100 and 130 men fell dead or wounded on the Mole itself in thirty minutes. Still, it could be shrugged off. Keyes urbanely described the losses as 'light compared to those that the Army continually suffers in similar enterprises . . .'. It was as good an excuse as any.

At Ostend, nineteen were killed and thirty wounded.

By the time *Iris* docked, Keyes was clutching the telegram from Buckingham Palace which told him that he had been created a Knight Commander of the Order of The Bath. The honour arrived before it was clear if the operation had succeeded.

The haste with which communiqués were issued to the national and foreign press suggests that the Admiralty had already decided that one single man on the Mole, one single ship into the harbour, would count as a gallant British victory. Whether this was the influence of Wemyss, the desire of Lloyd George for a morale-boosting victory at any price or a conspiracy to humble the generals is not clear. It is certain that no time was wasted in trumpeting a glorious feat of arms.

On the morning of 24 April 1918 the *Mona's Herald* on the Isle of Man published a brief statement which they clearly received at a very early stage the previous day:

The Admiralty announced that naval forces, this morning, raided Ostend and Zeebrugge. Scanty information to hand so far is to the effect that the operation met with a considerable measure of success. Five obsolete cruisers, filled with concrete, were used as blockships and having been run aground, were blown up and abandoned by the crews in accordance with orders. A further report will be issued when our vessels, now returning, reach their bases. No report of casualties yet to hand.

The blocking of Ostend was a success. Zeebrugge was a triumph. No casualty reports dared mar the victory.

That same day, 24 April, hordes of reporters assembled at Dover. Keyes was, without question, the man of the hour. His action, small and easily comprehended, was romance personified. The journalists all had their own copy of the Press Bureau statement. This was not a proper communiqué but a ready-made article which could be put straight into the newspapers. Local journals in particular found such pieces extremely useful. They gave the impression that their very own reporters had been on the spot.

The Press Bureau release shows every sign of being compiled from Keyes' original submission to the Admiralty. The British public read how complete surprise was achieved. No mention was made of *Vindictive* running beyond her original location. Landing brows worked perfectly. Men swarmed ashore and 'nothing hindered the orderly and speedy landing by every gangway'. Germans fled when faced with British bayonets. 'The storming and demolition-parties upon the Mole met with no resistance from the Germans, other than the intense and unremitting fire.'

The statement is splendidly contradictory but in line with the persistent belief that the landing parties would rout a not very gallant enemy in hand to hand fighting.

The demolition parties carried out an orgy of destruction. Bombing parties worked their way up to the Mole extension but not a single German would stay and fight. One bombing party alone annihilated several machine-gun nests, the enemy fleeing before them.

Suitable heroics were much in evidence:

Lieutenant H. T. C. Walker had his arm carried away by a shell on the upper deck, and lay in the darkness while the storming parties trod him under. He was recognized and dragged aside by the Commander. He raised his remaining arm in greeting. 'Good luck,' he called, as the rest of the stormers hastened by; 'good luck!'

Nonetheless, twenty-four hours had wrought some changes. The failure at Ostend was carefully attributed to a freak change in the wind. That alone defeated *Brilliant* and *Sirius*.

The press took photographs. The reporters interviewed selected officers and men. Professor Sandford Terry, who edited *Keyes' Dispatches And Other Narratives of the Operations* in 1919, pointed out with the slightest touch of acerbity:

158

It is not surprising that the actors' accounts of a crowded and bewildering hour do little justice to its incidents and are blemished by exaggeration . . . it is necessary to discard as misleading those published in the public press on the morrow of the event.

These stories, which were eagerly devoured by an enthralled public, included the amazing tale of a seaman on *Daffodil* who destroyed the lamp on the lighthouse at the end of the Mole with a well-aimed grenade. This was doubtless before two Marines planted a Union Jack there. The two destroyers and two torpedo-boats anchored by the Mole became a veritable fleet, double-parked, whose crews begged for mercy as the modest tellers of tales stormed them. Many German sailors jumped overboard, drowning as a result, whilst British tars raced down into the hull, spun the seacocks and returned to the safety of the Mole before the vessels sank. It is depressing to discover from German records – which detail each vessel by its pennant number – that no destroyers were lost for several days either side of the action.

The canard about 'one thousand defenders on the Mole' was repeated and, the populace was assured, surprise had undoubtedly been complete for the craven Huns had fled, leaving the covers on their guns.

It was, therefore, no surprise that *The Times* should dismiss the German communiqué as 'a fine example in the camouflage of disagreeable news'. This became a great debate. The Germans simply did not rate Operation ZO as a major event. In comparison with the swirling imaginations of the Press Bureau and some of the participants, the announcement from Berlin of 24 April 1918 was positively restrained:

During the night of April 22–3 an enterprise of the British Naval Forces against our Flanders bases, conceived on a large scale and planned regardless of sacrifice, was frustrated. After a violent bombardment from the sea, small cruisers, escorted by numerous destroyers and motor-boats, under cover of a thick veil of artificial fog, pushed forward near Ostend and Zeebrugge to quite near the coast, with the intention of destroying the docks and harbour works there. According to the statements of prisoners, a detachment of four companies of the Royal Marines was to occupy the Mole at Zeebrugge by a coup de main, in order to destroy all the structures, guns and war material on it and the vessels lying in the harbour. Only about forty of them got on the Mole. These fell into our hands, some alive, some dead. On the narrow high wall of the Mole both parties fought with the utmost fierceness.

Of the English naval forces which participated in the attack, the small cruisers *Virginia* (*sic*), *Intrepid*, *Sirius* and two others of similar construction, whose names are unknown, were sunk close off the coast. Moreover, three torpedo-boat destroyers and a considerable number of torpedo-motor-boats were sunk by our artillery fire. Only a few men of the crews could be saved by us.

Beyond damage caused to the Mole by a torpedo hit, our harbour works and coast batteries are quite undamaged. Of our naval forces, only one torpedo-boat suffered damage of the lightest character. Our casualties are small.

The German casualties were unquestionably light. Schütte reported a loss of two dead and two wounded. German Admiralty figures admitted a total of ten killed and twenty-five wounded, totals which are confirmed by existing casualty returns as well as cemetery records.

Not surprisingly, Keyes did not refer to German losses or damage inflicted on the enemy in his official dispatch – a departure from a well-established tradition in the penning of such reports.

The sinking claims by the Germans are exaggerated but no more than the British equivalent in which the unfortunate ships moored by the quay were destroyed several times over.

The enemy version of events was dismissed out of hand. Keyes' venture had, at a stroke, removed the U-boat menace, bottling up ships and men in Bruges. This was not how it rated with some observers. Captain Evans, the man who had resigned his post as Keyes' Chief of Staff, was emphatic that the canal was not blocked. He could, he declared, 'easily take the *Broke* past the blockships at high tide'.

The commander of the German torpedo flotillas was equally insistent. *Kapitän* von Storch testified, in 1927, that 'the large torpedo boats at Zeebrugge could pass the block ships and . . . so could the submarines . . . the military object of the bottling up attempt was not attained'.

Neither was British Admiralty Intelligence convinced. Although they had intercepted a signal from Ostend Wireless Station advising all Flanders boats not to use Zeebrugge, this was swiftly countermanded. Four hours after the attack, another message was overheard. It referred to 'passing the two blockships' although this could have been a position report referring to *Sirius* and *Brilliant* on the sandbanks by Ostend.

Admiral von Schröder reported to Berlin that the channel was not closed. 'Submarine warfare,' he advised 'would be neither obstructed nor delayed by the English onslaught.'

Despite the public acclaim, some of the Royal Marines did not believe

A CLEAN SWEEP!

JACK: " And the next job ? "

Newspapers throughout Britain carried this triumphant cartoon. As well as the Zeebrugge Raid, the Royal Navy claimed the destruction of ten German minelayers in the Kattegat in April 1918. *(Courtesy Northumberland Gazette)*

that they had succeeded. Lieutenant Lamplough, who had led 9 Platoon with considerable gallantry, was of the opinion that:

> . . . as far as our objectives were concerned, i.e. capture of the battery at the seaward end of the Mole and the damage to material on the Mole, the operation was a failure.

Chater, the adjutant, agreed:

> We had failed to gain any of the objectives which had been laid down in our orders. We felt our part of the operation had been a complete failure. We had lost many good men with what seemed to us no result. We felt extremely despondent.

Within hours of the attack, German engineers put a temporary bridge across the destroyed viaduct. The silt on the western side of the block-ships was cleared after removing the wooden piles of two piers on the western bank of the channel. In three weeks, Zeebrugge resumed its role.

Fritzchens Zeichnungen
zum Brief des Onkels aus Zeebrügge.

Lieber Fritz!
Heute schnappe ich die Feder,

um Dir mitzuteilen, daß hier in letzter Zeit
die Wand mächtig gewackelt hat,

indem die Engländer in stark benebelte
Zustände versuchten,

uns nachts überraschender Weise
einzuwickeln.

Zuerst schossen ihre Monitore große Trichter
in den Strand,

dann kam ein Kasten vollgepfropft mit
Tommys längsseit der Mole

die sich sofort ausschifften

und uns aufrollen wollten,

wobei sie sich ganz eilig in den Finger
schnitten,

The magazine for the German Navy & Marines on the Flanders coast featured this pastiche of a children's comic strip. The invaders fled when faced with, amongst other weapons, white mice. *(Openbaare Biblithek, Brugge)*

bem wir ihnen prompt den Zaun ...ichen

und ihnen etwas vorbliesen, daß sie vor Angst ins Wasser sprangen.

Unsere Maschinenkanonen spuckten weiße Mäuse,

...andgranaten tanzten dazwischen

und die Batterie-Geschütze fraßen mehr Munition als je vorher,

worauf Tommy uns nicht mehr riechen konnte und mit langer Nase abhaute.

Seitdem regnet es dauernd Fliegerbomben,

daß man nicht ohne Schutz über die Mole gehen kann

(Zeichnungen von Rich. Fiedler.)

und sich nur im Stahlhelm wohl fühlt.

Worin ich bis zum nächsten Mal verbleibe

Dein treuer Onkel

Richard Policke.

Until then, as *Kapitän* Schülze confessed, 'the passage was impossible except at high tide'.

On 25 April, *UB-16* worked her way past the blockships. She was only about eighty-four feet long with a single officer and thirteen men. She was, though, reasonably typical of the boats in the Flanders Flotilla. While Keyes had been planning his attack, many of the destroyers had gone north to German ports. There lived the real menace to Britain's supplies – the big U-boats, displacing 1000 tons or more. They were the grey wolves who patrolled the Atlantic. Zeebrugge, for all its claim to be the 'Pirates' Lair', had become a harbour for the small coastal submarines.

As Captain Stephen Roskill, the official Naval Second World War historian, has shown, Zeebrugge's role was seriously overrated by the British in 1918. Only about one third of merchant shipping losses could be attributed to the Flanders Flotilla. That was dropping all the time. The new minefield and other Allied defences were making life very difficult for the Flanders boats. One captured officer informed his hosts that it was a point of honour to volunteer for the Flanders bases because their wastage was so high.

Almost as a reproach to Keyes, the Bruges complex sent more boats to sea. In January 1918, seven boats had been on patrol out of a total of thirty. During April, eight out of twenty-six were at sea. In May, eight out of twenty-five.

In June, nearly half of the Flanders boats were harassing British shipping or laying mines – eleven out of twenty-three. The number dropped to eight from a flotilla of twenty-four in July but numbers crept up again in August. Ten boats out of twenty-two were active.

As the land war turned against the Germans, the Flanders bases lost importance. September saw their strength down to eighteen boats. Seven were on patrol. On 1 October 1918, Ostend wireless station ordered the eight boats at sea to make for German ports. The five remaining in the Bruges area were to put to sea if serviceable. Failing that, they were to be scuttled.

These figures were not, of course, known at the time although Admiral Hall probably had some idea. Messages came from Belgian spies at Ostend and Zeebrugge with some regularity. As far as the War Cabinet, the press and the British public were concerned, however, the U-boat menace had been crushed in a single, thrilling act of dash and gallantry.

The Royal Navy certainly enjoyed the accolades. Public perception of their work had grown steadily more sour since the Battle of Jutland.

In that fight, the public had been annoyed that Jellicoe had failed to destroy the entire German Fleet in a single half-hour. This was not the stuff of Nelson. Although the Kaiser's ships had retreated and stayed in port ever since, the Grand Fleet also spent its days and nights at anchor at Scapa Flow. Britannia might rule the oceans but the population demanded proof, not rationing.

While most people had friends or relatives fighting and dying in Flanders mud or the dust of the Levant, sailors apparently enjoyed an extremely restful life in safe anchorages far, far away from shot and shell.

Zeebrugge changed all that. A *Punch* cartoon showed the ghost of Drake congratulating Keyes. 'Bravo, Sir! Tradition holds. My men singed a King's beard, and yours have singed a Kaiser's moustache.' Keyes and his men had swept the seas clear of German raiders.

One of the more useful ploys of the Ministry of Information was to produce a monthly war supplement for the myriad of local newspapers up and down the land. The header title was reproduced with reasonable accuracy so that readers could believe, if they so desired, that their own local journalists had compiled the pages. Official photographs showing cheery and dauntless Tommies and lion-hearted and jovial Frenchmen were a staple fixture.

On 4 May 1918, the authorized version of the Zeebrugge and Ostend operation reached every reader in the land. *Iris* and *Daffodil* were quietly dropped from the narrative. There could, of course, be little glossing of the casualty list. Too many people passed on rumours of tremendous slaughter. Even so, in contrast to the enemy's propaganda, the British story was true adventure.

From the destroyers, 'the German sailors came up in swarms to attack us, but they found themselves face to face with British bayonets. With a cheer our men charged them. . .' The eighty yards of bare concrete which had to be crossed was not emphasized.

Another account, stunning in its falsehood, revealed that:

> . . . the six big guns at the top of the Mole in the entrance to the harbour had been abandoned by their crews when they saw that we must land. We destroyed them and then pressed forward, throwing hand grenades and bayoneting the enemy. Some of our officers carried heavy sticks, like entrenching tools, for hand-to-hand fighting. The number of black eyes and bruises is sufficient evidence of the extent of this close fighting. We made our way along the Mole, a place about a mile long and eighty yards wide. Halfway down it were barbed wire entrenchments and machine guns which

165

swept the entire width. We captured that position. The work of demolishing the enemy guns having been completed, in came the blockships and then the landing party returned.

The inference is plain. *Vindictive* landed her men in exactly the intended spot. The assault teams did their work precisely as Keyes had envisaged when he presented his plans to the Admiralty two months earlier.

The narrative account is also very clear that 450 men, the full complement of *Vindictive*'s storming parties reached the Mole. It is true enough that the approved account confesses that only two landing brows operated but this, in turn, was presented as an extra proof of the gallantry of the men who went ashore.

As we have seen, though, the losses on board *Vindictive* on her approach to the target were horribly high. Survivors told the same tale time and time again – 'only 12 out of 40 got to their feet' or 'we were the only three out of a team of eight'. Even allowing for exaggeration, even assuming mistakes, such comments suggest a minimum casualty rate of forty per cent amongst the storming parties. It is very likely that little more than 200 Marines and seamen made it onto the Mole.

Every ship in the Grand Fleet, bar one, which provided volunteers was notified of casualties. The exception was HMAS *Australia*. All of her five seamen with the landing parties got on shore. None were even wounded although their comrades were as impressed as the Germans by their pugnacity. The five stokers escaped unhurt from the battered *Thetis*. Edgar, on board *Iris* was also unscathed. Strangely, the press account stresses a factor which no survivor mentions. The Ministry of Information claimed that the whole affair took place in torrential rain.

If Keyes was able to dismiss the casualties as light in comparison to those of the Army in similar circumstances, he made up for it with wholesale recommendations for decorations. He saw no reason to observe any ratio of awards to numbers engaged. It is no disparagement of the incredible gallantry shown by the men who were at Zeebrugge to state that many of them would have received nothing at all if Operation ZO had taken place near Albert, by Cambrai or the outskirts of Ypres. Valour was commonplace in the bloody fields of Flanders.

Keyes demanded eight Victoria Crosses; there were twenty-one admissions to the Distinguished Service Order. Twenty-nine Distinguished Service Crosses were cited. Sixteen Conspicuous Gallantry Medals and 143 Distinguished Service Medals went to Marines and ratings. Two hundred and eighty-three participants were mentioned in dispatches. Fifty-five officers were awarded special promotion for services in action. Two of the Victoria Crosses were posthumous awards. In 1918, there were only two distinctions which could be awarded after death. The Victoria Cross was one; the other was a Mention in Dispatches.

It says much for Keyes' empathy as a leader that he personally badgered the Sovereign to approve two immediate awards. A bar to the Distinguished Service Cross went to Sub Lieutenant Lloyd, whose blood had seeped with such terrible slowness into *Iphigenia*'s White Ensign. He was still clinging to life the next morning. So, too was Sub Lieutenant James Wright, the badly-wounded second in command of *ML 282* which had done so much heroic work in rescuing the crews of *Intrepid* and *Iphigenia*. He received an immediate DSC. Neither officer was expected to live. Lloyd died soon afterwards. Wright survived to wear his decoration.

Seven men may have become casualties for every minute spent on the Mole. Decorations came for every ten seconds of the action.

Keyes had to fight very hard to achieve his wishes. The honours and awards he demanded were well in excess of those that many Army divisions in Flanders achieved in four years of fighting. There were battalions which had lost as many men in as short a time but their purgatory was not salved with a crateful of medals. Keyes stuck to his guns. Decorations legitimized an action. They gave it the trappings of success. Nations rarely give bravery medals for failure.

Opposition was dismissed as jealousy. Some queried why the men who had run aground outside Ostend received coveted awards. Others claimed that a disproportionate number of Keyes' friends were nominated. Officers did rather better than the men.

Keyes had disparaged a supposed convention, allegedly in force at the Dardanelles, of limiting awards to one medal and one Mention in Dispatches for every 600 men engaged. He believed firmly that medals meant a great deal to 'so many good fellows'. He further considered that the Navy came off worse when it came to medals than did the Army. The awards for the Zeebrugge Raid were, perhaps, an attempt to redress the imbalance.

To achieve his prodigal ends, Keyes allegedly simply failed to attend an investiture to receive his own knighthood. After several non-appearances, the Sovereign enquired why the hero of Zeebrugge was always absent. Informed, the Royal word went forth. The full list of awards was duly approved.

There is, however, a curious element in the whole affair. Normally, a commanding officer, or the senior surviving officer, of a unit makes recommendations for awards. A platoon commander makes a recommendation to the company commander and so on, all the way up the line. In the case of the 4th Battalion, Keyes personally took a hand.

The Victoria Cross has a special provision. If it is impossible to single out a particular individual for the very highest decoration, the survivors of the action vote on who should receive the distinction. As the Marines' adjutant, Captain Chater later revealed, Keyes bypassed the whole system:

> On 25th April a telephone message was received from V A's Office, Dover (Vice Admiral Keyes) that the Bn was to elect <u>one</u> member to receive the VC on behalf of the Bn and that Admiral Keyes would come to Deal and address the Bn before it dispersed and announce the name elected to receive the VC. This was later confirmed by telephone from the RMO, who referred to the Royal Warrant for the VC then printed at the end of the Navy List, but we never referred to this because we had too many other things to do in the limited time. In any case they did not apply, because we were told to elect only <u>ONE</u> VC whereas the Royal Warrant provides for the Officers to elect one representative and the rank and file to elect one representative, which would have meant <u>TWO</u>.
>
> On the afternoon of 26th April the Bn paraded in the Drill Field behind the Officers' Mess. The Adjutant addressed the Bn and explained they were to elect one representative to receive the VC. Small slips of paper were issued and the Bn was ordered to break off, so the men could talk amongst each other, and given half-an-hour at the end of which each Officer, NCO and man must write the name of the one he thought most deserving on the paper and hand it in. The CO and the Adjutant withdrew to the office, leaving the Senior Company Commander (Captain Bamford) to supervise the collection and counting of the voting slips. An hour or so later Captain Bamford came into the office (which was the Mess Drawing room) looking very embarrassed and handed to the CO the paper, which is now in the Corps Museum at Eastney. It was straightway reported to the VA's Office at Dover, that Captain Bamford had been elected to receive the VC as representative of the Bn.
>
> At 0900 hrs on 27th April the Bn paraded on the North Parade. At 0915 hrs Vice Admiral Keyes arrived and was received on the edge of the parade by the CO and Adjutant. As he got out of his

car he said there are to be Two VCs, who is to receive the second one? The CO and Adjutant withdrew and after a brief talk told the Admiral that the second VC should go to Sergeant Finch. He then walked on to the parade ground, took the salute, addressed the Bn and announced that Captain Bamford and Sergeant Finch would be awarded the VC as representatives of the Bn.

From the above it will be seen that the election of the VCs was most irregular and certainly not in accordance with the Royal Warrant, nevertheless it proved to be completely acceptable to all ranks, and I was never aware of any feeling of dissatisfaction or grievance.

The citations, which form the permanent record, are both in some way incorrect. Captain Bamford was <u>not</u> selected by the Officers, but by all ranks of the Bn. The Officers, who discussed the matter before the voting, voted for Lieutenant T F V Cooke, who led the assault along the top of the sea wall and was twice wounded. He received the DSO and a brevet. Sergeant Finch was <u>not</u> firing a Lewis gun in the foretop. He was firing a two pounder pompom, and it was the noise and encouragement given by this gun firing over our heads (all other guns were below the level of the Mole and so could not fire) that made so many of the men (both RMA and RMLI) vote for Sgt Finch.

The Kaiser had no such petty concerns. As part of his round of inspections, he had spent two days with Admiral von Schröder on a round of visits to the three Marine divisions. On 23 April, he had gone sightseeing in Bruges, accompanied by a small retinue of some twenty officers. *Vizefeldwebel* Tellgmann photographed the occasion.

The scheduled visit to Zeebrugge took place on 24 April. The All-Highest had plenty to see. He noted the superficial damage to the torpedo-boats, gazed at the spot where a British missile had gouged into the concrete harbour wall, studied the blockships and offered a few affable words of praise – 'the pluck shown by all ranks' – to an unresponsive Captain Palmer, rigidly at attention as only a Marine can be. Palmer pointedly ignored the outstretched Imperial hand. Whatever Private Clist may have thought, Palmer knew his duty. Officers of His Majesty's Royal Marines did not shake hands with the enemy. The hovering official cameraman was denied a great propaganda picture.

Harry Wright – now Prisoner of War No 98008 – and his men reluctantly paraded, wooden-faced, for Wilhelm's perusal. As with Captain Palmer, so with the men. Nobody could ever claim they cooperated with

169

their captors. The Supreme War Lord gave instructions that they were to be well treated.

He presented medals, a duty of which he was particularly fond, to the heroes who had so thoroughly repulsed the enemy. *Oberleutnant* Rodewald received an Iron Cross First Class. *Kapitänleutnant* Schütte received a signal mark of Imperial favour. Wilhelm invested him with the Knight's Cross with Swords of the Royal Order of the House of Hohenzollern. The presumptuous English had been sent packing with their tails between their legs. The Kaiser was a happy man.

In Whitehall, the British Admiralty was also pleased. The British Government was elated. Lloyd George was ecstatic. The British public, saccharin supplies available once more, was greatly cheered to learn that the U-boat war was essentially over.

Keyes was not so content. He considered the job was only half done. Ostend had not been blocked. Ostend could still send submarines to sea. Bruges remained active. As soon as he learned that the Ostend operation was unsuccessful, he resolved to finish the task and mount a new attack. He would have to move quickly. That necessary combination of night-time and high tide ended on the 27 April.

But, Keyes was determined to do it.

CHAPTER FOURTEEN

Not everybody was convinced that another attempt to block Ostend was either wise or necessary. Admiralty Intelligence was one organization which counselled against it. They believed, on the evidence of their mysterious sources, that the Bruges-Ostend canal was closed to almost anything that floated with the possible exception of a flat-bottomed punt. There was, in their opinion, 'no shred of evidence that the Canal . . . was used for the passage of submarines'.

Keyes did not agree. Interestingly, confirmation of his view came several years later from our old friend *Kapitän* Schülze of the Intelligence Staff of the *Marinedivisionen* in Flanders:

> For about three weeks, until a passage had been dredged beside the block ships, the big destroyers had to go to sea by way of the Ostend canal. In order to make use of this canal its water level had to be raised by means of locks.

Either the Admiralty's Belgian reports lost much in the translation from Flemish or the wily *Kapitän* was indulging in a gentle bout of mischief-making.

Keyes was determined to press ahead even though there were some in the Navy who were less than enthusiastic about the whole Zeebrugge affair. Keyes was, to put it mildly, totally disconcerted during a visit to the Admiralty when he was assailed by two extremely senior admirals. Sir Arthur Wilson, who had won his Victoria Cross on land as a member of the Naval Brigade in the Sudan in 1884, and Sir William May were 'most unpleasant about the Zeebrugge show, the latter was quite rude and said it had no military value'.

Sir Arthur's strictures could, perhaps, be ignored. He had, after all, been totally opposed to the Royal Navy having submarines. They were, he observed, 'underhand, unfair and damned un-English'.

Keyes could console himself with the flood of congratulatory messages that had poured into his office. One of the first to send his personal commendation was King George V. Lloyd George was not far behind him. Admirals, old shipmates, the Archbishop of Canterbury, schoolchildren by the hundred, ordinary citizens all penned letters of lavish praise. It was the perfect answer to those who thought him 'weak and unreliable with . . . a mediocre standard of professional knowledge'.

Keyes' single-minded purpose in going back to Ostend was to stop the Germans from clearing the Bruges shipping via the Ostend-Bruges Canal. Admiralty Intelligence could bleat as much as they wished about the outlet being only seven feet deep. Keyes was not prepared to give them the benefit of the doubt.

With only four days in which to work, Keyes badgered anybody and everybody for help. The only vessel immediately available was the war-battered *Vindictive*. Keyes informed the Admiralty that he would use her to block Ostend.

If the planning for the Zeebrugge Raid was hurried, that for the second Ostend attack was perfunctory. Keyes, in fact, handed over the operational details to Commodore Lynes at Dunkirk who did what many officers have done when handed a squalling infant – adapt the existing plan.

Preparing *Vindictive* for her new role was, of necessity, rushed. She had to be filled with concrete, cement and rubble. Shredded metalwork on funnels and housings must be replaced. New wiring and navigation equipment was necessary. The dockyard staff worked round the clock to get everything completed within the four short days.

Shovelling 200 tons of cement and assorted debris into the after magazines and upper bunkers needed a lot of labour. That particular difficulty was solved by the helpful intervention of Major General Sir William Hickey who had recently arrived in Dover as the Garrison Commander. His soldiers spent time filling bags with cement. When that was done, they heaved them on board *Vindictive*.

Appointing a suitable crew took no time at all. Both Godsal from *Brilliant* and Hardy of *Sirius* together with all of their officers had immediately volunteered to make a second attempt. Commander Godsal was the senior. Keyes gave him command. Lieutenant Victor Crutchley and Petty Officer Joseph Reed, all from *Brilliant*'s crew joined him. Sub Lieutenant Angus MacLachlan was also in the group on the clearly specious grounds that his kit had been delivered, by accident, to the ship. He felt it his duty to stay and look after it.

Engineer Commander William Bury, who had sailed to Zeebrugge with *Vindictive*, asserted his right to stay with her. His four Engine Room

Artificers also volunteered to sail with the old cruiser on what could well be her, and their, final mission.

Keyes had decided that the crew would be no more than four officers and thirty-nine men. It was therefore by chance, and not design, that a specialist navigator joined the team. Lieutenant Sir John Alleyne was given the task of proving *Vindictive*'s newly installed compass. He was appalled, as any navigator would have been, to discover that the gyro compass was out of date and that the ship carried no reliable sounding apparatus. He promptly volunteered to take the ship to Ostend. Keyes agreed.

Alleyne had spent two years with the Dover Patrol as navigating officer of the *Lord Clive*. He served his time amongst the shoals and currents of the Belgian coast. He was also well alert to the possibility of buoys mysteriously moving to new locations. It is a legitimate criticism that nobody considered specialist navigators necessary on the first venture. That neglect cost dearly. The fault was firmly that of Keyes.

Vindictive's complement – and the extra men to serve as the steaming crew – were quickly found amongst the sailors of Chatham and the Dover Patrol.

Like Keyes, Commodore Lynes was anxious for the second attack to take place as soon as possible. He believed, with justification, that an immediate try would probably catch the enemy off-guard. He had stuck closely to the original plan but had made significant changes. It was clearly more than an idle possibility that the Germans would be prepared for another effort.

Lynes paid, in his own words:

... particular attention ... to perfecting the navigational arrangements; numerous small, but important, improvements were introduced into the smoke gear, and the alternatives for guiding the blockships into the entrance were made so numerous as to reduce chance of failure, in that respect, to the smallest possible dimensions.

Vindictive was ready in time. The weather broke. On that afternoon of 27 April, strong northerly winds allied with rough seas made it very plain that the enterprise would have to be postponed for two weeks when tide and darkness would be right once more.

Commodore Lynes sent his plan to the Admiral for approval. It was entitled 'VO' which a casual observer might think stood for 'Vindictive Ostend'. Keyes approved it before the Board of Admiralty suggested that another blockship be added to the force. HMS *Sappho*, serving as a depot ship at Southampton was available. The delay caused by the weather gave time for her to join the team.

Keyes instantly agreed to double his strike force. Lynes incorporated the extra vessel into his orders. The plan's title was amended. It became, surprisingly, Operation VS.

Lieutenant Commander Hardy and his eager volunteers took over *Sappho*. She arrived at His Majesty's dockyard, Chatham and the yard workers swung into action. The first possible date for the attack was 9 May 1918. *Sappho* sailed triumphantly into Dover harbour with hours to spare.

Keyes had demanded a stream of reconnaissance photographs from the willing machines of the newly-formed Royal Air Force. He believed that they showed clearly that the Imperial German Navy's torpedo craft and submarines were firmly bottled up in Bruges. This was not totally incorrect.

However, he failed to notice that the enemy's engineers were busy dismantling the wooden piers in the Zeebrugge canal entrance close to where the blockships lay. Once removed, these gave sufficient space for the torpedo-boats and submarines to go to and fro, tide permitting. Interpreting aerial photographs is a specialist art. It appears that the 1918 Dover Patrol had no expert in the subject.

Zeebrugge would soon be back in action although Keyes did not, seemingly, realize it. Ostend was untouched. Ostend would be dealt with.

Admiral von Schröder read Keyes' mind. Confident in the abilities of his gunners, he nonetheless poured in more troops to boost the beach and harbour defences. The men in the giant *Tirpitz*, *Preussen* and *Deutschland* batteries were anxious to test their skills on more stupid Tommies.

More to Keyes' taste was the news that nine German destroyers from the High Seas Fleet were on their way south. The *Flotille Flandern* which had been denuded of destroyers in the earlier part of the year, asked for their temporary return.

He decided, very properly, to send a force to shield the blockships from possible interference by these new players on the field. The monstrously large silk standard was again raised in *Warwick*. Accompanied by *Whirlwind*, *Velox* and *Trident*, the Vice Admiral Dover Patrol set off in high hopes of meeting the enemy.

The two blockships left for Dunkirk. Dusk was in the air when Lynes received word that the latest air reconnaissance of Ostend showed a disconcerting feature. All the buoys in the vicinity had vanished. Lynes immediately ordered a additional flight. Captain Ronald Graham of 213 Squadron took the duty. He duly returned, landing by the light of goose-neck flares, to confirm the news. He got back in time for Lynes to arrange to lay a special light buoy.

The weather was perfect for the operation. A gentle wind, ideal for the deployment of the smokescreen, blew from the north-west. The sea was calm, perfect for the coastal motor boats and launches. The clear skies were absolutely right for the diversionary bombing. The monitors and the siege guns in Flanders would also enjoy the placid weather.

Lynes' plan did not envisage heavy shelling of Ostend before the arrival of the blockships. The enemy were accustomed to an 'evening hate', be it by shells or bombs. The full weight of artillery and bombing would be held back until the enemy reacted to the arrival of the block-ships.

At 22.45 hours, *Vindictive* and *Sappho* reached Dunkirk. The steaming crews were put ashore. There would be no overloading of rescue launches because of stowaways on Operation VS. Peculiarly, Commodore the Honourable Algernon Boyle, Keyes' Chief of Staff, had decided that Lieutenant Alleyne should also disembark at Dunkirk. The wisdom of removing a navigating officer when there was not a single marker buoy to be found in the area of Ostend harbour is doubtful. Alleyne prudently vanished until *Vindictive* was again under way.

At 22.30 hours, the destroyers *Moorsom*, *Myngs* and *Nugent*, the launches and the monitors *Prince Eugene*, *Sir John Moore* and the small *M 27* left to take up their station. At 23.30 hours, Commodore Lynes in the destroyer *Faulknor* followed the two blockships and the escort of coastal motor boats out of the harbour.

Glory is a fickle mistress. She often sidesteps those who wish to embrace her the most warmly. At 23.58 hours, *Sappho* suddenly lost way, her speed sagging to a miserable six knots. A manhole joint in the side of her boiler had blown. For Lieutenant Henry Hardy, Sub Lieutenant Edward Berthon, Sub Lieutenant Alfred Knight, Engineer Lieutenant William McLaren and the seamen volunteers from Chatham, Operation VS was over.

Lynes could have called off the operation at that point. The strike force had been halved. He decided, though, to carry on. The original plan had envisaged one blockship. He had one blockship. The Commodore signalled Commander Godsal that he had every confi-dence in him. *Vindictive* steamed on.

Faulknor raced ahead of *Vindictive*. Four and a half miles north-west

175

of the entrance to Ostend Harbour, she placed an Aga buoy. The small craft moved towards the harbour five minutes later. *Vindictive* was seven minutes away from making her final turn in towards Ostend. Lynes left to join the other destroyers. Everything now depended on Godsal.

Vindictive reached the Aga buoy at 01.37 hours. She turned onto the final leg. Eight minutes more to reach the correct position of the Stroombank buoy now temporarily marked by a coastal motor boat.

By 01.43 hours, German searchlights were roaming edgily across the sky. Lynes ordered his planned heavy bombardment. The monitors coughed into action moments before seven Handley Page bombers from 214 Squadron dropped their first bombs. During the next three-quarters of an hour, six 550-pound, fifty-three 112-pound and twenty-six 25-pound bombs fell in the general area of the coastal batteries in an attempt to spread dismay and confusion.

On schedule, *Vindictive* passed the Stroombank motor boat on her port side. Speed came down to twelve knots. The smokescreen worked perfectly, forming a lane between the eastern and western sections. Two miles and fifteen minutes to the harbour entrance. Sir John Alleyne, lacking a more sophisticated instrument timed the run with his own watch.

Three minutes later, *Vindictive* hit thick fog. Mixed with the smoke, it formed a choking, opaque mixture. The minutes ticked by. Godsal reduced speed. Thirteen minutes after passing the Stroombank, he altered course to the west and cautiously moved, as he hoped, parallel to the shore.

The small craft, in the interim, were suffering problems of their own. Lieutenant Arthur Welman, the Flotilla Commander, was in *CMB 22*. His job was to fire red rockets when he located *Brilliant* and *Sirius*. These would be an extra navigational check. They might even distract the enemy. At about 01.50 hours, Welman heard the sound of waves to starboard. As *CMB 22* turned out of danger, the fog lifted enough to show the superstructure of a ship.

It was neither of the two blockships. A German torpedo-boat had been lying in wait. Its searchlight pointed a cold accusing finger of light at the motor boat. A pom-pom cracked with vicious intent.

The British craft replied with four angry Lewis guns. The bullets raced down the searchlight beam which promptly went out. With 200 yards between them, the torpedo-boat turned and made for Ostend.

Fiercely conscious of time slipping by, Welman called off the search for the two wrecks. He ordered *CMB 22* eastward, dropping smoke-floats on the way. Without warning, ahead of them, heavy firing began.

It is likely that the torpedo-boat had raised the alarm to defenders who had been warned to expect another attack similar to that of 23 April.

Lieutenant Archibald Dayrell-Reed and Lieutenant Albert Poland commanded *CMB 24A* and *CMB 30B* respectively. As zero hour – 02.00 hours – approached, they were close to the harbour entrance. The fog had passed them by but the enemy was well alert. A machine gun stammered into frantic action. Dayrell-Reed went left. He saw the outline of the eastern pier on his right. *CMB 24A* took a curving route south at full speed chased by machine-gun bullets. Dayrell-Reed turned directly towards the harbour and into the enemy fire, now augmented by pom-pom shells. With two hundred yards to go, the boat was pointing directly at the western pier. Dayrell-Reed fired his torpedo at the machine guns nestling on the pier and turned away. The explosion stopped, at least temporarily, the machine-gunners. The pom-pom continued. *CMB 24A* made smoke to mask the eastern batteries before turning to clear the entrance in advance of *Vindictive*'s arrival.

Lieutenant Poland played follow-my-leader, a hazardous game when the enemy fire was intense. He got within 700 yards of the pier before firing. Another explosion but the German guns continued to make life extremely unpleasant.

Three coastal motor boats had remained with *Vindictive*. One, *CMB 23*, was designated the 'last resort'. She plodded behind the block-ship with infinite patience. The other two escorts, *CMB 25BD* and *CMB 26B* had the task of dropping calcium light buoys and firing flares to light the way into Ostend.

Despite the fog, they pushed ahead leaving *Vindictive* to grope her way towards the harbour. Lieutenant Cuthbert Bowlby in *CMB 26B* sighted the eastern pierhead directly ahead of him. He promptly fired a torpedo, increasing speed as he did so.

The water was shallow. The range was short.

Bowlby ran over his own torpedo at the moment it exploded, presumably by hitting the seabed or some submerged object. The seams of *CMB 26B* opened wide. The sea hurried in. The engines stopped. The electrics failed. Bowlby, splashing in cold ankle-deep water, managed to plug the leak. The chief motor mechanic, E. W. McCracken, persuaded the port engine to work, albeit reluctantly on just six of its cylinders. Bowlby decided it was time to go home. *CMB 26B* managed three miles before the complaining port engine stopped completely. Out of the immediate danger zone, they were eventually rescued by HMS *Melpomene*.

Lieutenant Russell McBean in *CMB 25BD* had let his partner go ahead. He decided he would be better placed in closer contact with *Vindictive*, a sensible decision which, in fact, failed to work as he had hoped. At 02.00 hours, McBean found himself in the middle of a collection of large waterspouts as enemy shells landed across the canal mouth in a hostile barrage.

The Lieutenant, ahead of *Vindictive* and on her right, weaved hastily out of danger. When he looked again, *Vindictive* was still on his left but the canal entrance had disappeared.

McBean went cautiously ahead and then to his right. *Vindictive* vanished into the murk. The motor boat attracted the attention of some aggressive gunners. McBean circled, fast and noisily. He suddenly ran into clear air. The Ostend piers were visible – and *Vindictive* was steaming well to the east of them.

CMB 25BD chased after her. Green flares shot upwards as McBean tried to gain Godsal's attention. The blockship finally started to turn.

McBean charged towards the eastern pier into a hail of enemy fire. His own Lewis guns fired frantically as he loosed his port torpedo. Once it was running, McBean swung hard about and went for the western pier. More heavy fire stitched across the water towards *CMB 25BD*. With 250 yards to go, McBean fired the starboard torpedo. Bullets smashed into the boat. The hull shuddered under the impact. McBean was badly wounded. His chief motor mechanic died instantly. Sub Lieutenant George Shaw, the second-in-command, left his Lewis guns and guided the boat out of the harbour. She left as *Vindictive* at last approached the entrance.

Godsal had gingerly turned about at 01.58 hours and cautiously steamed back to the west.

At 02.00 hours, when *Vindictive* should have been entering the harbour, the eight destroyers – *Faulknor, Moorsom, Nugent* and *Myngs* to the east and *Broke, Matchless, Mansfield* and *Melpomene* patrolling to the west of Ostend – fired star shell to light the way as *Vindictive* groped for the shore. Nobody on board the cruiser saw either the star shell or the expensive flares which 214 Squadron was dropping with enthusiasm.

Either the flares or the star shells, or possibly both, brought the already alert shore batteries into action. Shellfire crashed out towards the sea. Godsal still held his westerly course. Sure that he had passed the harbour, he turned again towards the east. *Vindictive* was now some twenty minutes behind schedule. Nobody saw McBean's green flares curving into the fog-shrouded night.

Godsal called upon the 'last resort', the single coastal motor boat which had stayed close to him throughout. A signal lamp flashed.

178

CMB 23 under the command of Lieutenant the Honourable Cecil Spencer laid and lit the fuse of a million candle-power flare before racing away into the night.

Thirty seconds passed. The world became daylight as the flare ignited. Godsal saw the harbour mouth hard on his left. Following orders, Lieutenant Crutchley passed the order 'preparatory abandon ship' to the engine room. *Vindictive* heeled over to make for the entrance. Her captain moved to the conning-tower to steer her in. Unfortunately, although Godsal could see the harbour, the German gunners could, in their turn, see *Vindictive*. Godsal ordered smoke. It was too late. As their comrades at Zeebrugge had done just over two weeks earlier, the Kaiser's sailors and marines put down a savage and unrelenting fire. *Vindictive* staggered in the water before settling down to her new course. She had 200 yards to go.

Ratings below decks who could be spared came topside in response to Crutchley's order. They took what cover they could, sprawling behind torpedo-nets, bundled up to provide some protection. Machine-gun fire raked the ship, splintering the wooden decks and ricocheting off metal fittings. The aged Gatling guns which had been acquired on the occupation of Belgium added their own distinctive, ear-shattering sound to the din.

The heavy gunners pounded away. A shell smashed into the after-control position severing communication with the conning-tower. *Vindictive* was too close to the western pier. To ram the bank on the same side, she had to move out into the channel before turning hard left. Commander Godsal stepped outside. He ordered a right turn to take the ship into the main channel. The bows swung. Seconds later, a shell exploded where Godsal was standing.

Worse followed. Alleyne, who had known Godsal's plan, fell with a critical stomach wound. He was unconscious. Only Crutchley was still on his feet, half-stunned. His Captain's last order had been a turn to starboard so he continued the good work. The eastern bank loomed ahead. Crutchley ordered *Vindictive*'s port engine full astern to try and bring the ship's bows round to increase the angle of approach.

The old cruiser had been prepared in a hurry. Her port screw was badly damaged at Zeebrugge when she pulled away from the Mole. It had not been repaired. Crutchley's crisp command had no effect. *Vindictive* pitched against the eastern pier at an angle of approximately twenty-five degrees. Crutchley ordered the crew to abandon ship. He and Bury blew the charges. The ship settled well clear of the central channel. Neither the canal nor the harbour were blocked.

Crutchley was a giant of a man. He could bellow very, very loudly when the need arose. His orders, audible even above the thunder of the German gunfire, quickly brought results. Alleyne was lowered gently into the skiff by Petty Officer Reed. Two wounded ratings joined him.

Acutely aware that he was the senior survivor, Crutchley searched the ship. His torch beam flashed into the control room. There was no sign that Commander Godsal had ever existed. The same was true of Angus MacLachlan and his mythical kit. The after-control position was a mass of twisted metal in the beam of Crutchley's flashlight. Crutchley reached the aft smoke canisters. They were unlit. As a final gesture, he set them going.

Crutchley walked back to the bridge. Beside *Vindictive*, *ML 254* waited. Crutchley lowered himself into the battered launch. A 15-centimetre shell had hit the fragile boat earlier. The First Lieutenant and one deckhand had died instantly. The coxswain was wounded and the Captain, Lieutenant Geoffrey Drummond, did his best to ignore a smashed thigh.

Crutchley confirmed that no living soul remained on *Vindictive*. Engines full astern, *ML 254* backed out towards the sea. Pom-pom and machine-gun rounds scythed across the water into the launch. Drummond was wounded once, then twice. *ML 254* reached the harbour entrance. Her bows turned towards the open sea. As she moved forward to safety, water rushed in through her badly damaged bows. Her head went down as the forward compartment flooded. Drummond, bleeding heavily, collapsed.

Crutchley took over. With some surviving ratings, he set to work, baling and pumping out the flooded compartment. Another sailor, handed the torch, was instructed to flash S O S to seaward. The launch, badly mauled, crawled through the fog. It was 02.55 hours.

The German gunners still had targets to destroy. Hamilton Benn and his opposite number in charge of the coastal motor boats, Lieutenant Welman, had patrolled as close inshore as they dared, laying smoke and more smoke for as long as they could.

Benn ordered two more of his tiny fleet, *ML 283* and *ML 128* into the canal to support *ML 276* and *ML 254* in their rescue work.

ML 276 was in the care of Lieutenant Roland Bourke. On the 23 April attack on Ostend, his vessel had rescued most of *Brilliant*'s survivors. As *ML 254* took *Vindictive*'s crew on board, Bourke raced up and down drawing the enemy's fire. Once he was sure that the leaking launch was through the canal entrance, he broke off the engagement to nose up to *Vindictive* to check that nobody had accidentally been left behind.

No replies came to his yells. *ML 283* and *ML 128* were busily giving covering fire, slowly withdrawing as they did so. Bourke decided, finally, to retreat, taking his craft in a curving race across the water towards the sea.

Somehow, above the whine of bullets, above the sound of ill-tempered shells, above the noise of his engines, he heard a shout. He turned back, braving a new hail of fire. His boat was now the only target. The gunners concentrated on this presumptuous intruder.

Bourke found nothing. As a last resort he went back to *Vindictive*. Dark in the shadows of the starboard bow, the remains of the skiff floated uneasily. Sir John Alleyne and two wounded ratings clung desperately to the waterlogged wreckage. Bourke took them on board, swung *ML 276* about and went furiously for the open sea. A 15-centimetre shell sliced into her but she kept going until she reached the welcoming fog. In all, she had been hit fifty-five times. Two of her crew died. One wounded man survived. At 04.30 hours, *Prince Eugene* came to her rescue and took her in tow.

ML 128 had two casualties, one dead, one wounded. *ML 283* was luckier but, like her sister craft, was severely scarred. Both launches made it home to Dunkirk.

ML 276, awash and stationary in the water, had not quite given up the fight. The rating flashed the torch. S O S – S O S – S O S. Crutchley bailed furiously but the launch could sail no more. Everyone wore their life jackets. It was simply a question of how many minutes were left before the boat sank under them. It was 03.05 hours. Survival might last as long as another fifty minutes.

On board *Warwick*, Keyes decided to patrol as close to the shore as he could. The German ships had not materialized. Clamped in the fog, the British destroyer moved slowly towards Ostend. The bombardment was heard clearly as *Warwick* nosed cautiously through the swell. The fog thinned. Sharp eyes saw a pin-prick of dots and dashes. S O S – S O S – S O S.

At 03.10 hours, *Warwick* came cautiously alongside the broken-down *ML 276*. It took thirty minutes to transfer the wounded. Dawn was getting closer and *Warwick* was well within range of the shore batteries. When the light grew strong enough, the enemy guns would make short work of a stationery target.

Warwick moved away at 03.45 hours. An explosive charge blew out the bottom of the gallant launch. Keyes took the deep water Ostend channel as the tide was falling. This channel took them through the net defence into a minefield. At 04.00 hours, *Warwick* broke her back seventy feet from the stern. She took a thirty degree list to port. The survivors from *ML 276* picked up their life jackets and awaited events.

Swift action kept the ship from immediate disaster but she was not yet saved. *Velox*, *Whirlwind* and *Trident* came to the rescue. *Whirlwind* took the damaged destroyer in tow. *Velox* was lashed alongside. *Trident* held station to the east. If nine German destroyers did appear, they could make a killing.

The wounded transferred to *Velox*. Should action stations sound, *Whirlwind* would slip the tow. *Velox* would part company with the flag-ship. All three undamaged ships would turn into the attack. But the Imperial German Navy did not appear.

Operation VS had ended. It had not been a success. The scheme had called for *Vindictive* to enter the harbour at 02.00 hours. Godsal's intentions were perfectly sound. He proposed to ram his command hard into the western bank by her bows. An incoming tide would then swing her stern across the channel.

The timing was completely wrong. High water in Ostend that night was at midnight. To block the channel, *Vindictive* should have been in position by 23.00 hours. As it was, she entered the harbour towards the end of the fast ebb-tide. Between 01.00 and 02.00 hours, the water fell three feet in the harbour. What made it worse was that *Vindictive* was well behind schedule. In real terms, a successful blocking was already impossible.

The planning of the whole affair is subject to query. Tide tables are usually quite easy to come by even in the Royal Navy. Perhaps the explanation is that the timings were ideal for the tide four days after 23 April but that nobody subsequently checked them. Lynes, who had extensive experience of the area, somehow overlooked such an elementary matter.

The valour, the enthusiasm, the courage of the men who sailed *Vindictive* to her final anchorage was in vain.

CHAPTER FIFTEEN

Congratulations poured in once more. Far from being a failure, the second Ostend affair was, by courtesy of the Press Bureau, another triumph for the Admiral 'with the Nelson touch'. The Germans had been humiliated on their own ground. Keyes made no obvious demur at the stream of telegrams that arrived at Dover nor at the glowing press coverage. Lloyd George and the War Cabinet set the tone:

> . . . the successful efforts you have made to deal with the submarine menace at the source. The blocking of Ostend last night puts the finishing touch to the gallant achievement at Zeebrugge.

Keyes promptly produced another impressive batch of recommendations for gallantry awards, proof positive that the raid had been a success. Three Victoria Crosses, a Companion of the Order of the Bath, a Companion of the Order of St Michael and St George, seven Distinguished Service Orders, three Bars to the Order, eleven Distinguished Service Crosses, two bars to the DSC, two Conspicuous Gallantry Medals, fifty-nine Distinguished Service Medals, three bars to the DSM and fifty-seven Mentions in Dispatches.

The public were enthralled.

The first German communiqué issued on the 10 May, was treated with disdain:

> At three o'clock on the morning of May 10, British naval forces, after a violent bombardment, again made a blockading attack on Ostend. Several enemy ships which, under the protection of artificial fog, tried to make their way into the harbour were driven off by the excellently directed fire of our coastal batteries. An old cruiser, entirely battered to pieces, lies aground before the harbour outside the navigation channel. The entrance into the harbour is quite free. Only dead were found aboard the stranded vessel. Two survivors had sprung overboard and were captured. According to

information so far received, at least two enemy motor-boats were shot away and one monitor badly damaged. The blockading attempt has, therefore, been completely foiled. Once again, the enemy sacrificed human lives and vessels in vain.

Captain Grant, Keyes' Intelligence officer, asked for a transfer. Keyes, he later stated, 'believed his own heroics'. Good men had died without need. Even allowing for Grant's antipathy towards his old Britannia classmate, the suggestion that the second Ostend attempt had achieved its purpose was too much to stomach.

Grant had been intensely irritated by his Mention in Dispatches. Keyes blandly stated that Grant had trailed round a number of ports, searching for suitable ferry boats. To aid him, he had a civilian advisor. Grant, a Seaman Branch officer of considerable experience, considered that the paragraph cast doubt upon his professional ability. He saw the statement, according to his story, before the Dispatch was published. He asked Keyes to remove it, stating that he had no wish to be associated with the whole business.

The Dispatch appeared without amendment.

The German Admiralty issued a second communiqué:

The second attempt of the English to get at the Flanders U-boat bases, which are getting more and more troublesome to them every day, found the German Marine Corps equally prepared as on the first attempt. It could be forseen that the English Admiralty would not be satisfied with one attempt. The reason why this time only an attack against Ostend took place cannot be judged. It is true that simultaneously with the attack against Ostend a strong artificial mist was developed by the English before Zeebrugge, but apparently this was done only in order to effect a diversion.

In the morning of May 10 at 2.45 the enemy opened fire from the seas and from the land against the German batteries at Ostend. A few minutes later a strong artificial mist was produced. When at two minutes after three two cruisers were sighted in the mist to the east of Ostend, [*this was a double sighting of* Vindictive *as she went back and forth trying to find the harbour*] the German heavy batteries immediately opened a well-directed target fire, an obstructive fire having been directed previously against the area before the entrance. One of the cruisers turned aside towards the west, the other towards the north. The latter could then be seen repeatedly in the mist and was again bombarded every time. At 3.43 a.m. she loomed up again before the entrance, and, taken under the

184

heaviest fire on all sides, sank outside the channel. In the meantime, the German batteries bombarded separate objects which could be observed at sea. A monitor, which was lying still and did not fire, and which clearly had been put out of action, was spotted at 4.13 a.m. but was immediately afterwards completely enveloped in a mist by the enemy. According to papers which have been found, the stranded cruiser is the *Vindictive*.

The German losses, as on the occasion of the first operation, are delightfully small.

For the Germans, who had anticipated a further attack, the casualty list was indeed minute. The cost of bloodying the English nose once more was three men dead and eight wounded, half of them severely so.

The 'monitor' was almost certainly *Warwick*. The German account, allowing for the different times between Britain and the occupied territory, hardly contradicts the British version. It need not be emphasized that the German statement that *Vindictive* was sunk outside the channel was a direct riposte to British claims that Ostend was completely blocked.

Keyes, of course, knew that the second attempt had failed. Wemyss agreed that another attack should take place. Keyes promptly began to plan a third try. *Sappho* and *Swiftsure* were earmarked as blockships. There was even some talk of repeating the Zeebrugge Raid as it was becoming clear that the port was back in use.

Some proof of this was provided on 25 May when an explosion sank the German destroyer *V 74* in Zeebrugge Harbour during the transfer of mines. They were for the submarines. Eleven men were killed and she was not raised for some weeks. It was painfully obvious that the port was functioning almost normally.

The unfortunate *V 74* was towed along the supposedly blocked canal to Bruges harbour for repair. German records make it clear that the Raid was a failure. During the last weeks of the German occupation, eleven destroyers, thirteen torpedo-boats and seven U-boats made their way back to Germany from Bruges.

With the Allied forces approaching ever closer, the Germans carried out Keyes' task for him and blocked the canal. In Bruges itself, any vessels still under repair were sunk. Destroyers *G 41* and *V 74* together with the submarine *UB 59* were the victims. Joining them were captured Allied vessels, *Princesse Josephine*, *Midland*, *Lestris*, *Niobe* and *Zuiderzee* with a host of smaller craft. The floating docks were destroyed.

Zeebrugge was also rendered useless. The Imperial German Navy scuttled *Brussels* and *Diomedes* with a number of barges and two submarines.

The lock-gates. a continuing target of RAF air attacks even after the supposed closure of the canal, were made useless by sinking the *Rio Pardo, Zaanstroom* and *Gelderland* between them.

It took two years to clear the wreckage and reopen the canal, a timescale which was triumphantly hailed by the British as proof that the Raid had been a tremendous success.

British Naval Intelligence, unhappy with the second Ostend attempt, made a new report. Admiral Hall and his department were positive that further sacrifices of life and loss of equipment could not be justified. It was also manifestly plain that the enemy expected more assaults. Failure was far more likely than success. Wemyss changed his mind. This time he would not be moved. He instructed Keyes that no more attempts were to be made.

Keyes, who apparently believed that caution was akin to cowardice and prudence the refuge of the craven-hearted, had no choice but to accept the direct order. He was slightly consoled by the glowing terms in which Lloyd George referred to the exploit. As *The Times* reported the Prime Minister's words:

> These are thrilling deeds that give new heart to a people, not merely for the hour, but when they come to be read by our children and our children's children, for ages to come. They enrich our history, they enrich the character of our people, they fertilize the manhood of the land.

More practical comfort came with the award of £10,000 voted to him by Parliament at the personal instigation of the Prime Minister.

Suggestions that the Zeebrugge and Ostend raids failed were downplayed. Even the British Official History, published after the war, maintained that the action had been a success. Many naval officers and others disagreed. In truth, the Zeebrugge and Ostend adventures are probably the only naval operations in British history whose results were falsified or intentionally ignored.

It is a matter of some debate as to whether the diversion did, in fact, succeed. The British version claims that the Mole end gunners were distracted long enough to allow the blockships to enter harbour. German accounts vehemently disagree. They stress with some force that *Thetis* was undoubtedly sunk. It was the Mole batteries which did the most harm. It does, of course, move the whole diversion in to the realms of futility if the Mole gunners were not dissuaded from their task.

Iphigenia and *Intrepid* sailed through with little damage but their captains, following orders faithfully, failed to exploit their luck.

It has been claimed that, even though the attacks did not achieve their primary purpose, their effect on morale was incalculable. British civilians were enormously cheered by the action; Germans were unduly depressed. Allied soldiers fought harder because of the Navy's example; the enemy's lost heart for the fight.

There is little evidence that Keyes was concerned about the effect on civilian morale. He did believe that the actions would enhance the Royal Navy in the eyes of the British Army. The Navy felt inferior to the Army for no other reason than that it was the men in khaki who were doing the fighting. Inter-service jealousy was a powerful motive.

It is difficult to find convincing proof that the British Army on the Western Front gained an immense boost to its spirits as a result of Zeebrugge. Most of them never heard about it until days or weeks later. The fighting soldiers were more concerned with the hordes of grey-clad enemy intent on killing them than the Navy's efforts – 'matelots mucking about' as one old soldier described it many years later.

German troops were equally unconcerned about the whole affair. The Tommies had tried something on and got a bloody nose for their pains. Breaking the Allied lines was far more important. German Army morale faltered when, amongst other things, they overran warehouses full of white bread, meat, coffee, tea, wine and spirits, leather boots, warm uniforms made of proper cloth and crates of medical supplies. If an allegedly beaten enemy had such largesse, it said little for the equipment of compressed cardboard, the paper bandages and miserable rations of the German soldier. Worse, every man knew that the Americans were coming.

The air services, too, had their own concerns.

'*Der Rittmeister ist gefallen.*' The stark announcement was a dagger at the heart of the propaganda effort. The German public and the *Luftstreitkrafte* took the death of Manfred von Richthofen badly. If the greatest of all could be plucked from the sky, death was inevitable for lesser mortals. On the Allied side of the lines, a distinct chirpiness invaded the Royal Air Force. With the bloody Baron gone, even the most newly joined pilot believed that there was a chance of survival.

It is undoubtedly true that British civilian morale was boosted enormously by the Zeebrugge Raid. Although there was no real defeatism in Britain, a distinct war-weariness pervaded everyday life. Good news, especially as the Western Front remained full of horrors, shone like a beacon of hope. Encouraged by Government, every paper

187

in the country ran morale-boosting articles and leader columns which were not always an example of shining truthfulness.

> The Canal is blocked by sunken ships full of concrete, the *Northumberland Gazette* proclaimed, and the lock gates are injured, if not destroyed. It will take the Germans a long time to clean up the mess. . . .
>
> . . . The Navy has sent a message of good cheer to the Army, and it has also reminded us slow-witted, home-staying folk that our 'sure shield' is not even dinted, for all the wild blows of the enemy. . . .

The same was claimed for the population of occupied Europe. Unfortunately, a glance through an admittedly small number of secret Belgian diaries of the time, reveals little of this apparent morale-booster. There is a growing concern about yet another cut in the bread ration. A lawyer noted that there had been a loud explosion in the direction of Zeebrugge. A third diarist wearily opined that the Germans would take Mount Kemmel and win the war.

The King and Queen of the Belgians were certainly impressed by the Zeebrugge and Ostend operations. Keyes collected another Order to add to his growing collection. It cannot be denied that any action, any event, which gave hope that one day the field-grey soldiers would retreat back to their homeland was much desired by those who were forced to tolerate their presence. The civilians in the occupied areas, however, knew only too well that their ordeal would end only when the German Army on the Western Front was beaten. They would not have too long to wait. Sir Douglas Haig would soon begin to methodically dismantle the enemy forces with considerable skill. Keyes' operations had been pin-pricks. Haig's final offensive would dismember the body.

The attacks had a rather more important result amongst the neutral nations. The Swedes, the Danes, the Dutch were already cautious about Wilhelm's Reich. Haig's 1917 offensive had the little-known side effect of persuading them that the Allies would not yield. Conversely, the vaunted *Kaiserschlacht*, the 'Emperor's Battle' which would win the war, had not brought the anticipated results. Despite the enormous effort by Ludendorff's troops, the Allies held.

Then came Zeebrugge. It would be absurd to claim that it alone changed minds but it helped shape opinion.

A number of papers in the uncommitted countries contented themselves with simply repeating the bulletins of both sides. The editor of the *Limburgs Koerier,* published in Maastricht, a handful of kilometres from the borders both with Germany and occupied Belgium, tended to emphasize the German case. Even so, there is a faint implication that the Allies were winning the war. Those Dutch citizens who crossed through the wire each day to labour for the Germans demanded more money. Paper reichsmarks bought progressively less guilders every week.

Neutrals, especially neutral bankers, did not give a moment's thought to any lack of military success at Zeebrugge. What they saw was that the British could move 167 ships across the North Sea to mount the attack without any interference. What was more, the German Navy made no reply. No destroyers slipped out of Ostend or Zeebrugge to harry the British when they left. No patrols policed the seas off Belgium to deter repetition. The German Navy had ceded control of the North Sea.

What the British had done once, they could repeat at will. What was more, even though the big sea-going U-boats never used Zeebrugge or Ostend, their record was becoming rapidly less impressive. If there was one priority for the men in grimy white sweaters, it was to disrupt the troopships bringing 100,000 US soldiers to Europe every month. They failed and failed lamentably. Neutral observers swiftly decided that Germany would lose the war; if not in 1918, certainly the year afterwards.

The result was inevitable. Bankers cut credit to the German Reich. Suppliers demanded gold in advance. It is only winners who are in a position to pay their debts. Victory slipped from the German grasp. The raw materials of an industrial war were outside their clutches.

The Germans considered the raids were simply of no importance compared to the struggles on the Western Front. Victory there would make pathetically small raids on second-rate ports irrelevant. They lost the propaganda war and it cost them dearly.

Zeebrugge and Ostend could, and should, both have been outstanding triumphs. Poor planning and a general atmosphere more properly associated with Victorian adventure stories bedevilled the enterprise.

Any commander can produce a plan. Any commander can carry out an operation. The difficult part is in anticipating problems, then countering them. Execution must be simple. The cost in life and material must be as low as possible. When an operation succeeds, it appears so easy that the spectator misses the hard work that went into it. A single neglected point can bring terrible casualties. It may also, paradoxically, transform a straightforward affair into something far more glorious and gallant than if proper care had been taken at the start. A disaster anticipated and averted receives little credit. Calamity alleviated by the bravery, the gallantry, the blood of the participants becomes a glorious chapter in the history books.

Using *Vindictive* was a mistake. Keyes claimed he wanted speed, a doubtful benefit, but this is a spurious point. If care had been taken, the smokescreen would have protected *Vindictive* right the way to the Mole. If care had been taken, the grapnels would have worked. If care had been taken, the pathetically inadequate landing brows would have been redesigned. If care had been taken, *Iris* would not have been stranded four feet lower than necessary.

Poor planning. Poor briefing.

The deck space of *Vindictive* was inadequate. The men, huddled closely together, were a compact target for even a single shell. Protection for them was, essentially, overlooked. It would, again, have been difficult to provide because the ship was simply not wide enough to take protective screens.

Better planning would have concentrated independent fire on the Mole batteries. Ignored, they were able to devote their efforts on *Vindictive* whose smokescreen failed at the critical moment. The orders issued to the motor launches and the coastal motor boats have, in the versions the author has seen, no reference to the impelling need for captains to keep a very close check on the wind. It was only by the greatest of good fortune that *Vindictive* was hidden during the last moments of her approach by the independent initiative of a single motor launch.

The landing brows were a failure. The chances of them being damaged by enemy fire were clearly high. Again, the clear impression arises that nobody, simply nobody, believed that the landing would be opposed. Keyes should have known better.

Even without enemy action, the brows suffered heavily as *Vindictive* rolled against the Mole. Again, this should have been anticipated. Even if every brow survived, there was no apparent comprehension that efforts to get ashore would be hampered by the swaying, moving gangplanks at a steep angle. No great sea-going experience was needed to realize that. Again, it was overlooked because nobody practised it. A single afternoon at a isolated spot would have made all the difference.

Similarly, the delays in dropping fifteen feet to the Mole could and should have been properly considered. Nobody rehearsed with ropes. Nobody tried to carry the heavy ladders. Even the stoutest quailed as enemy machine-gun fire swept across the quayside. To slow the process was, to use no stronger word, reprehensible.

190

The hold-ups simply meant death.

Admiral Sir John Fisher – 'Jackie' to the whole of the Navy and probably one of its finest admirals – cared little for Keyes. His opinion of the Zeebrugge operation was brutal:

> . . . no such folly was ever devised by fools as such an operation as that of Zeebrugge.
>
> . . . for sailors to go on shore and attack forts, which Nelson said no sailor but a lunatic would do is not only silly . . . but it's murder and it is criminal.

The men who went to Zeebrugge and Ostend fought because of patriotism and a belief in their King and their Country. They had ungrudging valour and a fierce sense of duty – qualities at which those who lack them find it easy to sneer.

Of the participants, Alfred Carpenter was awarded the Victoria Cross. So was Lieutenant Richard Sandford of *C 3*; his crew received lesser medals.

Lieutenant Commander Bradford, who climbed the derrick on *Iris* in a gallant attempt to fasten the Mole anchor also received the bronze award. It was the second posthumous Cross in the family. His younger brother had won his five months earlier as an acting brigadier general.

Lieutenant Commander Harrison, who led the doomed, desperate and pointless charge along the Mole, was similarly given a posthumous Victoria Cross.

Lieutenant Percy Dean, the commander of *ML 282* won the Cross for his incredibly gallant action in rescuing blockship crews at Zeebrugge. He survived to wear it for many years.

Able Seaman Albert McKenzie was the only rating to receive the country's highest award for gallantry. He was chosen for the honour by his fellow seamen. He was well on the way to recovering from his wounds when influenza struck. He developed pneumonia and died on 3 November 1918. He was buried at Camberwell Old Cemetery.

It is entirely appropriate that his great-nephew is the custodian of the medals of Leading Seaman William Childs who fought by his side on the Mole. These include the Distinguished Service Medal he was awarded for Zeebrugge.

Captain Bamford and Sergeant Finch of the Royal Marines were elected by their fellows as Chater described. Selection by one's comrades is perhaps even more valuable than the Victoria Cross itself.

Wing Commander Brock was never seen alive again. An unsubstantiated report placed him, wounded, supported by two Marines on his way back to *Vindictive*. A friend wrote to *The Times* to say that Brock would never have surrendered but fought on with his bare hands. Eventually, a tale circulated that Brock, protecting two wounded Marines, was last seen knocking out a burly German with a high quality uppercut in complete accordance with the Marquess of Queensberry's pugilistic rules.

The man who might have killed him, Hermann Künne, was honoured by Hitler's Third Reich. The nineteenth destroyer of the *Kriegsmarine* took his name on 22 December 1937. An unsentimental enemy sank it at Narvik in April 1940.

Photographer Franz Seldte was sickened by the state of Germany at the end of the war. He became leader of *Der Stahlhelm*, an ex-servicemen's organization which continued to honour the Kaiser and despised Bolsheviks, Jews and shirkers in equal measure. He, not surprisingly, fell in with another ex-soldier with similar views.

In 1933, Adolf Hitler chose Seldte to be in the first cabinet of the Third Reich. He later served as Germany's Minister of Labour throughout the Second World War. The former *Leutnant* died in 1947, a short while before he was due to take a centre stage position in the dock at the Nuremberg Trials.

Kapitänleutnant Schütte became the manager of a branch of the *Reichsbank* after the war. He was much admired. Even in post-monarchist Germany, a man with the Hohenzollern Order was respected. He died in 1923.

Keyes recommended another three officers for the Victoria Cross after the second Ostend action. Lieutenant Crutchley who took command on *Vindictive* was one. The others were Lieutenant Drummond of *ML 254* and Lieutenant Bourke of *ML 276* who had both displayed such courage in the harbour.

The Germans recovered what remained of Commander Godsal and Sub Lieutenant MacLachlan from the twisted ruins of *Vindictive*. The enemy buried them with full military honours, together with five other dead found on board the ship.

Keyes himself was clearly destined for the top of the tree. By November 1918, Wemyss was still First Sea Lord and the British representative at the armistice talks. Beatty would undoubtedly succeed Wemyss in due course. Keyes would eventually follow Beatty as the professional head of the Navy.

Keyes left the Dover Patrol to command the battlecruiser force based at Rosyth. After two years, he proceeded on half-pay for six months before going to the Admiralty as Deputy Chief of Naval

Staff. Beatty was First Sea Lord. Keyes' succession appeared assured.

In 1925, Sir Roger John Brownlow Keyes took command of the Mediterranean Fleet, a coveted post generally regarded as the precursor to returning as First Sea Lord. It was, though, a three-year tour. Beatty stepped down in 1927. Admiral Sir Charles Madden stepped into the job, an appointment widely regarded as simply a holding position until Keyes completed his tour in 1928.

There is some irony in the fact that Keyes became the subject of rumours on his return to England. Sir Charles Madden retained his post. Keyes became Commander-in-Chief at Portsmouth. During his first month in command, the rumours continued and grew. It was whispered that he played a game of favourites. It was said he was snobbish. The old story that many of the awards for Zeebrugge went to close friends surfaced again. Keyes' love of mixing with the wealthy became another stick with which he was beaten. Unless an officer had a string of polo ponies, promotion would be very hard to come by once Keyes was in charge. Untrue they were. And deadly.

When a socialist government won the General Election, any chances Keyes had of promotion promptly withered away. His political support vanished overnight. In June 1931, Keyes left active duty with the not inconsiderable rank of Admiral of the Fleet.

He became Conservative Member of Parliament for Portsmouth North. He wrote his memoirs. When Chamberlain resigned in 1940 and his old friend Winston Churchill became Prime Minister, Keyes was rewarded with an active service post.

He became Director of Combined Operations, attributable solely to his Zeebrugge experience. It was not to last. Keyes simply could not work as anything other than the head of the team. When the Chiefs of Staff refused to accede to his requests – especially his projected assault on Pantellaria, a totally insignificant island halfway between Tunisia and Sicily – he complained to Churchill, called them cravenhearted and suggested the country was better off without them.

Not even Churchill, fond as he was of mavericks and irregular forces, could back Keyes against the combined weight of the Chiefs of Staff. Keyes was shunted off into unimportant war work – visiting the Americans and advising them on how to invade Japanese-held islands.

He died on 26 December 1945.

It was suggested Keyes should be interred in St Paul's Cathedral. An Admiralty, touchy about prerogatives, pointed out that only Admirals who had defeated an enemy fleet in open battle received such an honour.

Roger Keyes was buried next to his old Zeebrugge comrades at St James' Cemetery at Dover.

Wemyss, inevitably, fell out with Lloyd George. Equally inevitably it was on a matter so trivial as to make one doubt the Prime Minister's sense of proportion. Lady Wemyss, a formidable champion of her husband, explained:

The Prime Minister had apparently planned a spectacular announcement of the Armistice which he hoped to make at the Guildhall Banquet on November 9th; baulked of this by the Armistice not being signed, he projected doing so in the House of Commons on the afternoon of the 11th – the news meanwhile being kept secret. This proved impossible after Wemyss telephoned the King who had announced the details to his entourage. The enthusiasm was concentrated at Buckingham Palace. Lloyd George's official statement in the House fell flat – hence his almost unconcealed fury.

Lloyd George preferred to ignore the unpalatable truth that officers take an oath of loyalty to the Sovereign and not to a political master. It is a procedure which has, from time to time, escaped other Prime Ministers. In this case, Wemyss and the King were both old classmates and shipmates. But Lloyd George could not bear to be thwarted.

Lady Wemyss recalled:

Shortly before his [Wemyss] departure for the Peace Conference, the Admiralty had been startled one morning by a quasi-official announcement in *The Times* of his resignation and the immediate appointment of Admiral Beatty in his stead, coupled with a most venomous article about Navy pay. An authoritative denial was immediately issued to the Press while Wemyss asked the editor of *The Times* to come and see him:

'I asked him,' Lady Wemyss quotes her husband as saying, 'why it was that *The Times* had made such a statement so authoritatively when there was no foundation for it. He replied that he never would have allowed it to be published had he not had it on the highest authority. He naturally declined to give me the source of his information, but so astounded was he to hear that I had not resigned, that I could have no illusions as to his statement.'

It was evident to even the most unsuspecting mind that some plot was afoot. Suspicion fastened on various people, amongst others the Prime Minister, but in an interview Wemyss had with

194

the latter shortly afterwards he disclaimed all participation in the intrigue, which he admitted having been aware of, and hoped Wemyss would continue to occupy his present position.

Having been rejected by the people, Lloyd George wrote his *War Memoirs*. He gave full vent to his hatred for Douglas Haig and other military leaders. His Celtic musings were carefully crafted to enhance his own reputation. A number of political leaders have since followed his example.

Daffodil and *Iris* went home to the Mersey. They received an enormous welcome. After extensive repairs and expensive refurbishment, they returned to service in 1919 with slightly different names. King George V agreed that they should be known as the *Royal Iris* and *Royal Daffodil*. The *Royal Iris* was sold to a Dublin company in 1932. In 1946, she passed into the hands of the Cork Harbour Commissioners and was renamed *Blarney*.

The *Royal Daffodil* stayed on the Mersey until 1934. She then returned to the Medway, running excursions from Rochester to Southend. She finally returned to Belgium in 1938, to a breaker's yard in Ghent.

The survivors of the Zeebrugge and Ostend attacks formed the Zeebrugge Association. Each year, on St George's Day, they paraded with pride. They had every right to do so. They were men who had done their duty to their Sovereign, honest men who had served their nation and were proud that they had done so with such great honour.

They had a standard, made of white silk. The design was really rather obvious. The White Ensign with a superimposed gold-coloured dragon. A dragon with a twisted tail.

CHAPTER SIXTEEN

The big trucks roar down the road to the port of Zeebrugge, day and night passing by the huge container parks each side. Few drivers know or even care about the events of St George's Day in 1918. It was, after all, a long time ago, and Europe is no longer a collection of warring states. The Pomeranian Grenadiers, the Spanish Swordsmen, the French Chasseurs, the English Musketeers who marched to war along the little lanes at the demands of kings and emperors are now just bones.

The Mole itself has been redeveloped. Still massive, still brooding, it is no longer the place where brave men charged across bare concrete against machine guns manned by other brave men. It is possible to take a boat ride around the harbour but the visitor needs a determined imagination to visualize what it must have been like all those years ago.

There are a few reminders of those who fought here on a misty, clammy night in April, 1918. A scenic walk to the west of the new quayside, St George's Way, leads to the memorial to the men of the Royal Marines and Royal Navy who created a legend at Zeebrugge Mole. Once a year, on the Sunday after 23 April, the local council gathers. There is a Service of Remembrance. Children lay flowers. Occasionally, the British Government sends some sailors or a handful of Marines but it is the Belgians who mark the occasion.

On the corner, just outside the entrance to the docks, is a large and imposing white building. For four years, it was home to the officers of the Imperial Navy. The U-boat aces of the Flanders Flotilla, the destroyer and torpedo-boat captains, the gun commanders, the administrative officers and the leader of part time stormtroopers had rooms here.

Travel eastward on the N34, *Kustlaan*, following the tramlines, for just over a mile. On the right is St Donaas Church, a red building with a slate roof. Most visitors miss the turning but it is simple enough to approach from the opposite direction.

Behind the red brick wall of the churchyard are a handful of the slain of 23 April. There is a memorial plaque to Wing Commander Brock on the wall. In grave No. 1 lies Captain Charles Tuckey of the Royal Marines. He failed to return to *Vindictive*. His friends hoped that he had, like Palmer, decided to remain with his men. He had served at Antwerp, the Dardanelles and in Ireland during the Sinn Fein Rebellion. He was twenty-three years old when he died as a member of the Machine Gun Company. It is no disgrace to describe him as a good Marine.

Germans greatly outnumber the British in the serene setting. The Imperial Navy used this graveyard throughout the War of 1914–1918. It is still an official German War Cemetery. Eight Germans who died that April night lie there. So, too, do the sailors killed when the mines on *V 74* exploded in May 1918. It is a reminder that dead fathers, sons, brothers and husbands are not confined to one side alone.

A short walk away is a street named *Admiral Keyesplein*. The man who led the Zeebrugge Raid is not yet forgotten. There is no memorial to *Kapitänleutnant* Schütte who was, in the end, on the losing side.

Bruges itself is determinedly medieval. Its information brochure points out that 'its many canals, streets, churches, almshouses and mansions with beautifully restored facades bear silent witness to a glorious past'.

The town holds, as the Kaiser knew, one of the minor wonders of the world. In the Church of Our Lady by *Mariastraat* is a statue of the Madonna and Child. It was commissioned by a worthy citizen from an ambitious nineteen-year old sculptor, known to history as Michaelangelo.

Bruges is usually awash with visitors, most of them from Britain if the Tourist Board is to be believed. The infamous canals to Zeebrugge and Ostend are now waterways for pleasure boats. They still run into the harbours. The curious visitor can make the trip for a modest sum. This was the route the U-boats took to the open sea.

Sadly, relics of the action are no longer to be easily seen. Zeebrugge's own museum, dedicated to the events of 23 April 1918, was lost in the redevelopment of the port. The Bruges Archives by the Information Office hold the items but an appointment is needed. Their catalogue includes both a Royal Naval and Royal Marines uniform with an assortment of other artefacts.

At Ostend, the visitor will find the largest single surviving reminder of Operation ZO. By the roadside, surrounded by neat grey bollards, linked by a chain, is the bow section of HMS *Vindictive* herself. Purists may wince at the restored paintwork but those are the very bows that nudged the quayside at Zeebrugge, which nosed into the harbour at Ostend.

Those who want to find other remnants of a daring glory without venturing on to the Continent can go to the Chatham Historic Dockyard or to the Royal Marines Museum at Eastney.

Chatham has, aside from *Vindictive*'s bell, one of the perilously narrow landing brows, part of a perforated funnel plate, a navigation light and the binnacle which held the ship's compass.

At Eastney, it is possible to gaze at Lieutenant Lamplough's helmet, still with its white painted band, a Lewis gun with a hole through the barrel which was in Sergeant Finch's foretop, some rather disagreeable blunt instruments and a treasure trove of other items. If imagination fails as to what that hour of fighting was like, there is a diorama of *Vindictive* alongside the Mole.

At both Dover and Liverpool every year, there is a commemoration of Zeebrugge on the Sunday closest to St George's Day. The Belgians are not the only ones to remember and reflect.

Grossly exaggerated claims of success, desperately inadequate planning, a deadly lack of attention to detail. So many years after, these faults should, perhaps for decency's sake, now count for little.

The Zeebrugge assault will ever stand as an memorial to superb gallantry. The driving force was Sir Roger Keyes. Posterity will always link his name with the Raid.

Keyes was not an uncaring man but, at heart, he possibly never stopped being a midshipman with a midshipman's values. Adventure never yielded to caution. It can be an endearing and valuable quality in young officers, It is, perhaps, less suited to an admiral with responsibility for others' lives.

For Keyes, British was best. Failure, accompanied by outstanding courage, became triumph. Charging along 100 yards of bare concrete towards well protected enemy machine guns was, in itself, a celebration of British courage. Clambering up a derrick swept by enemy fire was not a hopeless act but showed the world that British pluck always triumphed.

He was personally brave, a charismatic leader, single-minded, impetuous, foolhardy and an indifferent planner. His operations against the North Sea ports were no military success. They failed in their ultimate aim even though, for one glorious shining moment, there was the dazzling chance to destroy the Zeebrugge lock-gates. The failure, sadly, belongs to Keyes alone. No gallantry, no valour, no deeds of great bravery can hide that single unpalatable truth.

Nevertheless, that intrepid band of heroes who followed Roger John Brownlow Keyes will be long celebrated, and rightly so, for their actions on St George's Day 1918.

They gained their place in history. They deserve to be honoured for it.

BIBLIOGRAPHY

This is an extremely abbreviated list of the secondary sources that have been consulted in the compilation of this book.

Aspinall-Oglander, C. – *Roger Keyes*, Hogarth Press, 1951

Bacon, Admiral Sir Reginald – *The Dover Patrol*, Hutchinson, 1919

Bartz, Karl – *Zeebrugge. Der Englische Angriff auf die Deutsche U-Boot-Basis*, Im Deutschen Verlag Berlin, 1938

Bennett, J. T. – *Dover Patrol, Zeebrugge, Ostend*, Grant Richards 1919

Carpenter VC, A. F. B. – *The Blocking of Zeebrugge*, Herbert Jenkins, 1921

Compton-Hall, Richard – *Submarines and The War At Sea 1914–1918*, MacMillan, 1991

Cook, Sir Edward – *The Press in War-Time*, Macmillan, 1920

Corbett, Sir J. & Newbold, Henry – *Official History Naval Operations*, Longmans, 1931

Ewing, Alfred W. – *The Man of Room 40*, Hutchinson, 1939

Lloyd George, David – *War Memoirs*, Odhams 1938

Halpern, P. G. – *The Keyes Papers, 1914–1918*

Keyes, Sir Roger – *Despatches*, Oxford University Press 1919

—— *Memoirs*, Thornton Butterworth, 1934

Maxwell, G. S. & D. – *The Motor Launch Patrol*, Dent 1920

Patterson, A. Temple – *Jellicoe*, MacMillan, 1969

Pitt, Barrie – *Zeebrugge*, Cassell, 1958

Ryheul, Johan – *Marinekorps Flandern 1914–1918*, Uitgeverij Decock, 1996

Seldte, Franz – *Through A Lens Darkly*, Hutchinson, 1933

Terraine, John – *Business In Great Waters*, Leo Cooper, 1989

Turner, E. S. – *Boys Will Be Boys*, Michael Joseph, 1955

—— *Dear Old Blighty*, Michael Joseph, 1980

Warner, Philip – *The Zeebrugge Raid*, William Kimber, 1978

Wemyss, Lady – *Life & Letters of Lord Wemyss*, Eyre & Spottiswood, 1935

INDEX

203

207